Return Date

Staffordshire UNIVERSITY

This item is due for return or renewal on the date stamped below unless requested by another reader. Please check your post for recall notices

Please Return to Thompson Library, College Road, Stoke

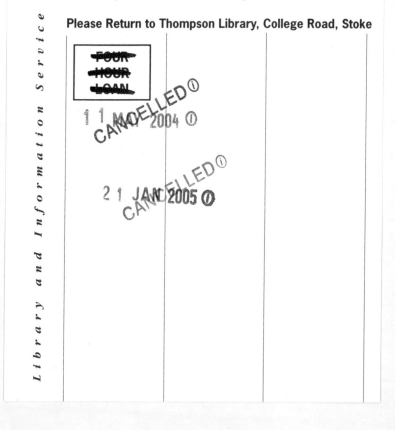

COLERIDGE AND THE SELF

MACMILLAN STUDIES IN ROMANTICISM

Stephen Bygrave
COLERIDGE AND THE SELF

John Turner
WORDSWORTH: PLAY AND POLITICS

Further titles in preparation

Series Standing Order

If you would like to receive future titles in this series as they are published, you can make use of our standing order facility. To place a standing order please contact your bookseller or, in case of difficulty, write to us at the address below with your name and address and the name of the series. Please state with which title you wish to begin your standing order. (If you live outside the U.K. we may not have the rights for your area, in which case we will forward your order to the publisher concerned).

Standing Order Service, Macmillan Distribution Ltd,
Houndmills, Basingstoke, Hants, RG21 2XS, England.

Coleridge and the Self

Romantic Egotism

Stephen Bygrave

MACMILLAN

First published 1986

Published by
THE MACMILLAN PRESS LTD
Houndmills, Basingstoke, Hampshire RG21 2XS
and London
Companies and representatives
throughout the world

Typeset by
Wessex Typesetters
Frome, Somerset

British Library Cataloguing in Publication Data
Bygrave, Stephen
Coleridge and the self: romantic egotism. –
(Macmillan studies in romanticism)
1. Coleridge, Samuel Taylor – Criticism and
interpretation
I. Title
821'.7   PR4484
ISBN 0–333–38851–8

Contents

v

Preface

This book is a study of Coleridge and the concept of 'egotism', the term he uses near the outset of his poetic career for a group of related concerns to do with the activity and powers of the self and their representation in poetry. I take the concept as a means of examining both the language of Coleridge's poetry and a number of problems related to the status of the self, the revaluation of which in the wake of Kant has long been recognised as a central feature in Romanticism. However, this truism conceals the extent to which the self is a problem for the Romantic writers: it is a problem having moral, metaphysical and political implications. Accordingly Coleridge's writings are considered in the light of the German idealist tradition as well as that of the British (mainly Scottish) enlightenment, although the focus of concern is always his poetry.

I attempt first to establish the importance of a concern with 'egotism' to a number of writers in the period and to define the nature of their concern; then to demonstrate problems associated with representation of the self in texts by Thomas Gray, Goethe and Schiller. The second part examines the representation of the self within what are taken to be two crucial cognitive metaphors: those of eyesight and of the circle. This leads to a consideration of strategies employed by and for the self within some of Coleridge's 'conversation poems' ('Frost at Midnight' is chosen for extended discussion). The final part sets the fascinated but morally ambivalent response evoked in Coleridge by the 'egotism' of Milton's Satan or of Napoleon against the analogous responses of Fichte, Hegel and Carlyle. Coleridge's own ambivalent response to such apparent manifestations of the absolute reproduces that oscillation everywhere evident in the language of his poetry.

Philosophically, Locke and Hume are sceptical of the 'theological' self of Descartes – but their alternative is, for Coleridge, part of the same problem. If the self is activity, what is its authority and what are the constraints upon it? Fichte and

Schelling ultimately find the transcendental self to be indefinable and can only restate the terms of this problem. Coleridge's location of an 'absolute self' in the divine is made problematic by the conviction that such an absolute can be known and represented. Linguistically, this division is paralleled in a division between subject and object, image and thing. Thus Chapter 5 below begins in epistemology but ends in language, and in Chapter 6 it is apparent that awareness of self is also awareness of separation, of the Fall. Little confidence can be placed in absolutes, which are unknowable as the self. One strategy Coleridge adopts for avoiding the stricture of 'egotism' within certain poems is the displacement of significance (by which I mean the responsibility for achieved meaning) onto others. This, as I try to show in Part III, is the true sense in which they are 'conversation poems'. So, one consequence of a revalued self is a need for validation. To go out of bounds is, as the Ancient Mariner found, to go without a pilot. I suggest that 'egotism' is an act of extending the bounds of (poetic) language to create a new consensus that we can now see as different in kind rather than in degree from that out of which it grew.

This then is a book about concepts, and I have tried not to underestimate the difficulty of the concepts with which I deal. Though it is a study of a single author, I suppose the book is ambitious to say something about Romanticism, egotism and representation of the self in general. I have not dealt explicitly with 'Selfhood' in Blake, nor with such figures as Shelley's Prometheus (though I hope Part IV might be of genealogical help). Had I done so, I do not know where I should have begun or ended but in language, as I have done. Still, the book proceeds by teasing out, eliciting and sometimes by wrenching Coleridge's meanings, and this may make it a difficult read. If I were starting again – which in a sense I am – I should begin at the point I think I reach somewhere around the geographical centre of the book, with the reading of 'Frost at Midnight'.

Each of the four parts centres on a poem (perversely enough, in Part I, on a poem by Thomas Gray not by Coleridge). Since the book may already bear too obviously the scars of its genesis (as a PhD thesis at Cambridge) I have not further weighted the notes by referring much to other critics of the poetry, though my differences with many of them are implicit. I have learned from all of them I have read, but particularly from John Beer, Kenneth

Burke, Geoffrey Hartman and David Simpson. I should also mention a book that appeared too recently to be assimilated here: Paul Hamilton's *Coleridge's Poetics*.

For what often seemed as grim and lonely a business as Hegel's 'Calvary of the Spirit' it is chastening to record how much the writing of this book depended on others. My parents were supportive above and beyond the call of kin: thanks. My debt has grown to John Beer, who was a model of tact and patience as supervisor of the research on which the book is based. Rosemary Ashton and John Casey, who examined the thesis, made some helpful suggestions. Dr Ashton also acted as the reader for Macmillan. I should also like to thank two friends who, amongst many other things, typed earlier versions of the first three parts: Anne Millman and Pete de Bolla. I was emboldened and stimulated by John Barrell's 1980–2 research seminar on the eighteenth century. I also profited from many late-night discussions with Steve Clark and Peter Rawlings, who read proofs and made valuable comments on a later draft. Without encouragement from David Simpson and Robert Woof the book might never have been started. Now it is finished it is for Frances Loe, to whom the work shall justify itself.

S. B.

Acknowledgements

The author and publishers would like to thank the following for permission to use copyright material:

Cambridge University Press, for the extracts from *Hegel: Lectures on the Philosophy of History: Introduction – Reason in History*, translated by H. B. Nisbet;

The Macmillan Press, for the extracts from Kant's *The Critique of Pure Reason*, translated by N. Kemp Smith;

Oxford University Press for the extracts from Hegel, *Phenomenology of Spirit*, translated by A. V. Miller, *The Letters of Samuel Taylor Coleridge*, ed. E. L. Griggs, and *Coleridge: Poetical Works*, ed. E. H. Coleridge;

Princeton University Press and Routledge & Kegan Paul, for the extracts from *The Collected Works of Samuel Taylor Coleridge*;

Frederick Ungar Publishing Co. Inc., for the extracts from Schiller's *'Naive and Sentimental Poetry' and 'On the Sublime': Two Essays*, translated by Julius A. Elias.

List of Abbreviations

To keep down the number of notes, works to which constant reference is made are cited within parentheses in the text, using the following abbreviations.

AR Coleridge, *Aids to Reflection, in the Formation of a Manly Character on the General Grounds of Prudence, Morality and Religion* (London, 1825).

BL [*CC*] Coleridge, *Biographia Literaria*, ed. James Engell and W. Jackson Bate, 2 vols (1983), in *CC*.

CC *The Collected Works of Samuel Taylor Coleridge*, general editor Kathleen Coburn (with Bart Winer), Bollingen Series LXXV, in progress (London and Princeton, NJ, 1969–). (Cited by work: see under the relevant abbreviations.)

Church and State [*CC*] Coleridge, *On the Constitution of the Church and State*, ed. John Colmer (1976), in *CC*.

CL *Collected Letters of Samuel Taylor Coleridge*, ed. Earl Leslie Griggs, 6 vols (Oxford, 1956–71).

CN *The Notebooks of Samuel Taylor Coleridge*, ed. Kathleen Coburn, Bollingen Series L, in progress (London, New York and Princeton, NJ, 1957–). (Transcriptions from the notebooks follow the practice in this edn.)

EOT [*CC*] Coleridge, *Essays on His Times*, ed. David V. Erdman, 3 vols (1978), in *CC*.

Friend [*CC*]   Coleridge, *The Friend*, ed. Barbara E. Rooke, 2 vols (1969), in *CC*.

HW   *The Complete Works of William Hazlitt*, Centenary Edn, ed. P. P. Howe, 21 vols (London and Toronto, 1930–4).

KL   *The Letters of John Keats*, ed. Hyder Edward Rollins, 2 vols (Cambridge, Mass., 1958).

Lectures 1795 [*CC*]   Coleridge, *Lectures 1795 on Politics and Religion*, ed. Lewis Patton and Peter Mann (1971), in *CC*.

LS [*CC*]   Coleridge, *Lay Sermons*, ed. R. J. White (1972), in *CC*.

MiscCrit   *Coleridge's Miscellaneous Criticism*, ed. Thomas Middleton Raysor (London, 1936).

PL   Coleridge, *The Philosophical Lectures, 1818–1819*, ed. Kathleen Coburn (London, 1949).

Prelude   *The Prelude 1799, 1805, 1850*, ed. Jonathan Wordsworth, M. H. Abrams and Stephen Gill, Norton Critical Editions (New York, 1979). (References give the date of the version cited, followed by book and line references.)

PW   *The Complete Poetical Works of Samuel Taylor Coleridge*, ed. Ernest Hartley Coleridge, 2 vols (Oxford, 1912).

QCW   Thomas De Quincey, *Collected Writings*, ed. David Masson, 14 vols (Edinburgh, 1889–90).

ShakCrit   *Samuel Taylor Coleridge: Shakespearian Criticism*, ed. Thomas Middleton Raysor, 2nd edn, 2 vols (London, 1960).

TT   *Specimens of the Table Talk of Samuel Taylor Coleridge*, ed. H. N. Coleridge, 2nd edn, rev. (Oxford, 1836).

Watchman [*CC*]   Coleridge, *The Watchman*, ed. Lewis Patton (1970), in *CC*.

WPr   *The Prose Works of William Wordsworth*, ed.

W. J. B. Owen and Jane W. Smyser, 3
vols (Oxford, 1974).

WPW   *The Poetical Works of William Wordsworth,*
ed. Ernest de Selincourt and Helen
Darbishire, 5 vols (Oxford, 1940–9).

For other works cited, full details appear in the Bibliography, and
in the Notes on first reference. For the more frequently cited,
references are thenceforth provided in the text, wherever possible.

PART I
The Birth of the Self

1   Querulous Egotism

The charge of 'querulous egotism' Coleridge anticipates for his
Poems *on Various Subjects* (1796) leads him to an early and explicit
claim for the poetic possibilities of 'egotism'; for, rather than
refute the charge of a disabling presence of self, he defines egotism
precisely as an enabling quality for his own poetry and an affective
quality in reading other poets (*PW*, ii, 1135). The Preface to his
first volume then adumbrates what comes to be a structural
principle in Coleridge's poetry, and contributes to a debate which
it is the concern of this book to study. He claims 'egotism' to be the
natural and necessary condition of the lyric poem, as roundness is
that of the circle (ii, 1136). As he goes on, dropping the pejorative
modifier 'querulous', he is already tending towards a con-
ceptualisation of the term, while retaining a sense of its older,
non-technical usage. In his own writings, the term and the
concept are charged with this ambivalence. On the analogy of the
ratio of 'affective' to 'enabling' suggested above, I shall try to
show Coleridge's ambivalence towards 'egotism' operating both
morally and at the level of poetic language. The wider importance
of the term and the concept is suggested by a cluster of first usages
of 'egotism' and its cognates between 1780 and 1830 – the period
we designate 'Romantic'.

The *OED* ascribes an early use of the word 'egoism' to the Scots
'commonsense' philosopher Thomas Reid, writing 'of the
sentiments of bishop Berkeley': 'I am left alone, as the only
creature of God in the universe, in that forlorn state of *Egoism*, into
which, it is said, some of the Disciples of Des Cartes were brought
by his philosophy.'[1] Here 'egoism' is a passive state – the 'forlorn'
one into which Reid is committed by Berkeley's doctrine of no
proof of objective existence outside the mind. The word 'Egoists'
was applied, says Reid, to those of Descartes's disciples who
remained fixated on the uncertainty of everything but their own
existence[2] – a technical sense of 'egoism' which is employed by
Coleridge too.[3] In general, 'egoism' comes to refer to a passive

state – thinking about oneself, where 'egotism' is active – talking about or asserting oneself: the morally ambivalent quality for the Romantics of Shakespeare's Edmund and Milton's Satan, or of historical figures such as Napoleon or Milton himself.[4] The *OED* cites Addison from 1714, using 'egotism' to denote a specific breach of decorum in writing – too frequent a use of the word 'I' – or, in Dr Johnson's definition (which cites the same passage from the *Spectator*), 'The fault committed in writing by the frequent repetition of the word *ego*, or I; too frequent mention of a man's self, in writing or conversation.'[5] In the same year as Coleridge's first preface a review in the *British Critic* of Mme D'Arblay's *Camilla* censures the novel for its use of 'Gallicisms, such as *egotism* for selfishness'.[6] Hugh Blair's *Lectures on Rhetoric*, which went through several editions in the late eighteenth century and was a university textbook, is generally descriptive rather than prescriptive, but Blair resists 'conceit' as he sees the term shift from Johnson's sense of it as a trope (of 'metaphysical' poetry) to that of an affective quality. Blair restates as an imperative the pejorative definitions offered by Addison and Johnson:

> Conceited Writers . . . discover their spirit so much in their composition that it imprints on their Style a character of pertness; though I confess it is difficult to say, whether this can be classed among the attributes of Style, or rather is to be ascribed entirely to the thought. In whatever class we rank it, all appearances of it ought to be avoided with care, as a most disgusting blemish in writing.[7]

Adam Smith, in a conjectural essay affixed to the second edition of his *Theory of Moral Sentiments*, claims that the 'original' languages were synthetic, composed of propositions which were integral representations of events, as opposed to analytic, which distinguish subject, predicate and copula, and that therefore the first verbs were impersonal:

> Impersonal verbs, which express in one word a complete event, which preserve in the expression that perfect simplicity and unity, which there always is in the object and in the idea, and which suppose no abstraction, or metaphysical division of the event into its several constituent members of subject and attribute, would, in all probability, be the species of verbs first invented.[8]

Verbs became personal only 'by the division of the event into its metaphysical elements' and the personal pronouns thus 'express ideas extremely metaphysical and abstract':

> The word *I* . . . is a general word, capable of being predicated, as the logicians say, of an infinite variety of objects . . . the objects of which it may be predicated do not form any particular species of objects, distinguished from all others . . . what they call, a common term; and to join in its signification the seemingly opposite qualities of the most precise individuality, and the most extensive generalization. (II, 444)

Smith accords no special status to the demotion of the 'I': the word is an example of the 'metaphysical division', the degeneration into prolixity, disagreeableness to the ear and rigidity of modern languages. What all these examples suggest (as do the *OED*'s definitions, where the phrase 'too much' recurs) is that the presentation or representation of the self in 'egotism' is always an excess. The significance of the status accorded to 'egotism' in Coleridge's preface is in his suggesting a positive revaluation.

The *OED* also has two citations of Coleridge. In the first, he clearly ascribes to 'egoism' more active power than is apparent in its other examples and indicates excess rather by the nouns than the adjective: 'The thirst and pride of power, despotism, egoistic ambition'.[9] He is using 'egoism' interchangeably with 'egotism'. There is a second, technical sense of 'egoism', but it belongs not to eighteenth-century discourse (Johnson does not record the word at all) but to our own commentary upon its discourse. We refer to the 'psychological egoism' of Hobbes and Mandeville, and to the continuing eighteenth-century moral debate in their wake as a debate over whether egoism or altruism is the dominant impulse in human actions. Here Shaftesbury, in his 'benevolent' optimism, can exemplify the terms of the debate. Selfishness, originated by the 'Self-Passions', is defined as acting on self-interest to the detriment of public good: 'if there be found in any Creature a more than ordinary Self-Concernment, or Regard to private Good, which is inconsistent with the Interest of the Species or Publick; this must in every respect be esteem'd as ill and vitious affection'.[10] It is the 'constant relation to the Interest *of a Species*',[11] a 'natural sympathy', such as filial affection, which prevents man acting solely for himself and, since conscience is a part of his nature too, leads to his happiness. Coleridge contributes to this debate, notably in the *Opus Maximum* manuscript, but it is transmuted in a debate about 'egotism' conducted in his writings.[12] The transmutation is visible in the *OED*'s second citation of Coleridge, from the tenth of the 1818 series of lectures on poetry. For an eighteenth-century tradition of which Addison stands as an exemplar, egotism is a quality that is personally unattractive and socially undesirable, and will remain so in poetry while the reader is not challenged by, or tempted to sympathise with, values that threaten that assurance. Coleridge's ambivalent attitude towards the affective capacity of 'egotism' is a moral one. He begins in moral criticism of the literary character and ends in praise for the literary work from which he is inseparable:

> The character of Satan is pride and sensual indulgence, finding in self the sole motive of action. It is the character so often seen *in little* on the political stage. It exhibits all the restlessness, temerity, and cunning which have marked the mighty hunters of mankind from Nimrod to Napoleon. The common fascination of men is, that these great men, as they are called, must act from some great motive. Milton has carefully marked in his Satan the intense selfishness, the alcohol of egotism, which would rather reign in hell than serve in heaven. To place this lust of self in opposition to denial of self or duty, and to show what exertions it would make, and what pains endure to accomplish its end, is Milton's particular object in the character of Satan. But around this character he has thrown a singularity of daring, a grandeur of sufferance, and a ruined splendour, which constitute the very height of poetic sublimity.   (*MiscCrit*, p. 163)

Here the terms of the debate on 'egoism' ('lust of self in opposition to denial of self or duty') are transmuted by poetry. Although he recognises the morally intoxicatory power of 'egotism', Coleridge is sure of Milton's 'object' prior to reading him. However, far from being the instrument of a moral intention which requires only that evil be made credible, 'poetic sublimity' may serve to make the reader question whether the effect is in accord with the intention. If the literary character can at best be read off symbolically ('in little') against the historically 'real', that may provide a criticism not of the literary work but of the 'real'. As Keats observes in the letter to Woodhouse in which he distinguishes 'the wordsworthian or egotistical sublime' from his own, Shakespearean, practice, 'What shocks the virtuous philosopher delights the camelion Poet' (*KL*, I, 387). Coleridge dissociates himself from 'the common stock of men' but cannot hold himself immune to the 'singularity', 'grandeur' and 'splendour' of Satan as Milton presents him. The ambivalent regard Coleridge has for such an overreacher is something I shall discuss in Part IV below but it is an ambivalence which charges the single word.

The phenomenon of new words, or of words acquiring new (often their modern) meanings in the Romantic period has been often noticed.[13] As an instance of the regard attaching to single words we could cite the case of the Bristol shipowner who, according to J. Dykes Campbell, changed the name of a vessel from 'Liberty' to 'Freedom' because 'Liberty' bore the stigma of French republicanism,[14] or Coleridge's own (1803) footnote to his 'Ode to the Departing Year' which speaks of 'The Name of Liberty, which at the commencement of the French Revolution was both the occasion and the pretext of unnumbered crimes and horrors' (*PW*, I, 161n). Euphemism, a disguise for the unpalatable, may become 'perjury'. In his 'Fears in Solitude' Coleridge is bitter about 'all our dainty terms for fratricide' (I, 260). The single word often provides an instance of the pervasive management of opinion by the ruling class. One tendency of radical writings of the 1790s is to focus attention on its distortion of words. Let me give a cento of entries from Pigott's *Political Dictionary*:

Enquiry, – according to the modern construction, signifies Sedition.
Justice, – obsolete.
Heresy, – an abjuration of nonsense and superstition.
Heresy, – the rights of man, and the promulgation of truth.
Rights, – those claims which belong to us by nature and justice. They are quite obsolete and unknown here.

There is thus a wonderful self-reflexiveness in one definition: '*Irony*, – a mode of speech, in which the meaning is contrary to the word; as Pitt is a great and worthy character . . . Edmund Burke a man

of the most virtuous consistency.'[15] (This concern relates too to
the definition by 'desynonymising' in chapter 4 of the *Biographia*
and elsewhere.) Although our own sense of 'egotism' is that of
Addison rather than that of Coleridge, the 'ego' words bear less
obvious stigmata of contemporary controversy than do those
normally cited. A comparison with an earlier period may suggest
some explanations.

   The cluster of first usages of compounds of 'ego' around the late
1700s and early 1800s is perhaps comparable to the new lexicon of
introspection which enters the English language in the period of
Shakespeare's plays. I am thinking of such words as 'identity',
'characterisation', 'conscious' 'idiosyncrasy' and 'individuality'.
The *OED* cites nearly thirty new compounds with 'self' in the
period 1580–1610.[16] Sir Edward Dyer's 'My mind to me a
kingdom is', written in 1588, classically exemplifies the notion of
an inner territory to be explored which may be as rich as the
external new-found lands. He writes from within a momentum of
scientific discovery – Gilbert's discovery of magnetism, Harvey's
of the circulation of the blood – which is also in force in the period
of the Industrial Revolution. That the fractured syntax of
Hamlet's   soliloquies   is   psychologically   convincing   is   a
commonplace, but in the 'To be or not to be' speech, for instance
(to take the most commonplace), he speaks twelve lines entirely of
infinitives, without using the word 'I'. That an increase in
consciousness may imply a surplus of disabling self-consciousness
is something I shall discuss in regard to a novel by Goethe and a
poem by Gray, but from this example it will be remembered that
Hamlet's turning-inward discovers an unstable self, one that is
potentially a rogue and peasant slave besides exemplifying what a
piece of work is a man. (Marjorie Hope Nicolson even claims that
Hamlet embodies the collapse of Shakespeare's own assurance in
the old morality and cosmology, leading to his retirement).[17]
Hamlet can, at any rate, be seen to embody a paradox of
expansionist momentum and collapsing assurance which is
analogous to that in the later period. Just as the crisis of
Renaissance humanism – man's struggling to become the subject
of his own history – can be detected in its linguistic self-
consciousness, so the neologisms and new compounds of 'ego'
words in the latter period evince a new or newly-heightened
concern with the self. Kant claims that his critical philosophy has
effected a decentring, a 'Copernican revolution'. However, this is

a revolution discernibly under way in British writing before British writers had heard of Kant.

Here the reasons are complex: philosophical, in that Locke and Hume cast into doubt the assurance of a stable and continuous divinely ordained identity; 'historical', in that the repressive legislation and censorship introduced in the aftermath of the American and French Revolutions make social authority distrusted; and, perhaps, in the case of Coleridge, biographical, in that the failure of the Pantisocracy project, the estrangements from Southey and Wordsworth and the unconsummated desire for Sara Hutchinson combine to disillusion him of the ideal of a community of like-minded people. These are large issues, but there is a clear progression in the contraries of retirement from and engagement with late eighteenth-century English society which can be seen 'in little' in the words in which it describes itself. In 'egotism', the contraries are retained. Even as Coleridge, within his Preface, tries to force its amelioration, the word bears rather the wounds than the scars of its older, non-technical usage.

Coleridge diagnoses the 'symptoms' of Hamlet's 'aversion to real action' as an 'overbalance in the contemplative faculty' (*ShakCrit*, II, 272). This is akin to the 'egotism' he finds in Milton. Since Hamlet and *Hamlet* are, in Coleridge's reading, not so much metonymic of as synonymous with each other, the dichotomy of Shakespeare and Milton alluded to by many writers is a collapsible one: egotism indeed fulfils the enabling function claimed for it in Coleridge's Preface. Yet to speak of the enabling influence of other writers is of course to collapse also a distinction between enabling and affective qualities. The suggestion of disease in this comment on Hamlet is one that will be met with again as something rotten in the state of the *Zeitgeist* and which all flesh is heir to. The moral ambivalence of the concept arises from this indistinctness.

In his Preface, Coleridge posits 'egotism' as a mediating instrument for the poet. At first the intensity of experience may be too violent to allow him to write, but then 'the mind demands amusement and can find it in employment alone; but full of its late sufferings it can endure no employment not in some measure connected with them' (*PW*, II, 1144). This associationist 'employment' is the act of composition, and the passage at once recalls the more famous account of the genesis of a poem from the Preface to the 1800 *Lyrical Ballads*:

Poetry is the spontaneous overflow of powerful feelings: it takes
its origin from emotion recollected in tranquillity: the emotion
is contemplated till by a species of reaction, the tranquillity
gradually disappears, and an emotion, similar to that which
was before the subject of contemplation, is gradually produced,
and does itself actually exist in the mind.   (*WPr*, I, 148)

Some at least of this passage is by Coleridge himself,[18] but, if at
first there appears to be a contradiction between the mediating-
power of 'egotism' and 'the spontaneous overflow of powerful
feelings', there is as much of a contradiction within the second
passage alone. Unless 'powerful feelings' are very different from
untranquil emotions, 'spontaneous' and 'gradual production' are
mutually contradictory. To resolve the contradiction, the
statement 'poetry *is*' must, in the light of the claims that follow,
mean something like 'is the (final) product of'; the final product of
a mediating process which can reconstruct experience and
achieve its deferred significance. The most striking difference
between the passages of 1796 and 1800 is the later stress on
memory; but memory itself, as Hazlitt recognises in 'On the
Principles of Human Action', is inextricable from egotism: 'As an
affair of sensation, or memory, I can feel no interest in anything
but what relates to myself in the strictest sense' (*HW*, I, 1). So,
what the 1800 passage adds to Coleridge's earlier account is the
suggestion that memory is abundant recompense. Meaning is
deferred. Memory can re-present experience with its sensory force
abated; and random present experience may discover itself
retrospectively. The self is submerged grammatically – in a
passive rather than reflexive construction ('the emotion is
contemplated') – as within the associationist process. The 1800
Preface is of course itself the product of retrospective
understanding, rather self-consciously 'theoretical' and, it will be
noted, this 'overflow' must therefore always be promissory.

Coleridge goes on (in a passage added to his Preface in the
edition of 1797) to claim egotism as more than a trait of the
author's temperament which is merely the neutral and necessary
prerequisite of literary production: 'If I could judge of others by
myself, I should not hesitate to affirm, that the most interesting
passages in our most interesting Poems, are those in which the
Author develops his own feelings' (*PW*, II, 1144). Coleridge's

syntax is tentative: the double subordinate clauses preceding the claim make for an effect which is markedly unegotistical. This betrays the residue of a non-technical sense as he adumbrates 'egotism' as an affective quality. Coleridge does hesitate to judge of others by himself, and yet the affective value of egotism is not as a record but a 'development' of the consciousness of an individual (an author), in the manner suggested by placing the passages from 1796 and 1800 against each other above. The concept must escape the condemnation; so Coleridge goes on to distinguish the nascent concept from 'one species of Egotism which is truly disgusting; not that which leads us to communicate our feelings to others, but that which would reduce the feelings of others to an identity with our own' (II, 1144–5). The moral distinction is illuminated by a remark in the *Friend*: 'To *fill* a station, is to exclude or repel others – and this is not less the definition of moral, than of material, *solidity*' (*Friend* [*CC*], I, 296). While this recalls the way in which Milton's poetic practice is contrasted to Shakespeare's in the *Biographia*, it contrasts in turn with the more complex and, again, ambivalently regarded egotism of Coleridge's own practice: temporal shifts between a dramatic present, a remembered past and a willed, potential future all apparently occurring within the consciousness of the poet (the structure of the poem) do not exclude or repel the reader, who cannot possibly fill the same station, but, on the contrary, rely on his or her inclusion and attraction.

The ambivalence of egotism – at once a flaw in, and power of, the self – is the reflex of a debate still wider than that over egoism and altruism. Its status must depend on the concept of the self, and its ambivalence is signalled within the seminal statement of modern Western philosophy. Descartes's *cogito, ergo sum*, though it gives primacy to the knowing subject, submerges the subject in an inflection of the verb. Descartes, detaching the act of his own doubting from anything external to itself, makes 'I am' the inevitable corollary of 'I think', with God as the omniscient voice who articulates the sentence. His is the *ergo* which both articulates and divides knower and known. A second important consequence of Descartes's Latin is that the statement disguises the problem of the transitiveness of the English verb 'to be'. The 'I AM' in Coleridge is the infinite, original voice of God, and the necessity for predication – and, for Coleridge, of interlocution – will be shown as a problem that recurs. Commitment to the *cogito* then, is to a subject which possesses itself directly and unmediated, in a 'moment' before or above time. This is not to say that the Cartesian *ego* has unmediated knowledge but that the mediation is effected through the medium of internalised 'ideas' rather than through the operation of internal 'categories': 'There are some objects that we can contemplate without being logically committed to the existence of anything other than the ego. These objects are ideas . . . an idea is any object that can be contemplated by a thinking being without existential commitment to anything except that being.'[19] Cartesian doubt, 'this self-determined indetermination' (*BL* [*CC*], I, 258), did not extend to this subject, and Shaftesbury, doubting such a subject in a very Lockean manner, only concludes, 'To the force of this reasoning I confess I must so far admit as to declare that, for my own part, I take my being upon trust.'[20]

Coleridge states his particular objections to the Cartesian formulation in a footnote to the *Biographia* (I, 275–8): does it make for a conditional, empirical self, confirmed only by its activity, or does 'I am' imply 'I am, as many are', a dedication of the soul to the absolute I AM which is God? For Coleridge, there is a 'dependence, or rather . . . inherence' of the former in the latter: of, we might say, the empirical in the metaphorical. The power of the self resides in its very capacity for being subsumed, a power to be necessarily asserted against the mechanism of Newton and Locke which, maintaining a dichotomy of subject and object, and therefore between the individual and society, the soul and God, could see egotism only as wayward and socially destructive. For Descartes, such a dichotomy is divinely ordained, while Coleridge, in the *Biographia*, insists on the necessity for dismantling 'the absolute and essential heterogeneity of the soul as intelligence, and the body as matter' (I, 129) in order to arrive at the individual relationship with God recorded as a goal in the seventeenth-century divines. While he is wary of 'egotism' for reasons already suggested, 'relationship' always entails relationship *to* some other; entails verification or confirmation of 'intuition' which might otherwise become solipsism. This entailment has a direct bearing on Coleridge's poetic practice and will be dealt with in Part III below. In Chapter 2 it will be examined in terms of the faculty of 'conscience'. He defines faith as 'fidelity to our own being', and says of the knowledge of his own conscience (a faculty coinstantaneous with consciousness): 'I know that I possess this knowledge as a man, and not as Samuel Taylor Coleridge.'[21]

It is in his literary (auto)biography however that Samuel Taylor Coleridge complains of the reception of 'Christabel', and goes on, 'I had the additional misfortune of having been gossiped about, as devoted to metaphysics, and worse than all, to a system incomparably nearer to the visionary flights of Plato, and even to the jargon of the Mystics, than to the established tenets of Locke' (*BL* [*CC*], II, 240). In the four 'philosophical' letters to Wedgwood, with copies to Poole (*CL*, II, 679–703), Coleridge attempts to correct a view of those tenets as innovatory by stating Locke's debt to the rationalist method of Descartes, who is the principal antagonist. If Descartes 'was the first man who made nature utterly lifeless and godless' (*PL*, p. 376), Locke and Hume, following him, made much the same of the self. The nature of Coleridge's departure from Locke can be gauged from two statements which, placed together out of context, might appear congruent. Locke states that 'personal identity can by us be placed in nothing but consciousness (which is that alone which makes what we call *self*)',[22] while Coleridge requires no 'other predicate of self, but that of self-consciousness' (*BL* [*CC*], I, 276). The emphases of the syntax alert us to the difference. Postulating 'consciousness' as the unifying faculty in identity enables Locke to solve the problem of personal identity only empirically, in individual cases: 'Where-ever a Man finds what he calls *himself*, there I think another may say is the same *Person*' (*Essay*, p. 346). The self is, for Coleridge, a given; for Locke, a construct. In Locke 'consciousness' is interchangeable with 'thinking', and he defines a person as 'a thinking intelligent Being, that has reason and reflection, and can consider it self as it self, the same thinking thing in different times and places' (p. 335). 'Personal identity' then is no more than a species of the identity perceived between any material objects.

Thus the relation between the conscious self and personal identity remains unproblematic for Locke. The classic objection is by Bishop Butler: 'And one should really think it self-evident, that consciousness of personal identity presupposes, and therefore cannot constitute, personal identity; any more than knowledge in any other case, can constitute truth, which it presupposes.'[23] Although it might be objected to this objection that Butler does not say what self this is evident to, he points out the absurdity of contending that 'he is the same person' means 'he can remember that he is the same person'.[24] Locke's definition of a person indeed implies memory as central to self-construction. His interest in personal identity is in the sense of a person's being identical with another, past person, not in the ontological sense of what a person is. The concept of memory as constitutive of that bodily continuity which, he argues, is 'personal identity' again remains unproblematic, especially by comparison with the strata of memory produced within 'Frost at Midnight', for instance.

Clearly, there is also a distinction to be drawn between Locke's 'consciousness' and Coleridge's 'self-consciousness'. For Locke, in states of sleep or madness – when not 'thinking' – the person cannot be said to exist: 'a Being that . . . can consider it self as it self . . . does [so] only by that consciousness, which is inseparable from thinking' (*Essay*, p. 335). Hume, similarly, equates the egotism of poetry with the dissociation of madness: 'and this is common both to poetry and madness, that the vivacity they bestow on the ideas is not deriv'd from the particular situations or connexions of the objects of these ideas, but from the present temper and disposition of the person'.[25]

Hume also relegates the self to the position of a secondary inference in the system of human understanding. In the chapter 'Of Personal Identity' in *A Treatise of Human Nature* the logical result of his initial empirical idealism – the contention that knowledge consists of and can only be gained through sense impressions – emerges in his view that the self, as an object, is a chimera. We become aware of a self, says Hume, only through sense impressions: 'But there is no impression constant and invariable. . . . It cannot therefore, be from . . . impressions . . . that the idea of self is deriv'd; and consequently there is no such idea' (pp. 251–2). The consequence follows so readily for Hume because ideas are the fading memories of sense impressions, and when these are removed Hume is 'insensible of *myself*, and may truly be said not to exist'.[26] Yet, of another's insistence that he does indeed exist, 'All I can allow him is, that he may be in the right as well as I, and that we are essentially different in this particular' (p. 252). This suggests the crux of Hume's problem with causation. 'Identity' is the relationship between perceptions. The self is merely a retrospective construct of the imagination, which is to say, for Hume, an illusion: 'identity is nothing really belonging to these different perceptions, and uniting them together; but is merely a quality, which we attribute to them, because of the union of their ideas in the imagination, when we reflect on them' (p. 260). Memory is again the chief source of the persistence of the illusory idea of the self, acquainting us with or deceiving us with the principle of causation: 'memory not only discovers the identity, but also contributes to its production' (p. 262). Wishing to deny the existence of self precedent to, and independent of, consciousness of particular 'impressions', Hume is driven, as was Locke, to the admission of its existence as a necessary fiction, and there is a cunning retraction of his position in this chapter in the Appendix (pp. 633, 635–6).

For both Locke and Hume, then, even the existence of the self is at best an embarrassment. As Coleridge notes, 'Defences & proofs *ab extra* of personal Identity well ridiculed in the song of the little old woman & her little dog – If it is not me, he'll bark & he'll rail – But if it is me, he will wag his little Tail' (*CN*, i, 1235). He finds it easy enough to ridicule the empiricists for giving a dog a bad name, but the contrary implication – the necessity for consciousness of the self as intuition – is fraught with difficulty. Egotism has, potentially, the capacity for actively spanning that fissure which in the Cartesian *Cogito* is occupied by an unknowable God. Locke and Hume only reproduce that fissure and their dismissal of a metaphysical self implies a dismissal of any possible power. They underwrite, in other words, the fairly trivial strictures of 'egotism' which we saw, for instance, in Addison: what Goethe will call a 'disease' may be no more than unease.

This tertiary difficulty is demonstrated by an early note of Coleridge's in which the remark 'poetry without egotism comparatively uninteresting' is followed by a memo to himself to 'write an Ode to *Meat and Drink*' (*CN*, i, 62). In his anecdotal *Essay on the Literary Character* Isaac D'Israeli says that 'consciousness of merit characterises men of genius; but it is to be lamented that the illusions of self-love are not distinguishable from the realities of consciousness'.[27] The posthumous *Anecdotes and Egotisms* of Henry Mackenzie, author of *The Man of Feeling* and whom Scott called 'our Scottish Addison', turn out to be, rather, the gossip of a Scottish Aubrey. The 'egotisms' are simply first-person anecdotes usually apologised for in advance: 'if I may be forgiven the egotism ... insignificant as I am'.[28] The trivial, pejorative connotations of the term represent a threat to its technical usage and such connotations may dominate it in Coleridge's own usage, as when he apologises for the 'inanity and egotism' of the letter informing Poole of his marriage (*CL*, I, 161). For some of his readers this was the abiding impression left by Coleridge's work. Emma Darwin, on reading Mrs Sandford's *Thomas Poole and his Friends* (1889), recorded that 'Every word of Coleridge's letters revolts me, they are a mixture of gush, mawkish egotism, and what seems like humbug.'[29] If, more than a half century after his death, the response to Coleridge's writings has progressed only from 'querulous' to 'mawkish', the accusation of egotism has stuck.

I cannot here go into the ways in which a claim for the positive value of 'egotism' affects the economic debate on individualism and I can only leave implicit its implied challenge to man's social responsibilities in Locke's formulation of government. For Locke, the law of nature does, however, justify a concern with all mankind. A person's obligations are 'moral' as well as prudential, and thus in joining a civil society it is to be understood that 'the fundamental natural law which is to govern even the legislative itself is the preservation of society and (as far as it will consist with the public good) of every person in it'.[30] Locke's very syntax here mimes the hierarchical superiority of 'the legislative itself', who are ascribed sole access to the imperatives of 'public good': and his parenthesis brackets a multitude of sins. (It is worth drawing close attention to Locke's prose here, because of the similarity of such disingenuousness to that sometimes apparent in Coleridge's – though to suggest the superiority of the legislative in 1690 is *radical*.) Leaving aside for now the question of Coleridge's own political views,[31] his earliest political writings do attack a passive obedience to social authority. Like Pigott, he does so characteristically by means of the rhetorical *contrarium*. The *Watchman*, between the sixth and seventh issues of which the 1796 *Poems* appeared, urges on its readers the Johannine injunction to know the truth that the truth may set them free. So, defending his published 'disapproval' of Godwin, he remarks that 'it is pleasant to observe with what absurd anxiety this little monosyllable [I] is avoided', and goes on, 'You condemn me as prejudiced – O this enlightened age! When it can be seriously charged against an Essayist, that he is prejudiced in favour of gratitude, conjugal fidelity, filial affection, and the belief of God and a hereafter!!' (*Watchman* [*CC*], pp. 195–6). It is the prejudices of the establishment of the 'age' that have deviated from first principles which it and Coleridge equally regard as sacrosanct: 'In the Dictionary of aristocratic Prejudice, Illumination and Sedition are classed as synonimes' (*Lectures 1795* [*CC*], p. 52). More crudely, Coleridge can demonstrate the folly of the Anglo-French war by juxtaposing a column listing its 'OBJECTS' against what is 'OBTAINED' (*Watchman* [*CC*], pp. 108–9), a series of direct opposites obviously incapable of reconciliation. It is significant, however, that the validity of Locke's social thought quite as much as of his epistemology is assumed by the aesthetics of the sublime against which, as I shall show in Chapter 5, Coleridge is implicitly in reaction. Burke's sublime and beautiful are derived respectively from the principles of '*self-preservation* and *society*'.[32] It is significant too for the next generation's view of his political 'apostasy' that De Quincey should use the phrase from the Preface in his recollections of Coleridge. In the course of a long digression on Richard Watson, the pluralist and absentee Bishop of Llandaff (the addressee of Wordsworth's *Letter*), De Quincey refers to the Bishop's 'querulous egotism' (*QCW*, II, 198).

I have tried to show the essential unity of concern in some earlier texts which Coleridge's Preface joins, despite the ostensible kinds of their discourses – political, philosophical, moral and so on. In doing this, of course, I might be making what philosophers call a category mistake, 'the presentation of the facts of one category in the idioms appropriate to another'.[33] If so, it is a mistake I shall repeat. The authority or decorum of discourse is the principle behind those examples of the prohibition or demotion of the 'I' with which I began. My concern is with the formal problems raised by the counter-assertion of an authority for the self. With these last two examples in mind, what Coleridge advances in that 1796 Preface as a literary concept may be seen as more pervasively and, specifically, more politically significant than it seems.

A more serious charge would be that I have treated Hume as a metaphysician rather than a moralist and Locke as a social theorist rather than a philosopher. In the cases of both Hume and Locke admission of the self as an embarrassingly recalcitrant function makes for a hiatus between their discussions of such a function and its articulation in their explorations of the limits, respectively, of morals and of the understanding. Coleridge himself writes of Kant's having liberated him from such empiricist limitations, but the effect of the presentation of self by Kant,

Fichte and Schelling – who all assign formal functions to what they call the self – is, I shall argue, to leave a similar hiatus. There are passages in Kant's *Critique of Pure Reason* which seem to offer the self as a kind of *Ding an sich*: an element which is irreducible but inarticulate. The *Ding an sich* was the point at which Fichte and Schelling discerned a point of leverage in the Kantian system. Kant's claim was that all elements should be capable of being articulated by the categories. Yet the *Ding an sich* can only be known in the forms of its representations. Although such an element can be dismissed as supplementary or aberrant (as Locke and Hume dismissed it), to take no more account of it within a philosophical system is to risk staging Hamlet without the Prince. Coleridge's 1796 Preface – and essays on egotism by Hazlitt and by Leigh Hunt – call attention to such risk, albeit within a non-technical vocabulary. Neither Locke nor Hume assuages such worries. Nor, finally, does Kant. I believe that it is Hegel who most convincingly deals with the implication that activity implies an agent: the self in Hegel projects ends for itself in which dualism is rather superseded than continually dissolved. Looking briefly at Coleridge's various definitions of two moral agencies, 'the will' and 'conscience', may help by more than analogy in the problem of defining the analogous activity of the self which he calls 'egotism'.

2 The Crucible and the Fire

And God said unto Moses, I AM THAT I AM: and he said, Thus shalt thou say unto the children of Israel, I AM hath sent me unto you. (Exodus 3:14)

Coleridge later calls this egotistical activity, in distinguishing it from mere volition, 'the will' – 'the true and only strict synonime of the word I, or the intelligent self' (*Friend* [*CC*], II, 279). It can be known only in the process of its own operations, knowing 'its own State in and by its Acts alone' (*AR*, p. 89). Within the associationism of David Hartley, which had seemed to Coleridge to provide a viable exit from the closed systems of Locke and Hume, it is illogical to suppose that the association of ideas has as its first cause an act of the will: 'Since . . . all Love and Hatred, all Desire and Aversion, are factitious, and generated by Association; *i.e.* mechanically; it follows that the Will is mechanical also.'[1] It is the element of the will that Coleridge insists must be added to Hartley, to 'control, determine, and modify the phantasmal chaos of association' (*BL* [*CC*], I, 116). One way in which 'the secondary imagination' is distinguished from the primary in the *Biographia* is by its coexistence 'with the conscious will' (I, 304). The will is an 'obscure Radical of the Vital Power' (*CL*, V, 406), the 'mysterious Ground of all things visible and invisible' (VI, 641), and as such the fallen state of man can be attributed to a disease of this faculty. The assertion of the will can usurp free will. In *The Statesman's Manual*, the egotistical perversion of the will 'in its utmost abstraction and consequent state of reprobation' (*LS* [*CC*], p. 65) is connected with the fallen angel Satan and with Napoleon, linked in much the same terms as in the passage quoted on page 6. I shall consider in Part IV the ambivalent response this draws from Coleridge, but in his later references to the will he has

19

identified some of the conditions for the ambivalence attaching to egotism.[2] Situating a moral sense on this 'mysterious Ground' could make it prey to the notorious subjectivism of Hume, for whom 'morality . . . is more properly felt than judg'd of' (*Treatise*, p. 470 [III. i. 2]).[3]

One way out of this dilemma is to hypostatise a moral tribunal which is static and substantial rather than active – something akin, in other words, to the theological self deconstituted by the scepticism of Locke and Hume. Such a hypostatisation is 'the conscience'. In the fifth and sixth essays of the *Friend*, Coleridge attempts to prove that truth is a 'right notion' of a speaker's intention and not a mere correspondence of signifier to signified. This proof is 'without reference to *consequences*' and distinguishes truth from gossip and calumny, '*Tell-truths* in the service of falsehood'. The only ground for truth can be the 'principle of self-consistence or moral integrity' (*Friend* [*CC*], I, 49). The conscience then knows but is unknowable, a 'Moral Being' as he writes in a long addition to Derwent Coleridge's copy of the three-volume *Friend* of 1818. Whether beginning from sensory evidence or an idea of the infinite,

> All *speculative* Disquisition must begin with Postulates, which the Conscience alone can at one authorize and substantiatione, and from whichever point the Reason may start . . . it will find a chasm, which the Moral Being only, which the Spirit and Religion of Man can alone fill up.   (*Friend* [*CC*], I, 523n)

If the moral criterion is not the consequence of particular actions then reliance on this 'Conscience' must be an act of faith: 'surely morality, which is of equal importance to all men, ought to be grounded, if possible, in that part of our nature which in all men may and ought to be the same: in the conscience and the common sense' (I, 314). That 'surely' is more imploring than certain. He does offer definitions of this 'part of our nature': the 'law of Conscience or universal *selfless* Reason' (I, 424n) which 'is neither reason, religion, or will, but an *experience* (sui generis) of the coincidence of the human will with reason and religion' (*LS* [*CC*], p. 66). However, the question remains as to what faculty is to be the arbiter of such an experience if not the experience itself.

In the remark from the *Friend* quoted on page 11, the analogy between the material and moral 'filling of a space' challenges the

heterogeneity of body and soul. Coleridge illustrates this when he
repeats word for word the *Biographia*'s description of the Cartesian
fission in the lectures on philosophy of 1818–19 (*PL*, p. 349), by
quoting Raphael's exposition of a world picture to Adam in
Paradise Lost.[4] It is a picture of nature as a dynamic organism to
which Coleridge would subscribe (he uses it too as epigraph to
chapter 13 of the *Biographia*), and which he sees Descartes as
having rejected. For him Descartes, and not Locke,

> was the first man who made nature utterly lifeless and godless,
> considered it as the subject of merely mechanical laws. And
> having emptied it of all its life and all that made it nature in
> reality, he referred all the rest to what he called 'spirit',
> consequently 'the faculty of spirit' in relation to this
> 'matter'.   (*PL*, pp. 376–7)

Like Descartes, however, the Milton passage insists on the
hierarchical dichotomy, or 'heterogeneity' of body (material,
space-filling) and soul or spirit (moral, thinking) of the second
sentence above. I shall turn in the next chapter to the way in
which such a dichotomy is analogous to the dichotomy, in Keats's
terms, of the protean (Shakespearean) and egotistical (Miltonic)
poet, but this is itself indicative of the need Coleridge insists on for
the 'balance or reconciliation' in the poet of 'opposite or
discordant qualities' (*BL*, [*CC*], II, 16). First he lists those pairs
of apparent opposites which, 'in ideal perfection', are to be
reconciled, then enters the qualification that 'harmony' is not
inconsistent with 'subordination' – for the imagination which
reveals itself as this balance 'still subordinates art to nature; the
manner to the matter; and our admiration of the poet to our
sympathy with the poetry' (II, 17). In moving 'from notional to
actual' we discover the result of their 'interpenetration' only 'in
the process of our own self-consciousness' (I, 299). While Raphael
at once goes on to assign 'intuition' to the angels and 'discourse' to
those below, Milton's 'discursive reason' is analytic and not
synthetic, offering the possibility that the process may be from
'body up to spirit'.

Even laying aside until the next chapter the difficulty of
distinguishing the poet from the poetry, the stance to which
Coleridge is committed by this 'notional' refusal of a subject–
object dichotomy is one that is ambivalent morally and difficult

practically. For Fichte, in the Introduction to *The Science of Knowledge* (*Wissenschaftslehre*), 'when all existence of or for the subject is taken away, it has nothing left but an act'.[5] Schelling derives his proposition from Fichte: 'Through the act of self-consciousness, the self becomes an object to itself.' The self is 'originally mere activity', and becomes an object only retrospectively as reconstructed 'for myself', for the philosopher. Fichtean 'freedom' is limited by this opposition.[6] Later Schelling deals with the apparent paradox of the 'empirical' and the *a priori* being the same. What, he asks, is the site of the *a priori* if not the self?

> For were it not wholly our own production, our knowledge would be either all given to us from without . . . or there would be nothing left but to suppose that some of it comes to us from outside, while the rest emerges from ourselves. Hence our knowledge can only be empirical through and through in that it comes wholly and solely from ourselves, *i.e.* is through and through *a priori*.   (p. 152)

It cannot be 'all given to us from without', owing to the necessity and universality of the Kantian categories: 'the self produces everything from itself'. Thus the self is not a kind of substrate, in which case everything would have to be produced backwards, or teleologically, in a circle (p. 153), but an object. There is then an absolute identity of 'mind' and 'nature': the categories *are* reality (p. 154). Such a solution, however, does not escape the dilemma Fichte recognises in his account of external knowledge as the positing of an opposition:

> So far as its being and determination are concerned, the opposing force is independent of the self . . . it exists *for the self* only insofar as it is posited *by the latter*, and otherwise has no existence for the self . . . the ultimate ground of all consciousness is an interaction of the self with itself, by way of a not-self that has to be regarded from different points of view. This is the circle from which the finite spirit cannot escape, and cannot wish to escape, unless it is to disown reason, and demand its own annihilation.   (*Science of Knowledge*, p. 248)

In striving for such different 'points of view' the self must remain as activity. Coleridge's assertion of the identity of subject and object in the *Biographia* (*BL* [*CC*], I, 276–80), which, as his daughter shows,[7] is a direct translation from Schelling, and for which 'the words spirit, self, and self-consciousness' will be used interchangeably (I, 272–3), is a programmatic restatement of the earlier, more tentative deduction,

> During the act of knowledge itself, the objective and subjective are so instantly united, that we cannot determine to which of the two the priority belongs. There is here no first, and no second; both are coinstantaneous and one. While I am attempting to explain this intimate coalition, I must suppose it dissolved. (I, 255)

This dissolution is a difficulty in the notebooks. Just as Hamlet's syntax fractures in soliloquy, in making the self the object as well as the subject of his consciousness, both scrutineer and scrutinised, Coleridge can discover himself only fragmentarily. He was himself inclined to see the nature of his achievement as fragmentary, and therefore a failure (*LS* [*CC*], p. 114n2) but, as in some of the major poems, the achieved object *is* the fragment, which imposes difficulties on the reader as well. Southey believes that it is 'the very essence of passion to speak in hints and fragments',[8] and Coleridge that the very essence of the 'man of education' is revealed by

> the unpremeditated and evidently habitual *arrangement* of his words, grounded on the habit of foreseeing, in each integral part, or (more plainly) in every sentence, the whole that he then intends to communicate. However irregular and desultory his talk, there is *method* in the fragments. (*Friend* [*CC*], I, 449)

So, although Coleridge nowhere propounds the fragment as a literary form in itself, as does Friedrich Schlegel, we are not to understand the fragments by reference to some actual or imaginary prior conception but to interpret them as autonomous, as actually and not potentially 'whole'.[9] The relevance of this principle to reading 'Kubla Khan' and 'Christabel' is clear, to say nothing of the differing organisations of fragments which constitute the two versions of 'Dejection'. Rewriting the *Cogito* as 'Sum quia sum; I am, because I affirm myself to be; I affirm myself to be because I am' (*BL* [*CC*], I, 275) is a theoretical commitment to a tautology.[10] If the self is activity, whether 'being' or 'becoming', writing may only offer fragments of that process.

In the 'Dissertation' Smith adduces the observation that a child at first speaks of itself in the third person in support of his contention that originally such 'abstract propositions' as 'I' were expressed by conjugation of the verb (*Theory*, II, 444). At the beginning of the late *Anthropology* (1798) Kant by-passes the problem of 'personal identity' in a manner similar to Hume:

> The fact that man can have the idea [*Vorstellung*] 'I' raises him infinitely above all the other beings living on earth . . . any language must *think* 'I' when it speaks in the first person, even if it has no special word to express it. For this power (the ability to think) is *understanding*.[11]

The 'I' then is the most necessary of fictions, the site of the categories or, as he puts it in *The Critique of Pure Reason*, the 'vehicle of all concepts',[12] and he therefore admits it to the list of transcendental concepts almost by default. When the child, speaking of itself initially in the third person, comes to represent the 'I' to himself, this is the beginning of reason: 'Before he merely *felt* himself; now he thinks himself.'[13]

In Locke and Hume we saw a denial of the self as substance. The inference that the 'I' which thinks is a substance or soul is one of the 'paralogisms' of which Kant disposes in *The Critique of Pure Reason*:

> [The] bare consciousness which accompanies all concepts . . . is known only through the thoughts which are its predicates, and of it, apart from them, we cannot have any concept whatsoever, but can only revolve in a perpetual circle, since any judgment upon it has already made use of its representation . . . consciousness in itself [*das Bewusstsein an sich*] is not a representation distinguishing a particular object, but a form of representation in general.   (pp. 331–2 [A346, B404])

The 'I' is not an unknowable *Ding an sich* but a formal function: *Bewusstsein an sich*. In the second edition Kant says,

> The unity of consciousness, which underlies the categories, is . . . mistaken for an intuition of the subject as object, and the

category of substance is then applied to it. But this unity is only unity in *thought*, by which alone no object is given, and to which, therefore, the category of substance, which always presupposes a given *intuition*, cannot be applied. Consequently, this subject cannot be known. (p. 377 [B422])

For Kant the self has an epistemological function: the understanding 'itself is nothing but the faculty of combining *a priori*, and of bringing the manifold of given representations under the unity of apperception'. This unity of activity is the site of the categories through which understanding becomes possible, and thus the 'principle of apperception is the highest principle in the whole sphere of human knowledge' (p. 154 [B135]). However this decision leaves such a site as a shadow area. Writing of the *a priori* representation of 'intuition' Kant says, 'it must be possible for the "I think" to accompany all my representations' (p. 152 [B131]): the transcendental analytic thus rests on the necessity of a possibility. As opposed to what he calls the 'empirical idealism' of Descartes, Kant's interest in the 'I think' is 'anthropological' and not 'psychological'; in the *cogito* itself and not in the *sum* which it predicates: 'The proposition 'I think', is . . . here taken only problematically, not in so far as it may contain perception of an existent (the Cartesian *cogito, ergo sum*), but in respect of its mere possibility . . .' (p. 332 [A347, B405]).

In one of his few explicit references to Kant, Hegel recognises that the Kantian 'Ego' is an epistemological function:

Kant, it is well known, did not put himself to much trouble in discovering the categories. 'I', the unity of self-consciousness, being quite abstract and completely indeterminate, the question arises, how are we to get at the specialized form of the 'I', the categories?

The terms of the problem have shifted from 'personal identity' to 'self-consciousness' and the solely formal status of the 'I' is, to Hegel, unsatisfactory. Like Fichte, to whom he assigns the 'great merit of having called attention to the need of exhibiting the *necessity* of [the Kantian] categories and giving a genuine *deduction* of them', he would distinguish this 'absolute' from any individual, empirical self. Thus, for Hegel, Kant's system is one of 'subjective idealism' in which

The 'I' is as it were the crucible and the fire which consumes the loose plurality of sense and reduces it to unity. . . . At the same time we must note that it is not the mere act of *our* personal self-consciousness which introduces an absolute unity into the variety of sense. Rather, this identity is itself the absolute. The absolute is, as it were, so kind as to leave individual things to their own enjoyment, and it again drives them back to the absolute unity.[14]

The second chapter of the *Anthropology* is 'On Egoism'. Where Kant sees 'egoism' only as excess, usurpation (*Unmassung*) this becomes, for Hegel, the absolute self he calls *Geist*. For Kant this usurpation occurs after the child's capability of self-representation: 'From the day a human being begins to speak in terms of "I", he brings forth his beloved self whenever he can, and egoism progresses incessantly.'[15]

Epistemologically necessary, the activity of the self is not morally neutral, and both sides of this coin are reflected on within, as they are reflected by, Coleridge's writings. The Cartesian 'heterogeneity' perpetuated by Locke and Hume clearly permits writing only a subordinate role – writing could only be a pale reflection of another pale reflection, 'thought' – which he intuitively rejects. Even Shaftesbury's 'trust' in an indeterminate is congruent with a *Logos*, the force of which, as both 'speech' and 'reason' was reasserted by neoclassicism.[16] There are dissentient voices of course. As early as 1710, in section 20 of the Introduction to *The Principles of Human Knowledge*, published that year in Dublin, Berkeley writes that 'passions' can be 'immediately' aroused 'upon the perception of certain words, without any ideas coming between'. 'Immediate': unmediated. The replacement of the serial mediation of 'things' by 'ideas' into 'discourse' will also have consequences for external authority claimed by language, as Berkeley also recognises.[17] The possibility which then arises of conflict between the Word and the words is something that will be considered in Chapter 6. It is a possibility of conflict which is problematic within a developing 'aesthetics'. The disruption of such consonance at the moral level is a consequence of the problematising of the 'passions' – unmediated outbursts of the 'natural' self. (The fashion for aesthetic Primitivism is an example of the attempt to accommodate them.) Hume's conflation of a dichotomy of 'reason' and 'passion' is directly relevant here: 'a

passion is an original existence . . . [which] contains not any
representative quality, which renders it a copy of any other
existence or ramification' (*Treatise*, p. 415 [II. iii. 3]). A shift
towards self-consciousness noticed in the differences between
Locke and Coleridge and sketched in Kant is noticed in literary
language too. While words can only be 'tokens' of ideas or
impressions which are themselves representations of the objects of
nature, taking the poem as an object is liable to disturb the surface
of an, ideally, homogeneous discourse. Such a disturbance is
registered by Burke. Under the rubric 'Poetry not strictly an
imitative art', he writes that 'nothing is an imitation further than
as it resembles some other thing; and words undoubtedly have
no sort of resemblance to the ideas for which they stand'
(*Philosophical Enquiry*, p. 173 [v. vi]). Then, interrupted by no more
than the heading for the next section, he goes on,

> Now, as words affect, not by any original power, but by
> representation, it might be supposed, that their influence over
> the passions should be but light; yet it is quite otherwise; for we
> find by experience that eloquence and poetry are as capable,
> nay indeed much more capable of making deep and lively
> impressions than any other arts, and even than nature itself in
> very many cases.

One of the reasons Burke gives for this derived, representational
power will be considered in Chapter 9 below. Another is
'sympathy':

> We take an extraordinary part in the passions of others, and . . .
> we are easily affected and brought into sympathy by any tokens
> which are shewn of them; and there are no tokens which can
> express all the circumstances of most passions so fully as words;
> so that if a person speaks upon any subject, he can not only
> convey the subject to you, but likewise the manner in which he
> is himself affected by it. (p. 173 [v.vii])

The conflict can be discerned also in the Latin lectures Robert
Lowth gave as Professor of Poetry at Oxford between 1741 and
1750 (translated into English in 1787). In treating of 'the Sublime
in General', Lowth opposes the 'language of the Passions' to that
of 'Reason'. The distinction is certainly that the former employs a

greater 'amplification', 'magnification' and 'exaggeration', but this is in fact a truer 'imitation': 'The mind, with whatever passion it be agitated, remains fixed upon the object that excited it'; and thus 'passion' is not the usurpation of the moral self but linguistically creative,

> illustrating the subject [object] with splendid imagery, and . . . employing new and extraordinary forms of expression, which are indeed possessed of great force and efficacy in this respect especially, that they in some degree imitate or represent the present habit and state of the soul. Hence those theories of Rhetoricians, which they have so pompously detailed, attributing that to art, which above all things is due to nature alone.[18]

That Burke and Lowth are here at odds in the relative priority they assign to 'nature' is, I think, less important than their common ground in what might be called a phenomenology of reading. Coleridge, then, is not being particularly revolutionary by writing in 1817 that 'language is framed to convey not the object alone, but likewise the character, mood and intentions of the person who is representing it' (*BL* [*CC*], II, 142). For Lowth, in the language of the passions 'conceptions should burst out in a turbid stream, expressive in a manner of the internal conflict' (*Lectures*, I, 308), but as will be seen in Chapter 6, he is concerned that the stream should not burst its banks.

Coleridge's notebooks, begun two years before the 1796 Preface, offer a prospective rather than retrospective representation of the growth of a poet's mind, 'the history of my own mind for my own improvement' (*CN*, II, 2368). Generalising, he again defers the achievement of the act's significance to a future time which cannot be located since it is a continuing process. That there should be a 'moment' to be located as the beginning of self-consciousness is, however, a necessary fiction, since such a moment must also be the moment of intellectual genesis: 'The moment, when the Soul begins to be sufficiently self-conscious, to ask concerning itself, and its relations, is the first moment of *intellectual* arrival into the World, – Its *Being* – enigmatic as it must seem – is posterior to its *Existence*' (III, 3593). The 'Soul' is brought into 'Being' by its own nascent consciousness of itself, yet then to regard it as fixed and dead would be a ludicrous inversion of the Cartesian hierarchy: the soul's arrival is not at a terminus. If self-consciousness is that which enables the self to be, then egotism enables it to do, the soul's activity. Here we are close to Kant's self as 'the vehicle of all concepts' and to Hegel's self as becoming – 'the understanding is thought, the pure "I" as such' [19] – to which Coleridge moves, but as an apostle of the transcendental philosophy Coleridge had the sense of himself as a voice crying in the wilderness, and it was an influence felt only gradually and painfully in England.[20] Indeed, until some time in the new century a much greater influence seems to have been operative in the other direction, from English to German.

So, this self or soul is still neither the empirical self of Locke and Hume nor the transcendental ego of the post-Kantians, and my evidence for what Coleridge puts in place of that empirical 'identity' which he intuitively suspects – even amidst his enthusiasm for Hartley – is necessarily drawn from much later writings than that earlier, tentative claim for what constitutes the chief interest in writing. Nor, in writing, is it merely the case that Coleridge 'goes beyond' Burke and Lowth. Perhaps it took Kant and Wittgenstein to teach us that 'passion', the yearning for expansion, must be a yearning for new bounds. For Coleridge, as for Wittgenstein, these bounds are linguistic. The breakdown of a subject–object dichotomy necessarily affects the relation of reader and text, of which it is a paradigm, and we can now turn to some literary implications of Coleridge's claim for 'egotism'.

3 Protean and Egotistical

The ambivalence with which 'egotism' is regarded stems from the relationship of enabling and affective qualities: in literary terms, egotism is not only a means of writing but also an effect upon the reader. Keats comes to see poetry as internally generating its own moral values, but the intentional aspect of perception which he finds asserted in Wordsworth and Milton is eventually deadening. Kant says that 'Egoism can take three forms of presumption [*dreierlei Unmassungen*]: presumption of understanding, of taste, and of practical interest; that is, egoism can be logical, aesthetic, or practical.'[1] Just as the received sense of 'egotism' is of something personally, stylistically and socially undesirable in moral terms, so the intrusion of 'egotism' into the moral autonomy of the poem is potentially destructive. The archetype of the egotistical poet for the Romantics is Milton, but their reading of his poetry cannot but be affected by their response to the historical Milton. Indeed, they could claim Milton's own authority for the observation that 'poets generally put something like their own opinions into the mouths of their best characters'.[2] Thus they read the blinded, libertarian Samson, imprisoned under a new and repressive regime, as a heroic self-portrait.

Dr Johnson's life of Milton similarly suggests that the man is the work or, at least, that the egotism he continually finds in the man is the motive force of the poetry. He says, for instance, of *The Reason of Church Government*, that

> in this book [Milton] discovers, not with ostentatious exultation, but with calm confidence, his high opinion of his own powers; and promises to undertake something . . . that may be of use and honour to his country. . . . From a promise like this, at once fervid, pious and rational, might be expected the *Paradise Lost*.[3]

Johnson is at once fascinated and repelled by Milton's

personality. He says of Milton's commanding his daughters to read to him in languages they did not understand, 'it is hard to determine whether the daughters or the father are most to be lamented'[4] Primarily he has no sympathy for Milton's politics, which he sees as contradicted by Milton's own domestic authoritarianism. Finally for Johnson, the consistency of Milton's personality is in its egotism:

> Milton's republicanism was, I am afraid, founded in an envious hatred of greatness, and a sullen desire of independence; in petulance impatient of controul, and pride disdainful of superiority. He hated prelates in the church; for he hated all whom he was required to obey. It is to be suspected, that his predominant desire was to destroy rather than establish, and that he felt not so much the love of liberty as repugnance to authority.[5]

I have quoted from the account of Milton's life rather than that of his *Paradise Lost* and it is perhaps not surprising that Johnson's conclusions as to Milton's 'character' should involve some prejudgement of his poetry. Isaac D'Israeli's reminder of the difference between the two itself occurs in an essay concerned not with the work but the character. He writes of 'the little alliance between the literary and personal dispositions of an author. . . . The impiety of Satan, might equally be attributed to the poet. . . . A poet is a painter of the soul; if he seizes its deformities, he is a great artist but not therefore a bad man.'[6] It is the 'therefore' which is insidious. What might this mean when applied to an author long dead, such as Milton, who is alluded to here? The name signifies both a body of work and a historical individual which, historically at least, bore some relation.

De Quincey's essay 'On Milton' (1839) plays with the notion of the contract existing between writer and reader: 'the feudal relation of fealty (*fidelitas*) may subsist between them' in either order. De Quincey still mocks the written flattery of 'the reader', but his playful opening is not merely playful, for it is the example of Milton that calls this stable relationship into question: 'The man erred, and his error terminates in itself. But an error of principle does *not* terminate in itself: it is a fountain, it is self-diffusive, and it has a life of its own.' So, although De Quincey's avowed purpose – to which he moves in the second part of his essay – is to refute Addison and Johnson's strictures of an indecorous mixture of dictions and mythologies, his fundamental interest is in coming to terms with Milton's presence: 'Milton is not an author amongst authors, not a poet amongst poets, but a power amongst powers; and the "Paradise Lost" is not a book amongst books, not a poem amongst poems, but a central force amongst forces' (*QCW*, x, 396–9).

There are analogues too for the opposed, Shakespearean presence as Proteus which I shall look at in Keats and Coleridge. William Richardson distinguishes imitation from description by the passive inferiority of the latter, comparing a passage from *Le Cid* to a soliloquy from *Hamlet*: 'Shakespeare imitates, Corneille describes'.[7] Richardson continues by attempting to define such imitation: it 'can never be effectuated, unless the poet in some measure becomes the person he represents, clothes himself with his character, assumes his manners, and transposeth himself into his situation'. In then enumerating the qualities necessary to doing so, Richardson prefers 'affection' and 'imagination' to 'sympathy', concluding that 'nothing affords a stronger evidence of the active, versatile nature of the soul, and of the amazing rapidity of its motions, than these seemingly inconceivable and inconsistent exertions'.[8] It is these sympathetic, self-annihilating qualities which are possessed pre-eminently by Shakespeare: 'Possessing extreme sensibility, and uncommonly susceptible, he is the Proteus of the drama; he changes himself into every character, and enters easily into every condition of human nature.'[9] More polemically, in August Wilhelm Schlegel's *Vorlesungen* of 1809, the view of Shakespeare as a 'careless pupil of nature' is countered by the assertion that he has 'the capability of transporting himself so completely into every situation . . . that he is enabled, as plenipotentiary of the whole human race, without particular instructions for each case, to act and speak in the name of every individual'. Shakespeare is Promethean, but 'from the diversity of tone and colour, which he assumes according to the qualities of objects, a true Proteus'.[10]

In the 1797 Preface, Coleridge's sense that the ascription of 'egotism' need not be pejorative was justified by reference to Milton, and in a notebook entry of 1801 he bolsters his defence of the word:

Milton in his prose works – &c – and those in similar

circumstances who from prudence abstain from Egotism in their writings, are still egotists among their friends – / It would be unnatural effort not to be so / & Egotism in such cases is by no means offensive to a kind & benevolent nature. . . . (*CN*, I, 904).

That the immediate historical pressures that led to the production of Milton's prose works should have forced him to suppress his inherent egotism is itself a biographical inference, but the 'unnatural effort not to be' egotistical recalls the description in the 1796–7 prefaces of the forcible attempt to escape from the egotism of the 'violent emotions of sorrow . . . [which] is a painful and in general an unavailing effort' (*PW*, II, 1136, 1144); and, as for those who not from political 'prudence' but from a sense of social or literary decorum suppress and pretend to abhor egotism, 'Observe, watch those men – their habits of feeling & thinking are made up of *contempt*, which is the concentrated Vinegar of Egotism' (*CN*, I, 904). (Egotism must therefore once have been wine – perhaps the Satanic 'alcohol of egotism' [*MiscCrit*, p. 163, cited in Ch. 1].) If, as I shall argue, egotism as a quality of the 'poetical character' is an opposite with which the protean spirit of Shakespeare can be reconciled, then we may accept Coleridge's claim that his own egotism derives from an impulse to become one with his subject, and his readers, or auditors:

Egoistic Talk *with me* very often the effect of my love of the Persons to whom I am talking / My Heart is talking of them / I cannot talk continuously of them to themselves – so I seem to be putting into their Heart the same continuousness as to me, that is in my own Heart as to them – . . . . (*CN*, I, 1772)

This observation seems to be an empirical analogue of the later claim for the 'interpenetration', the oneness of subject and object. At the same time it calls up the other possible result of egotism: that it will in fact distort perception and hinder the process of interpenetration. The emphasised '*with me*' egotistically insists on Coleridge's possible uniqueness while at the same time suggesting that this very uniqueness may detract from the authority of the observation generally.

In a note quoted above Coleridge says that egotists are boastful 'often because they introduce <real or> apparent novelty – which

excites great opposition – <personal> opposition creates reaction (which is of course a consciousness of power) associated
with the *person* reacting' (I, 904). He distinguishes once more
between egotism as a psychological characteristic and as Satanic
or Napoleonic action; a distinction between man and work which
is not always made by those of his contemporaries who accuse him
of egotism. For example, Hazlitt was prepared, in reviewing
the *Biographia* in August 1817, to condemn Coleridge as 'a
disappointed demagogue . . . indulging his maudlin egotism and
his mawkish spleen' (*HW*, XVI, 106). In the later biographic
portrait of Coleridge in *The Spirit of the Age*, while still regarding
'egotist' as a condemnatory epithet Hazlitt praises him in
personal terms: 'Mr. Coleridge talks of himself, without being an
egotist, for in him the individual is always merged in the abstract
and general' (*HW*, XI, 31). Such a merger is for Hazlitt
antithetical to egotism, and in his attitude to Milton too he
represents the spirit of the age in regarding Keats's 'egotistical'
and 'protean' as opposites incapable of reconciliation.

Although the prefaces of 1796–7 insist on egotism as a property
of lyric poems, in history or epic it 'is to be condemned . . . only
when it offends against time and place' (*PW*, II, 1136, 1144), and
in the 1797 Preface the example Coleridge adduces of a poetry
which is affecting by virtue of its 'egotism' is extracted from epic.
The blind Milton hailing the light *in propria persona* is taken to be
self-evidently affecting: 'I should almost suspect that man of an
unkindly heart, who could read the opening of the third book of
the Paradise Lost without peculiar emotion' (II, 1144). More than
twenty years later he returns to the passage with a more complex
understanding of his response:

> The apostrophe to light at the commencement of the third book
> is particularly beautiful as an intermediate link between Hell
> and Heaven; and observe how the second and third books
> support the subjective character of the poem. In all modern
> poetry in Christendom there is an under consciousness of a
> sinful nature, a fleeting away of external things, the mind or
> subject greater than the object, the reflective character
> predominant. In the *Paradise Lost* the sublimest parts are the
> revelations of Milton's own mind, producing itself and evolving
> its own greatness; and this is truly so, that when that which is

merely entertaining for its objective beauty is introduced, it at first seems a discord. (*MiscCrit*, p. 164)[11]

The first thing to be said here is that Coleridge makes metonymic use of the Milton passage, for instance in 'This Lime-tree Bower my Prison'. Milton claims a superior insight as more than compensating for his loss of eyesight:

> So much the rather thou, celestial light,
> Shine inward, and the mind through all her powers
> Irradiate, there plant eyes, all mist from thence
> Purge and disperse, that I may see and tell
> Of things invisible to mortal sight.
>
> (*Paradise Lost*, III. 51–5)

For all that the sensory (and temporal) 'displacements' of Coleridge's poems serve, as I shall show, to liberate him from closed systems such as those of Locke and Hume, they are all antedated by this passage from Milton's invocation of 'thoughts, that voluntary move / Harmonious numbers'.

Secondly, there is an admiration in the Coleridge passage not for the specific means (whether blindness or a pan of boiling milk spilled on the foot) by which such sublimity is achieved, but for the spirit in which it is done; for the activity of mind rather than for that of the mind of Milton. Compare Payne Knight:

> it is not with the agonies of a man writhing in the pangs of death, that we sympathise, on beholding the celebrated group of Laocoon and his sons; for such sympathies can only be painful and disgusting; but it is with the energy and fortitude of mind, which those agonies call into action and display: for though every feature and every muscle is convulsed, and every nerve contracted, yet the breast is expanded and the throat compressed to show that he suffers in silence.[12]

This late efflorescence of the sublime effect resembles Coleridge's response to *Paradise Lost*: 'the Objectivity consists', he says, 'in the universality of its subjectiveness'.[13] Knight's associationist 'sympathy' resembles too, in this respect, Fichte's *Egoismus*. Despite Coleridge's lampooning of the latter as 'all my I' in the *Biographia* (*BL* [*CC*], I, 157–60), Fichte's 'Ego' begins as the individual, empirical subject but ascends to the 'Idea', of which the individual subject is a limited mode: there is no recognition of the 'ego' without that active recognition of the 'non–ego' which is self-consciousness (*Science of Knowledge*, pp. 83–5). Milton's egotism is 'producing' and 'evolving' in the act of reading.

In saying that the lyric poem necessarily derives from 'egotism', Coleridge prefigures the more prescriptive account of the Schlegel brothers, who apply a subjective–objective dichotomy to poetry, holding the lyric to be the thoroughly subjective form, the epic purely objective, and drama a composite or intermediate form. Despite this, *Paradise Lost* is taken as the apotheosis of the 'subjective'. It is taken as metonymic of Milton himself – and vice versa. Milton possessed

> an Imagination to which neither the Past nor the Present was interesting except so far as they called forth and enlive[ne]d the great Ideal, in which and for which he lived, a keen love of Truth which after many weary pursuits found an harbour in a sublime listening to the low still voice in his own spirit.   (*MiscCrit*, pp. 159–60)[14]

Although he insistently generalises ('in all modern poetry in Christendom'), Coleridge is concerned not merely with the theoretical reconciliation of opposites but with analysing his responses to a text; and in his reading the 'subjective' in Milton's poetry is not a biographical inference (though complicated by that) but the product of such analysis. Where Coleridge goes on to speak of Milton's 'egotism' – these early prefaces being the first of many formulations – this tends towards an analysis of what Keats called 'the poetical character', in defining it as essentially opposed to Milton's (*KL*, I, 386).

The pervasiveness of the Romantics' dichotomy of the egotistical Milton and the protean Shakespeare owes much to the fact that, whereas Milton's biography is 'known', Shakespeare's (or Homer's) is not, but Coleridge's claim is that 'the sublimest parts' are precisely those which stand out as 'the revelations of Milton's own mind' while he insists that Shakespeare's plays are a seamless fabric in which 'character' stands to the play in the relation of the part to the whole (*ShakCrit*, II, 96).[15] Objectivity, by its nature, is not to 'fill a station' so as to 'exclude or repel others' but to take on, and into the creating self, numerous individual subjectivities:

> There is no subjectivity whatever in the Homeric poetry. There is a subjectivity of the poet, as of Milton, who is himself before himself in everything he writes; and there is a subjectivity of the *persona*, or dramatic character, as in all Shakespeare's great creations, *Hamlet, Lear* &c.   (*TT*, 12 May 1830)

The poetry creates a 'John Milton' who subjugates character to his own purposes – and this is egotism:

> In the *Paradise Lost* – indeed in every one of his poems – it is Milton himself whom you see; his Satan, his Adam, his Raphael, almost his Eve – are all John Milton; and it is a sense of this intense egotism that gives me the greatest pleasure in reading Milton's work. The egotism of such a man is a revelation of spirit.   (18 August 1833)

Shakespeare, on the other hand, has destroyed the subject–object dichotomy existing between the poet and his characters: 'Shakespeare is the Spinozistic deity – an omnipresent creativeness. . . . Shakespeare's poetry is characterless; that is, it does not reflect the individual Shakespeare; but John Milton himself is in every line of the *Paradise Lost*' (12 May 1830). These remarks amplify the distinction Coleridge makes between the two poetical characters at the end of his chapter on *Venus and Adonis* in the *Biographia*. Shakespeare's creativity derives not from an 'act of will' but from 'the inspiration of a genial and productive nature' (*BL* [*CC*], II, 19); and he goes on apparently to confute the early prefaces: 'I have found, that where the subject is taken immediately from the author's personal sensations and experiences, the excellence of a particular poem is but an equivocal mark, and often a fallacious pledge, of genuine poetic power' (II, 20). Like the praise twenty years earlier for poetry 'in which the author develops his own feelings' this is offered as a generalisation from experience; and, though 'most interesting' is not synonymous with 'excellent' or 'poetically powerful', the passages are mutually contradictory. Yet in both cases Coleridge is discussing the response to poetry, distinguishing here between intention and effect. The implication is also that those 'sublimest parts' of *Paradise Lost* in which Milton does speak in his own person are read as such precisely because they occur within the vast and potentially engulfing conception of the epic. Later in the *Biographia* Coleridge states that 'we can only *know* by the act of *becoming*' (*BL* [*CC*], II, 244), and this is the principle by which he distinguishes Shakespeare, who 'darts himself forth, and passes into all the forms of human character and passion, the one Proteus of the fire and the Flood' while 'all things and modes of action shape themselves anew in the being of Milton' (II, 27–8).

In 'On Genius and Common Sense', Hazlitt also distinguishes an egotistical Milton from a protean Shakespeare: in Milton 'you trace the bias and opinions of the man in the creations of the poet', while Shakespeare has 'the faculty of transforming himself at will into whatever he chose. . . . He was the Proteus of human intellect' (*HW*, VIII, 42); again, in *Lectures on the English Poets*, Shakespeare 'had only to think of anything in order to become that thing, with all the circumstances belonging to it' (*HW*, V, 48). De Quincey, in introducing Jean-Paul Richter to an English readership, does so in the context of the same distinction (*QCW*, XI, 266). Coleridge's distinction however, unlike those of Hazlitt and De Quincey, implies no moral disapproval of the Miltonic egotism, while Hazlitt blames Milton because 'he saw all objects from his own point of view' and praises Shakespeare as 'the least of an egotist that it was possible to be' (*HW*, V, 230, 47).

Referring to Leigh Hunt and Wordsworth, Keats writes that he prefers grandeur and merit which are 'uncontaminated & unobtrusive' (*KL*, I, 225). Keats shares Hazlitt's sense that these opposites cannot be reconciled and that the distinction entails a moral choice. In his more famous distinction, Keats recognises the 'Wordsworthian or egotistical sublime' while aligning his own poetical character with that of the Shakespearean 'camelion Poet', which 'is not itself – it has no self – it is everything and nothing – It has no character – . . . A Poet is the most unpoetical of anything in existence; because he has no identity – he is continually in for and filling some other Body – . . .' (I, 387), and thus is subject to no morality outside his art, within which he can take 'as much delight in conceiving an Iago as an Imogen'.[16] Clearly Keats has Shakespeare in mind when remarking that 'Men of Genius are those who have not any individuality, any determined Character' (I, 184). Shaftesbury anticipates Keats by more than a century when he writes of the characterless 'mirror-faculty' of Homer but, in a striking verbal anticipation of Keats, Shaftesbury's 'author who writes in his own person' and is 'no certain man, nor any certain or genuine character' is a coquette, attracting attention to himself, flattering the reader. In dialogue the 'I' and 'thou' of the author is 'annihilated' but the form is now dead: 'The ancients could see their own faces, but we cannot.'[17] In the *Friend*, Coleridge agrees: 'O! for one piece of egotism that presents itself under its own honest bare face of "I myself I", there are fifty that steal out in the mask of *tuisms* and *ille-isms*!' (*Friend* [*CC*], I, 26). Egotism can be a reciprocal activity, but Coleridge enjoins effort as the condition of such reciprocity. There may equally be a hindering egotism in the reader, blaming a lack of effort on obscurity or dullness on the part of the writer. When the reader likes a work it is because he or she can exclaim, 'this I can understand and admire. I have thought the very same a hundred times myself. In other words, this man has reminded me of my own cleverness, and therefore I admire him' (ibid.). Recombining these passages, the implication is again that it is precisely this bare-faced egotism which may succeed in breaking down the division between 'I' and 'thou', the dichotomy of subject and object as it pertains to the processes of reading and writing. (Such a reciprocal activity is relevant too to the metaphor of reading the language of nature discussed in Chapter 8.)

For Keats, determined characters produce determinate works of art and 'Men of Genius' are only chameleon-like, but Coleridge celebrates Shakespeare and Milton equally as occupying the twin 'glory-smitten summits of the poetic mountain' (*BL* [*CC*], II, 27). He alludes to the Wordsworthian egotistical sublime in the poem to his friend. Despite the loss of revolutionary hope recorded in the course of *The Prelude*, Wordsworth can regard the vision, 'Calm and sure / From the dread watchtower of man's absolute self' (*PW*, I, 405). Despite the claims made for the dramatic voice in the enlarged *Lyrical Ballads* Preface of 1802 (*WPr*, I, 138), Wordsworth himself accepts both the commonly made dichotomy and the place his poetical character occupies within it, aligning himself, in his Preface to the *Poems* of 1815, with 'the enthusiastic and meditative imagination' of Milton and Spenser, not with the 'human and dramatic imagination' of Chaucer and Shakespeare (*WPr*, III, 34–5).

Coleridge differs from Keats in his insistence that the protean faculty too is at the command of the will. A notebook entry summarises an (apparently) already written lecture on Shakespeare:

> That these feelings were under the command of *his own Will* – that in his very first productions he projected his mind out of his own particular being, & felt and made others feel, on subjects no way connected with himself, except by force of Contemplation – & that sublime faculty by which a great mind becomes that which it meditates on. (*Cn*, III, 3290).

Shakespeare's practice thus fulfils the theoretical desideratum of the *Biographia*: 'the act of contemplation makes the thing contemplated' (*BL* [*CC*], I, 251–2). Yet, even while Milton's egotism might seem to trap his practice within a single consciousness, however capacious, his epic also creates a dramatic character with the potential for subverting the magisterial authority of his own creator. Of course, such a view of Satan does not spring forth fully formed from the Romantics. When Johnson says, in the Preface to the *Dictionary*, that 'Words are the daughters of earth, and things are the sons of heaven', biblical language is applied to the disjunction of that 'original' unity of word and thing, an inextricable link between word and action which is acknowledged of Milton's God by his Satan: 'what he decreed / He effected' (*Paradise Lost*, IX.151). 'The language of poetry', as Hazlitt puts it, 'naturally falls in with the language of power (*HW*, IV, 214), and the attraction of Satan as an example may be as a way back to rather than out of such an objectification of desire, within a self which is subject and actor rather than object and patient. 'Power' a recurrent concern in Hazlitt, infects the language of poetry with problems from the languages of morals and of politics. These are problems of authority, however, which are better discussed in terms of Coleridge's own egotistical characters, from Robespierre and Osorio to Kubla Khan – whose 'decree' is similarly performative – and Napoleon. (I shall argue for the continuity of the fictional and the historical character in Part IV.) Such characters exert a fascination for Coleridge. However if Milton and his Satan are seen to be at odds in a reading of *Paradise Lost*, the contraries are reconcilable in terms of their shared egotism. While Coleridge is not, therefore, prepared to demote the Miltonic poetical character in favour of the Shakespearean, those contemporaries whose distinctions imply a moral hierarchy are apt to find in Coleridge's own character both a distorting egotism and a debilitating lack of will.

De Quincey, for example, complains of Coleridge's tendency 'to project his own mind, and his own very peculiar ideas, nay, even his own expressions and illustrative metaphors, upon other men, and to contemplate these reflex images from himself, as so many characters having an absolute ground in some separate object' (*QCW*, II, 185). This abuse of power, filling a space just so as to exclude or repel others, is redolent of attitudes to Milton; but if this egotistical mode is to be rejected there are concomitant dangers in the Shakespearean mode. Again, Hazlitt's is the clearest illumination. In 'My First Acquaintance with Poets' he quotes Coleridge himself from 1798, when 'some comparison was introduced between Shakespeare and Milton', as implying that Shakespeare's protean characterlessness is in fact an absence, a lack of character: '"he was as tall and as strong, with infinitely more activity than Milton, but he never appeared to have come to man's estate; or if he had he would not have been a man but a monster"' (*HW*, XVII, 120–1). This might be compared with Coleridge's judgement of the work of Milton, 'producing itself and evolving its own greatness', but it is, rather, suggestive of the way Hazlitt displaces the Shakespeare–Milton dichotomy onto Coleridge and Wordsworth in the same essay. He observes of Coleridge's walk

> that he continually crossed me on the way by shifting from one side of the foot-path to the other. This struck me as an odd movement; but I did not at that time connect it with any instability of purpose or involuntary change of principle, as I have done since. He seemed unable to keep on in a straight line   (XVII, 113)

and the inference Hazlitt draws from Coleridge's meandering gait is expanded a few pages later into the pedestrian dichotomy,

> There is a *chaunt* in the recitation both of Coleridge and Wordsworth, which acts as a spell upon the hearer and disarms the judgement. . . . Coleridge's manner is more full, animated and varied; Wordsworth's more equable, sustained, and internal. The one might be termed more *dramatic*, the other more *lyrical*. Coleridge has told me that he himself liked to

compose in walking over uneven ground, or breaking through
the straggling branches of a copse-wood; whereas Wordsworth
always wrote (if he could) walking up and down a straight
gravel-walk, or in some spot where the continuity of his verse
met with no collateral interruption.   (xvii, 118–19)

Hazlitt suggests the sporadic, fragmentary, pervious nature of
Coleridge's poetical (and political) character, distinguishing it
from the 'equable, sustained and internal' course of Wordsworth,
which brooks no interruption.[18] On the other hand, although
Wordsworth's voice is 'dramatic' in the sense he claims for the
Lyrical Ballads, it is a step away from the *self*-dramatising voice for
which Milton can be condemned.

The observations of Hazlitt and De Quincey can stand for those
of other contemporaries; the one reports Coleridge's egotism, the
other his characterlessness. In trying to effect a reconciliation of
opposites, he could be seen as falling between two stools. The
Miltonic–Shakespearean dichotomy is an indication of the
ambivalent status of egotism for many writers contemporary with
Coleridge, and metonymic of the Cartesian wound. Keats's letters
provide the sharpest delineation of the dichotomy between
identity-as and identity-with: a dichotomy which, following him,
I have called egotistical and protean.[19]

From Chapters 1 and 2 emerged a definition of self as
activity. The later adumbration of Milton as egotistical and
monolithic is opposed to a 'pure' activity (Shakespeare, negative
capability). Coleridge identifies this dichotomy, in the double
sense of that verb, both recognising and reconciling. The critical
shorthand becomes a problem of writing and of interpretation.
'Egotistical' and 'protean' imply and, I would suggest, involve
each other. As compared to, say, Johnson's, Coleridge's readings
of Shakespeare or of Milton are often no more than appropriations
in the name of different emphases: two sides of the same
(circulating) coin, as I shall argue in Chapter 6. Coleridge's own
doubts about the validity of egotism can help to explain the
ambivalent, vacillatory structure of 'The Eolian Harp' and 'Frost
at Midnight'; but first I shall briefly suggest some ways in which
two earlier texts are themselves affected by such ambivalence.

4 Who Wrote Gray's 'Elegy'?

The sense of egotism as indecorous which was noticed in Addison and Blair informs Gray's 'Elegy' more profoundly than at the level of local 'style', for it is written out of a tension implied by the rhetorical imperative and involving the presentation of the poet within the poem. Gray concludes an earlier version with a self-apostrophe, 'thou who mindful of the unhonour'd Dead / Dost in these Notes their artless Tale relate', which leads to a final Christian–Stoic reconciliation:

> No more with Reason & thyself at Strife
> Give anxious Cares & endless Wishes room
> But thro' the cool sequester'd Vale of Life
> Pursue the silent Tenour of thy Doom.[1]

This conclusion, as his editor comments,

> ultimately failed to satisfy Gray, partly because it was too explicitly personal for publication, but also no doubt because its very symmetry and order represented an over-simplification of his own predicament, of the way he saw his own life and wished it to be seen by society. A simple identification with the innocent but uneducated villagers was mere self-deception.[2]

In the final version, the pervading melancholy of Gray's concern with the prospect of his own annihilation is projected onto the rural society.

There remains a tension between the luck of the 'cool sequester'd vale' and the acknowledged repression of 'chill Penury' in village life; but a new tension is created within the decorous sententiae of the end-stopped quatrains: a tension between the soliloquy and the fact that its only audience can be the dead villagers, its ostensible subject (Gray calls the poem 'an elegy', another change from the earlier, Eton College manuscript, which has 'Stanza's' [*sic*]). Gray ascribes to the villagers a quiet heroism, 'far from the madding crowd', but the ambivalent praise for retirement is owing also to a bitter lack of faith in the possible reception of the poet's work by the literary culture of the madding crowd. The art of the panegyrist is contrasted with the villagers' retirement. They were

> Forbade to wade through slaughter to a throne,
> And shut the gate of mercy on mankind;
>
> The struggling pangs of conscious truth to hide,
> To quench the blushes of ingenuous shame,
> Or heap the shrine of Luxury and Pride
> With incense kindled at the Muse's Flame.[3]

Yet retirement implies a prior engagement: which entails that the tension is felt by the poet alone. The poet who is 'overheard' in the first twelve lines is an observer of rather than participant in nature and the villagers' lifestyle – which is presented in lines 17–28 as a pastoral reconciliation with nature. (I shall return to the analogy of spatial with psychological distance in Part III. Here of course the gap is primarily social.) Gray is an outsider within the rural society as well. Indeed, as the 'hoary-headed swain' evokes the poet figure at the end of the poem, the nearest he comes to filling a role within the rural society is as the village idiot:

> 'Muttering his wayward fancies he would rove;
> Now drooping, woeful wan, like one forlorn,
> Or craz'd with care, or cross'd in hopeless love.'

This 'rustic' poet too is an outsider, rapt in himself like Gray in the churchyard, yet distanced from him. We are unable to identify this poet figure because of the way in which he is addressed prior to the enquiry as to his 'fate': 'For thee, who mindful of the unhonoured dead / Dost in these lines their artless tale relate'. 'For thee', we are told, but 'thee' in this final version is less clearly Gray himself than the earlier 'thou' who is finally enjoined to accept obscurity. Is this a self-apostrophe, or is it addressed to the stonecarver who, although 'unletter'd', has incised the epitaph? 'These lines' could be either the lapidary epitaph or this poem written by Thomas Gray. If Gray is addressing himself there is a grammatical displacement. The only occurrence of the first-person pronouns is in the fourth line, 'And leaves the world to darkness, and to me'. While 'and to me' is made to seem syntactically superadded, almost an afterthought, it is of course foregrounded by its stanzaic position and, therefore, by rhyme.

In then going on to detail the 'homely joys and destiny obscure' of the vilagers, Gray implicitly sets theirs beside his own, paradoxically suggesting the promise of poetic immortality by its denial. The question whether he too may be a 'mute inglorious Milton' is never asked. It is the headstones not the 'Elegy' whose 'uncouth rhymes . . . the place of fame and elegy supply'. If, then, 'these lines' are not the lines Gray writes, ostensibly to elegise the villagers, but those written by a rustic poet, now himself in the oblivion of death, it must be the 'fate' of the dead stonecarver not of Gray which is related by the 'hoary-headed swain'. As a result, the identity of the 'youth' for whom 'th'unletter'd muse' has composed the epitaph is ambiguous.

Lest it be thought that I am playfully finding difficulties in a poem which, as Johnson says, finds an echo in every bosom, I shall here cite John Walker, from a rhetorical textbook which was reprinted nine times up to 1823. Walker assumes a sharp division between the voices of the 'melancholy' Gray and the 'indifferent' swain, in advising against accenting this second voice when reading the poem aloud:

> Nothing can be conceived more truly ridiculous, in reading this passage, than quitting the melancholy tone of the relator, and assuming the indifferent and rustic accent of the old swain; and yet no error so likely to be mistaken for a beauty by a reader of no taste; while a good reader, without entirely dropping the plaintive tone, will abate it a little, and give it a slight tincture only of the indifference and rusticity of the person introduced.[4]

Walker is referring to lines 93–100, the point at which Gray himself ostensibly 'quits' narration of his poem, displacing his own voice first onto 'some hoary-headed swain' and then onto the epitaph. The salient point here is that Walker's advice is contained within his chapter on prosopopoeia – defined as 'the investing of qualities or things inanimate with the character of persons'[5] – so Walker implicitly accepts that the villagers have as little animation as the gravestones, that the 'person introduced' merely ventriloquises for the poet who has withdrawn.

Assuredly, what Walker explicitly recognises is a homogeneity of tone which is more important than the voice of any individual 'character' in the poem. This is also the consensus reached by essays which the editor of a casebook on the 'Elegy' has grouped under the rubric of '"The Stonecutter" Controversy'.[6] The problem I have just elaborated is not one that can be 'solved', for the textual evidence, at least for this tension, is incontrovertible. The essay in that volume by Frank Hale Ellis points out that the stonecutter is evoked in conventional pastoral terms: 'The Stonecutter is not Thomas Gray', he concludes; 'he is Corydon *cum* Colin Cloute *cum* Jaques *cum* Lycidas.'[7] Ellis's New Critical orientation (he exposes something he calls the Biographical Fallacy) also leads him to assume a controlled, governing irony – so the 'me' of the poem is only 'the Spokesman'. Gray however is implicated in his own irony, as I hope I have shown. Although my own interest is in Coleridge's manner of dealing with what I take to be similar problems, there is room for more speculation as to the reasons for the withdrawal I have mapped in the 'Elegy'.

The withdrawal is strategic, displacing the responsibility for the achievement of signification onto a series of voices other than the 'me' of the fourth line, a progressive distancing which is indeed achieved by something like prosopopoeia.[8] This displacement of significance is a strategy that certain poems by Coleridge and Wordsworth deploy far from covertly. The 'Elegy', then, is a paradigm of the form to be taken by the 'conversation poems'. It moves from that single first-person singular into a kind of repressed dialectic of self and society, finally withdrawing from an assertion of the reintegration of the self at a higher level. The stance of withdrawn 'superiority' rationalises a political as well as metaphysical subject–object distance. Writers on society want at once to be involved in the picture as useful producers and to be possessed of a panoramic view of it: yet it is impossible to be convinced at once of right action and of 'an equal, wide survey'.[9] This of course is exactly the dilemma of Gray in the 'Elegy'. In Part III I shall suggest that, while this displacement results from a tacit acceptance of 'egotism', it results in turn in a questioning of it. Here, I want to show how in a work of German rather than of

English 'sensibility' the self is taken beyond the threshold of crisis.

In Coleridge's essay on the slave trade published in the *Watchman* for 25 March 1796, a slighting reference to 'the refined sorrows of Werter' goes to substantiate the assertion that 'Sensibility is not Benevolence. Nay, by making us tremblingly alive to trifling misfortunes, it frequently prevents it, and induces effeminate and cowardly selfishness' (*Watchman* [*CC*], p. 139).[10] But this sense is in fact comprehended by Goethe's novel. In the early ('Homeric') part of *Die Leiden des jungen Werthers* the concern with the 'feelings of an artist' vacillates between the resolve 'only to copy Nature for the future. Nature is inexhaustible, and alone forms the greatest masters', and a shackling self-consciousness, the feeling that the external world is 'but a dream': 'I examine myself; and what do I find? Alas! more vague desires, presages and visions, than I find of conviction, truth and reality: then all is chaos and confusion before my eyes; and dreaming like others, I let myself be carried away by the stream.'[11] In the German the first sentence reads, 'Ich kehre in mich selbst zurück und finde eine Welt!' (I return into myself and find a world).[12] Later Werther will find in the return to the self only vacuity, but this very vacuity enables him to identify himself with Christ:

> This is the voice of a creature oppressed beyond all resource, and who feels with terror that he cannot escape destruction – 'My God! My God! why hast thou forsaken me?' – Should I be ashamed to use this expression? – He who spreads out the heavens as it were a garment felt terror himself.   (II, 84)

The Homeric, dynamic nature which Werther has tried to render in his own painting as well as in the letters represents a harmony between internal and external worlds, between the actual and the ideal, symbolised in Werther and Lotte's mutual recognition of a rainy landscape as 'Klopstock!' (I, 63). The breakdown of this harmony is signified both by the breakdown of the epistolary style and by Werther's abandonment of Homer for Ossian. Coleridge adduces Ossian as well as Milton for his contention, in the Preface of 1797, that the egotistical voice is the one to which the reader responds, even in epic: 'the sweet voice of Cona [Ossian] never sounds so sweetly as when it speaks of itself' (*PW*, II, 1144). But the supplanting of Homer by Ossian goes with a supplanting of this immediate apprehension of nature by the attempt to supplant it in terms of a masculine, sublime consciousness. The unattainable Lotte, who had seemed like Homer's Nausicaa as well as surrogate mother, becomes the focus of an obsessive desire of which suicide is made to seem the inevitable outcome. Even the actual suicide is lingering and messy, in contrast to the clean, dignified, stoical suicide in the passage from Ossian Werther reads Lotte in their – emotionally almost orgasmic – final meeting. At their penultimate meeting, Lotte diagnoses the self-conscious and self-destructive character of Werther's obsession:

> 'Let me beg of you to be more calm; what a variety of pleasure and entertainment, your fine understanding, your genius and talents may furnish you! – Be yourself, and get the better of an unfortunate attachment to me, who can only pity you. Grant me a moment's patience, Werter! – Do you not see that you are deceiving yourself, that you are seeking your own destruction? Why must it be only me – me who belong to another? – I fear, I much fear, that the impossibility only of possessing me makes the desire of it so strong.'   (*Werter*, ii, 120–1)

If *Werther* embodies a kind of fall, then the import of a conversation Goethe had with Hegel, fifty years after first writing it, is that there can be a return, if not to prelapsarian innocence then to the fictive spiritual health of his fictional hero. To Goethe's *caveat* on the dialectic (that it could be used to invert morality), Hegel agrees:

> 'That does sometimes happen, but only with people who are spiritually sick'. . . . 'Well', said Goethe, 'I personally recommend the study of nature as preventive of that disease. For in nature we are dealing with something which is infinitely and eternally true, and which immediately rejects as inadequate everyone who does not show complete integrity and honesty in the way he observes and treats his subject. And I am certain that the study of nature would be a wholesome remedy for many a dialectical sufferer.'[13]

The germ of Schiller's treatise *On Naive and Sentimental Poetry* is in a long letter to Goethe dated 23 August 1794,[14] in which Schiller implies that the older poet and he represent respectively the 'naive' and 'sentimental' types of the poetical character. His reading of *Werther* is intended, he says, to exemplify 'how the naive poetic spirit proceeds with a sentimental theme'.[15] He notes how

> everything that nourishes the sentimental character is concentrated in *Werther*: fanatically unhappy love, sensitivity to nature, feeling for religion, a spirit of philosophical contemplation; finally, so that nothing shall be forgotten, the gloomy formless melancholic Ossianic world. If one takes account with how little recommendation, even in how hostile a manner actuality is contrasted with it, and how everything external unites to drive the tortured youth back into his world of ideals, then one sees no possibility how such a character could have saved himself from such a cycle . . . the poetic spirit is set in opposition to plain common sense, the ideal over against the actual, the subjective mode of representation over against the objective. (*Naive and Sentimental Poetry*, p. 138)

The slippage between *Werther* and Werther is akin to that between *Hamlet* and Hamlet in Coleridge: is it the work or the character who is the apotheosis of the sentimental? We need Schiller's summary: 'The poet either *is* nature or he will *seek* her. The former is the naive, the latter the sentimental poet' (*Naive and Sentimental Poetry*, p. 110). The terms correlate roughly with 'ancient' and 'modern' but, like other terms in those pairs of apparent opposites I have dealt with in Part I, they are points on a circle rather than linear opposites: 'The Romantic writers did not choose feeling, the many, the particular, change, and imperfection as the good members of each pair [of opposites]. . . . The Romantics' view becomes dipolar, an "either *and* or" way of looking at things. They kept *both* sides separate and together.'[16]

Schiller mentions Edward Young as the poet of *Night Thoughts* (*Naive and Sentimental Poetry*, p. 135). Young's *Conjectures on Original Composition* first appeared anonymously in the *Gentleman's Magazine* for 1759. A German translation published the following year led to its becoming more influential in that country than in England. In his treatise Young justifies writing 'naturally' while denying 'that you must either imitate *Homer* or depart from Nature'. For him, 'originality' is not an accident of time but an act of volition: 'may not this Paradox pass into a Maxim? *viz.* "The less we copy the renowned Antients, we shall resemble them the more." ' [17] For Schiller, in modern times nature must be an 'idea' and the poet can choose to move downward to individuality or upward to the idea. The naive poet – exemplified by Shakespeare as well as Homer – is at home in a nature corresponding with the Kantian *Verstand* rather than *Vernunft*: 'Nature, considered in this wise, is for us nothing but the voluntary presence, the subsistence of things on their own, their existence in accordance with their own immutable laws' (*Naive and Sentimental Poetry*, p. 84) – as for Perdita, the art itself is nature. Werther's desire to possess Lotte can then be seen as a desire to appropriate what lies out of bounds – or on the other side of the Cartesian divide. The forms of the sentimental poet then must be either satirical or elegiac – as modes of perception – and as an example of the latter Schiller adduces Ossian:

> The elegiac poet seeks nature, but as an idea and in a perfection in which she has never existed, when he bemourns her at once as something having existed and now lost. When Ossian tells of the days which are no more, and of the heroes who have disappeared, his poetic power has long since transformed those images of recollection into ideals, and those heroes into gods. The experience of a particular loss has been broadened into the idea of universal evanescence. . . .   (p. 127)

Ironically enough, in terms of *Werther*, Klopstock is also adduced as an example of the elegist. 'Subjectivism' – the very word is like a bell – is the necessary corollary of the sentimental:

> The mind cannot tolerate any impression without at once observing its own activity and reflection, and yielding up in terms of itself whatever it has absorbed. In this mode we are never given the subject, only what the reflective understanding has made of it, and even when the poet is himself the subject, if he would describe his feeling to us, we never learn of his condition directly and at first hand, but rather how he has reflected in his own mind, what he has thought about it as an observer of himself.   (pp. 129–30)

Schiller too implies that the self is irrecoverably lost to self-consciousness – irrecoverably because even redemption is not a return to innocence. I may seem to be assigning to a new object called 'egotism' the function which critics often assign to an object even more nebulous called 'Imagination'. However, as Keats's adumbration of the faculty of 'negative capability' suggested, we may be unimaginative, but it will be just then that we are conscious of the inherence of being 'ourselves'. There is a consciousness of self even in the moment of celebrating the Imagination which has interfused mind and 'nature':

> Imagination having been our theme,
> So also hath that intellectual love,
> For they are each in each, and cannot stand
> Dividually.
>
> (*Prelude*, 1805, xiii.185–8)

The final adverb evokes a ghostly third party which is party to this coalescence.

I hope to have shown that 'egotism' is more than the fact of Goethe and Werther sharing a birthday or Coleridge's employment of the first person. In terms of the two works by which I attempted to show the sense of its importance textually, Gray's fictional distancing of himself from the final version of the 'Elegy' is an attempt to stabilise that which his own questioning had destabilised; and Goethe shows Werther not retreating from the instability which his rejection of a shared apprehension of nature and society implies, but able to define himself outside that consensus only by self-destruction. Werther's self-destruction, like that of Gray's Bard, is only the end of his loss of self: for the modern, the 'naive' and 'sentimental' of Schiller's essay rejoin at such a point.

Schiller's essay begins by noticing human susceptibility to the appearances of 'nature' in a wide sense, which leads to an aphorism underlying all he will go on to say: '*They are what we were*; they are what *we should once again become*. We were nature just as they, and our culture, by means of reason and freedom, should lead us back to nature' (*Naive and Sentimental Poetry*, p. 85). The desire for such a return commits us to a circularity, of which what might be called the *locus Romanticus* is in Friedrich Schlegel: 'The romantic kind of poetry is still in the state of becoming; that, in fact, is its real essence: that it should forever be becoming and never be perfected.'[18] For Schiller, Werther is less the apotheosis than the 'dangerous extreme of the sentimental personality'

(*Naive and Sentimental Poetry*, p. 137). As Coleridge says of Hamlet, the 'due balance between the real and the imaginary world' is upset (*ShakCrit*, I, 37). The sentimental poet is forever seeking, like Werther, to attain the unattainable, to come full circle. We can do the same.

Coleridge describes Hamlet as

> a person, in whose view the external world, and all its incidents and objects, were comparatively dim and of no interest in themselves, and which began to interest only, when they were reflected in the mirror of the mind. . . . This admirable and consistent character, deeply acquainted with his own feelings, painting them with such wonderful power & accuracy, and firmly persuaded that a moment ought not be lost in executing the solemn charge committed to him, still yields to the same retiring from reality, which is the result of having, what we express by the terms, a world within himself.   (II, 192–5)

Crabb Robinson, calling on Coleridge during his lectures on Shakespeare of March 1813, finds him 'in raptures with [Goethe's] *Wilhelm Meister*'; and reports of his conversation, 'Hamlet he considered in a point of view which seems to agree very well with the representation given in *Wilhelm Meister*' (II, 251, 209). In Carlyle's translation (1824), Wilhelm says that ' "Not reflective or sorrowful by nature, reflection and sorrow have become for [Hamlet] a heavy obligation." ' The play is the character, the character a representation of ' "the effects of a great action laid upon a soul unfit for the performance of it. . . . He winds, and turns, and torments himself; he advances and recoils; is ever put in mind; at last does all but lose his purpose from his thoughts; yet still without recovering his peace of mind." ' [19] Walter Pater believes Coleridge to have more than a smack of Hamlet.[20] However, the fascination of such self-conscious figures is in balance with that exerted by those figures who have no such introspective doubts and are pure, but purely immoral, activity.

There is, except fictively, no birth of the self. The definition of 'egotism' is bound up with problems concerning the self and, as was perhaps inevitable with so fundamental a theme, several consequences have emerged. For example, Coleridge's claim that his reading of the Germans tended only to confirm ideas he had arrived at separately gains some credence from the consideration here of Burke, Lowth and Young on language and from Locke and Hume on the metaphysical self. Knowledge 'commencing with an *act*, instead of a *thing* or *substance*' (*BL* [*CC*], I, 158), which recognition Coleridge ascribes to Fichte, itself commences, perhaps, with them. The problem of 'egotism' has been treated as a problem which stems from internal and external constraints upon language. The external constraints are a series of prohibitions and demotions of the first person which may have consequences for the characteristically fragmentary and elusive surface of Coleridge's writings. I say 'may' because it is not my suggestion that, for example, the evasions of Gray's language in the 'Elegy' are attributable to the spectre of an object called 'egotism'. Rather, as Coleridge says of 'egotism' in one of his contributions to Southey's *Omniana*, 'the more decorous manners of the present age have disproportionate opprobrium to this foible, and many therefore abstain with cautious prudence from all displays of what they feel'.[21] It is the nature of these 'internal' constraints that will be investigated in Part II. Self-consciousness is not an *ab ovo* condition but it is the condition upon which and with which the poet must act. In Parts II and III I shall consider the activity and the deferral thereby entailed with reference to some poems by Coleridge.

PART II
The Circle of the I

Preamble

Coleridge's recognition of the affecting 'egotism' of the opening of *Paradise Lost* book III is certainly dependent on, and not merely confused by, a knowledge of Milton's blindness. In the next two chapters I want to show how such interests are comprehended within a more fundamental group of concerns. Wordsworth himself inveighs against that of which he is accused by Keats, 'that licentious craving in the mind / To act the God among external things' (*WPW*, III, 193). Chapter 5 will consider the way the eye, like the 'I', is distrusted for its capacity to disable the imagination; a seeming paradox (since the relative positions of 'mind' and 'nature' are inverted) which is in fact circular. Those who subscribe to the postulate of no authorising first cause are 'allegorised' by Coleridge as the blind leading the blind, for whom 'infinite blindness supplies the place of sight'. For him the authorising first cause is the imagination which 'contemplates' such a series 'as a continuous *circle* . . . [and] likewise supplies, by a sort of *subintelligentur*, the one central power which renders the movement harmonious and cyclical' (*BL* [*CC*], I, 266–7). The 'under consciousness' of the Fall that, for Coleridge, characterises 'all modern poetry in Christendom' (see Ch. 3 above) is a consciousness not merely of the 'sinful nature' of any individual self but of the powers of the self. In this passage from the *Biographia* such powers are said to 'supply' rather than to act for or to discover the 'central power'. The end of such a process would be a displacement of God by the individual imagination. Coleridge retreats from such implications but the metaphors of eyesight and of the circle here are crucial ones in the process. It is through them that I want to approach Coleridge's poetry.

Paradise Lost is a poem about the Fall as a retrospective and prospective fact of consciousness which challenges justification, but it is also a poem about the Fall both as a myth of origins and as the great metaphor, a metaphor upon which, for example, *Werther*

57

is predicated. The relation of myth and metaphor is a circular one, and Part I assumed a continuity: that, in spite of contradictions, a statement from a little-read passage of 1796 is reconcilable with one from a major prose-work of twenty years later. Parts II and III should confront that assumption. I shall examine the metaphor of eyesight and then, in approaching Coleridge's poetry with more respect for the actual history of its production, try and build on some insights afforded by Hartman, Abrams and Humphry House in order to show how these concerns function within one poem in particular. Before moving to such a reading (of 'Frost at Midnight') I shall examine the metaphor of the circle itself; but I begin with the simple homophone of my title for Part II. Wordsworth implies a relation of the eye to such a circular movement when he writes that the 'bodily eye'

> Could find no surface where its power might sleep;
> Which spake perpetual logic to my soul,
> And by an unrelenting agency
> Did bind my feelings even in a chain.
>
> (*Prelude*, 1805, III.166–9)

The image for that less tangible 'power' which displaces the insufficient 'surfaces' on which the physical eye alights is one of speech. The relation Wordsworth assumes between a moral 'agency' and his own restless eye lies behind my own assumption in Part II and will, I hope, prevent its being seen as my going off at a tangent.

5 That Despotism of the Eye

. . . sight is the keenest of our physical senses, though it does not bring us knowledge.   (Plato, *Phaedrus*)

The Understanding, like the Eye, whilst it makes us see, and perceive all other Things, takes no notice of it self: And it requires Art and Pains to set it at a distance, and make it its own Object.   (Locke, Introduction to *An Essay Concerning Human Understanding*)

The association of himself with the divine which Werther makes (and which I quote in Ch. 4 above) alludes to Psalm 104, in which the power of God is praised: 'Who coverest thyself with light as with a garment: who stretchest out the heavens like a curtain'. I return to this passage because Hegel quotes the same verse in connection with the sublime. He opposes what he calls an 'affirmative sublime' which is pantheistic and to be found in Indian poetry to a 'negative sublime' which is an apprehension of the Absolute in which 'the appearance falls short of the content'. Negative in regard to the particular, it is to be found in Hebrew poetry: 'While therefore we found in the imagination of substantiality and its pantheism an infinite *enlargement*, here we have to marvel at the force of the *elevation* of the mind which abandons everything in order to declare the exclusive power of God'.[1] The sense of an infinite power in which the human mind cannot participate but at which it can only wonder is a source of that ambivalence met with in Chapter 1. Hegel follows Kant, who opposes a 'positive' delight in the beautiful in nature to a 'negative' delight in the sublime, which is

a feeling of imagination by its own act depriving itself of its

59

freedom by receiving a final determination in accordance with a law other than that of its empirical employment. In this way it gains an extension and a might greater than that which it sacrifices. But the ground of this is concealed from it, and in its place it *feels* the sacrifice or deprivation, as well as its cause, to which it is subjected.[2]

I shall not press a suggestion of the homophone of 'I' and 'eye', but the sublime is largely an effect of the visual sense, and the determining capacity of each is, I shall show, regarded with great suspicion. Blake privileges the mind over 'ideas' of nature: 'We are led to believe a Lie / When we see [with] not Thro, the eye'.[3] Blake's pun conflates the fields of sense and self in order to advert us to their common danger.

Unable to satisfy his desire either within the self or in an amputated nature, Werther's hyperbolic outburst is a surplus or residue of signifying, the phrase going beyond the content. Wordsworth's 'eye' in the lines quoted in the Preamble (*Prelude*, 1805; III.166–9) is rather dissatisfied with than distrustful of the 'surfaces' which might absorb it. The 'perpetual logic' and 'unrelenting agency' to which he is committed by this refusal is not necessarily benign, moral. The 'negative Sublime' is the individual's recognition of intellectual incapacity before a divinity which reveals itself not as 'mind' but overwhelmingly as 'nature', the content going beyond the phrase. Whether refused by or refusing its objects, a residue or surplus of self is analogous to effects of the ocular metaphor discussed in this chapter: but to proceed will require another analogy.

'Sympathy', as it is defined by Adam Smith in his *Theory of Moral Sentiments*, is wholly commensurate with egoistic self-interest, the test being always 'when we bring the case home to ourselves'. Thus it can be brought within a system of 'natural' representations:

> Sympathy . . . does not arise so much from the view of the passion, as from that of the situation which excites it. . . . The compassion of the spectator must arise altogether from the consideration of what he himself would feel if he was reduced to the same unhappy situation and, what perhaps is impossible, was at the same time able to regard it with his present reason or judgement.   (I, 10–11 [I.i.1])

Sympathy then is to be within the limits of a 'propriety' arrived at by consensus: 'to us . . . he must appear to deserve reward, who appears to be the proper and approved object of gratitude; and he to deserve punishment, who appears to be that of resentment' (I, 166 [II.i.1]); there is 'beauty' in this propriety; and moral 'Virtue' is wholly empirical. Smith denies the existence of a 'moral sense' even as a recalcitrant remainder. Approval of any action stems always, he says, from correct motivation of the agent, sympathetic gratitude, correlation of an action with an ensuing benefit, or its promotion of individual or general wellbeing. (Our approval of the latter is like our admiration for the 'utility . . . [of] any well-contrived machine')[4]. Smith concludes,

> After deducting, in any one particular case, all that must be acknowledged to proceed from some one or other of these four principles, I should be glad to know what remains, and I shall freely allow this overplus to be ascribed to a moral sense, or to any other peculiar faculty, provided any body will ascertain precisely what this overplus is. (II, 356 [VII, iii.3])

In Coleridge and others there is frequently an assertion of 'overplus' or residue which by its nature (or rather by its not being nature) can be accommodated only with difficulty even to a system – language – rather more commodious than that of Adam Smith. The 'overplus' is something unsayable – even, in 'The Ancient Mariner' or 'Limbo', something unspeakable. In *The Prelude*, for instance, Wordsworth recalls that 'the soul – / Remembering how she felt, but what she felt / Remembering not – retains an obscure sense / Of possible sublimity' (1805, II.334–7). The current needs of the 'soul' are projected backwards. Potential sublimity is freed from reliance on the natural and immediate.

In the book of *The Prelude* which recounts the impairment and restoration of his imagination, Wordsworth speaks of his taste for the sublimely picturesque as instancing the tyranny of 'the eye / The most despotic of our senses', which was 'proud of its own endowments and rejoiced / To lay the inner faculties asleep' (1805, XI.171–99). Coleridge has some similar comments when finally refuting Hartley's mechanism in the *Biographia*:

> Under the despotism of the eye . . . . – under this strong sensuous influence we are restless because individual things are not the

objects of vision; and metaphysical systems, for the most part, become popular not for their truth but in proportion as they attribute to causes a susceptibility of being *seen*, if only our visual organs were sufficiently powerful.   (*BL* [*CC*], I, 107)

The despotism or tyranny of egotism is a danger analogous to 'that Slavery of the Mind to the Eye' (*PL*, p. 434). (The words are often used in the eighteenth century to denote the mastering of the moral impulse by the passions.) In the version of 'Frost at Midnight' in the *Poetical Register, 1808—9* 'the idling Spirit' has become a spirit in possession of will:

> . . . the living spirit in our frame,
> Which loves not to behold a lifeless thing,
> Transfuses into all things its own Will,
> And its own pleasures.
>
> (*PW*, I, 241n)

Here the 'Will' seems determined and in tension with the process of 'transfusion', leading to the suspicion that such a transfusion is pleasurable not for its recognition of a 'living spirit' in nature but for the ego's recognition of its own vivacity. It is a criticism made by Anna Seward of Wordsworth's 'I wandered lonely as a cloud' (*WPW*, II, 216), which she regarded as the product of 'an egotistical manufacturer of metaphysical importance upon trivial themes'.[5] Wordsworth himself would not classify it among his 'Poems of the Imagination' until the collected edition of 1815, in which he appends this note: 'The subject of these Stanzas is rather an elementary feeling and simple impression (approaching to the nature of an ocular spectrum) upon the imaginative faculty than an *exertion* of it' (II, 507). The imagination whose 'desires and demands' are described, in the Preface to that volume, as 'the plastic, the pliant, and the indefinite' (*WPr*, III, 36) is impressed upon rather than excursive. The affective dissatisfaction with the poem's egotism, felt by Anna Seward, is balanced by Wordsworth's dissatisfaction at the overmastering of his own imagination.[6] In the poem, significance is denied in the moment of experience – 'I gazed – and gazed – but little thought / What wealth the show to me had brought' – and that wealth is, rather, the accumulated interest of the 'inward eye'. The impact of such an 'ocular spectrum' had been too strong.

The eye can be a deceptive witness, as Othello found when he demanded 'ocular proof'. The almost tactile hold it can exert on the mind[7] can be evinced in a handful of utterances. Coleridge writes to Poole from Germany, describing the Harz mountains:

And now we arrived at Hartsburg / – Hills ever by our sides, in all conceivable variety of forms and garniture – It were idle in me to attempt by words to give their projections & their retirings & how they were now in Cones, now in roundness, now in tonguelike Lengths, now pyramidal, now a huge Bow, and all at every step varying the forms of their outlines; / or how they now stood abreast, now ran aslant, now rose up behind each other / or now ... presented almost a Sea of huge motionless waves / too multiform for Painting, too multiform even for the Imagination to remember them / yea, my very sight seemed *incapacitated* by the novelty & Complexity of the Scene. (*CL*, I, 513)

This may be compared with Keats's letter to his brother Tom from the Lake District:

What astonishes me more than any thing is the tone, the coloring, the slate, the stone, the moss, the rock-weed; or, if I may so say, the intellect, the countenance of such places. The space, the magnitude of mountains and waterfalls are well-imagined before one sees them; but this countenance or intellectual tone must surpass every imagination and defy any remembrance. I shall learn poetry here and shall henceforth write more than ever, for the abstract endeavour of being able to add a mite to that mass of beauty which is harvested from these grand materials, by the finest spirits, and put into ethirial existence for the relish of one's fellows. I cannot think with Hazlitt that these scenes make man appear little. I never forgot my stature so completely – I live in the eye; and my imagination, surpassed, is at rest. ... (*KL*, I, 301)

Each records pleasure at the 'variety' of 'these grand materials' in nature, but this life in the eye is the calm before a 'sublime' storm. Keats is writing before the abandonment of *Hyperion*, and his cheerful humanisation of a nature commensurate with or surpassing the imagination allows the possibility of a 'despotism of the eye' to feature only in the devil's advocacy of Hazlitt; only in the final admission here of the passiveness rather than catharsis of the imagination, the incapacity of Coleridge's eye, is there a suggestion of the collocation of 'egotistical' and 'sublime' which Keats finds in Wordsworth.

Wordsworth himself records the surpassing of *his* imagination when first seeing a (gowned) student on his arrival in Cambridge: 'nor was I master of my eyes / Till he was left a hundred yards behind' (*Prelude*, 1805, III, 8–9). He has, by this point, already adumbrated an attenuation of the senses as the ideal. Sound was 'most audible . . . when the fleshly ear . . . Forgot her functions, and slept undisturbed' (II. 431–4); and when 'bodily eyes / Were utterly forgotten . . . what I saw / Appeared like something in myself, a dream / A prospect of the mind' (II. 368–71). Similarly, in Coleridge's 'Hymn Before Sunrise', the 'silent Mount', though 'still present to the bodily sense', vanishes, until finally 'entranced in prayer / I worshipped the Invisible alone' (*PW*, I, 377). The implied imperative – for resistance to a 'despotism of the eye' – is resistance to a blindness caused by excess of sight, a determinate overmastering of the mind by the visual sense.

In one of the autobiographical letters to Poole, Coleridge speaks of himself at the age of eight: 'I never regarded *my senses* in any way as the criteria of my belief. I regulated all my creeds by my conception not by my *sight* – even at that age' (*CL*, I, 354). The egotistical child is father of the man. In Appendix C of *The Statesman's Manual*, written twenty years later, he explicitly distinguishes the 'vital Philosophy', which is a reconciliation of dynamic opposites, from the 'mechanic' philosophy, which

> demanding for every mode and act of existence real or possible *visibility*, knows only of distance and nearness, composition (or rather juxtaposition) and decomposition, in short the relations of unproductive particles to each other; so that in every instance the result is the exact sum of the component qualities as in arithmetical addition. This is the philosophy of death, and only of a dead nature can it hold good.   (*LS* [*CC*], p. 89)

The eye is displaced to the status of analogy in the state of true religion founded on Reason: 'As it is the image or symbol of its great object, by the organ of this similitude, as by an eye, it seeth that same image throughout the creation' (p. 90). The synecdoche 'eye' has become a capacity which can be named only metaphorically. The mind is no longer a mirror but is turned outward, in a revision of empirical 'vision'.

In the later tract intended to vindicate and explain his *New Theory of Vision*, Berkeley summarises its conclusion 'that *Vision is the Language of the Author of Nature*'.[8] The metaphor, not in itself new, makes possible a slippage from the visual into the aural. Berkeley has constant recourse to language as an analogy within his argument: a slippage, it might be said, from the picturesque to the conversation. He is reacting less to the particulars of Newton's work than to the positivism of optics in his wake.[9] Coleridge's attitude to the visual sense is affected by a distrust of its capacity for determinism, resulting in a similar slippage. The unnamed antagonist is again Locke.

For Locke, sight is 'the most comprehensive of all our Senses, conveying to our Minds the *Ideas* of Light and Colours, which are peculiar only to that Sense; and also the far different *Ideas* of Space, Figure, and Motion, the several varieties whereof change the appearances of its proper Object, *viz* Light and Colours' (*Essay*, p. 146 [II.ix.9]). Pictures on the retina become 'ideas' on the *tabula rasa* of the mind. Locke accepts the etymology of 'idea' (from Greek *eitho*, 'I see') to assimilate the sensory to the intellectual. By clear and distinct ideas Locke means, he says, 'some object in the Mind, and consequently *determined*, i.e. such as it is there seen and perceived to be'; and simple and complex ideas are, respectively, determined and determinate, when the mind has them 'before its view, and sees in it self' (p. 13 [Epistle to the Reader]). For all that sight may be 'the most comprehensive of all our senses', the visual metaphor is a means of imposing a limitation upon the understanding: 'when the Mind would look beyond those original *Ideas* we have from Sensation or Reflection, and penetrate into their Causes, and manner of production, we find still it discovers nothing but its own short-sightedness' (p. 312 [II.xxiii.28]). Although even the most 'sublime thoughts' have their 'rise and footing' in sensation or reflection,

In this Part, the *Understanding* is meerly *passive*; and whether or no, it will have these Beginnings and as it were, materials of Knowledge, is not in its own Power. For the Objects of our Senses ... obtrude their particular *Ideas* upon our minds whether we will or no.... These *Simple Ideas*, when offered to the mind, *the Understanding can* no more refuse to have, nor alter, when they are imprinted, nor blot them out and make new ones in it self, than a mirror can refuse, alter, or obliterate the Images or *Ideas* which, the Objects set before it, do therein produce (p. 118 [II.i.25])

As a nineteenth-century Coleridgean remarks of Locke, 'a metaphor, interpreted as a fact, becomes the basis of his philosophical system'.[10]

Appending a glossary of terms to his influential *Elements of Criticism*, Lord Kames (Hume's cousin) says,

The primary perception of a visible object, is more complete, lively and distinct, than that of any other object. And for that reason, an idea or secondary perception of a visible object, is also more complete, lively, and distinct, than that of any other object. . . . poets and orators, who are extremely successful in describing objects of sight, find objects of the other senses too faint and obscure for language. . . . man is endued with a sort of creative power: he can fabricate images of things that have no existence. The materials employed in this operation, are ideas of sight.[11]

Few writers are as explicit in acknowledging the Lockean foundations of their criticism, but most assume these foundations. In the prefatory Epistle to his *Essay* Locke calls himself an 'Under-Labourer' in the clarifying employment of Newton (p. 10). The aesthetics of the sublime, deriving from Lockean epistemology, are cognate with the positivism of optics after Newton which it is Berkeley's purpose to refute.

Boileau's French translation of Longinus's *Peri Hypsous* was published in 1674, the same year as the twelve-book edition of *Paradise Lost*. The coincidence is significant because the great exemplar of the sublime is Milton. The two eighteenth-century translations of Longinus – *On the Sublime*, by Leonard Welsted (1712) and by William Smith (1739) – take most of their parallels to illustrative quotations by Longinus from *Paradise Lost*, and Coleridge himself told his auditors that 'sublimity is the pre-eminent characteristic of the Paradise Lost' (*MiscCrit*, p. 164). As Samuel H. Monk has shown[12] an enormous number of speculative writings on the sublime succeeded Welsted's first

English translation of Longinus. His 'discovery', like that of Ossian, answers to an aesthetic need.

Addison's term, in the *Spectator* papers 'On the Pleasures of Imagination', is 'the Great', in which the eye can lose itself in vastness:

> Our Imagination loves to be filled with an Object, or to graspe [*sic*] at any thing that is too big for its Capacity. We are flung into a pleasing Astonishment at such unbounded Views, and feel a delightful Stillness and Amazement in the Soul at the Apprehension of them. The Mind of Man naturally hates every thing that looks like a Restraint upon it, and is apt to fancy it self under a sort of Confinement, when the Sight is pent up in a narrow Compass, and shortned [*sic*] on every side by the Neighbourhood of Walls or Mountains. On the contrary, a spacious Horison [*sic*] is an Image of Liberty, where the Eye has Room to range abroad, to expatiate at large on the immensity of its Views, and to lose it self amidst the Variety of Objects that offer themselves to its Observation   (*Spectator*, iii, 540–1 [no. 412])

For Addison, the freedom of the eye is due only to an extension of its field of view: imagination, soul and mind when shown an 'Image of Liberty' respond only with 'Stillness and Amazement'. 'Our sight', he says, 'is the most perfect and most delightful of all our senses', and, therefore,

> by the Pleasures of the Imagination, I mean only such Pleasures as arise originally from Sight, and . . . I divide these pleasures into two kinds: My Design being first of all to Discourse of those Primary Pleasures of the Imagination, which entirely proceed from such Objects as are before our eyes; and in the next place to speak of those Secondary Pleasures of the Imagination which flow from the Ideas of visible Objects, when the Objects are not actually before the Eye, but are called up into our Memories, or form'd into agreeable Visions of Things that are either Absent or Fictitious.   (iii, 537 [no. 411])

In *Spectator*, no. 413, Addison refers his readers to 'that great modern discovery' of primary and secondary ideas in book ii, chapter viii, of Locke's *Essay*. His own distinction of primary and secondary 'pleasures' of the imagination is followed by an assertion that all such pleasures are fundamentally visual: 'the Pleasures of the Imagination have this Advantage, above those of the Understanding, that they are more obvious and more easie to be acquired. It is but opening the Eye, and the Scene enters' (*Spectator*, III, 538 [no. 411]). To paraphrase T. H. Green, Locke's metaphor, interpreted as a fact, becomes the basis of his aesthetic.

Addison's 'greatness' thus easily mediates between his primary and secondary pleasures of imagination, between a 'natural' and 'rhetorical' sublime. As Kames admits in his chapter 'Grandeur and Sublimity', the terms have 'a double signification: they commonly signify the quality or circumstances in objects by which the emotions of grandeur sublimity are produced; sometimes the emotions themselves'.[13] And John Baillie says at the start of his *Essay on the Sublime*, 'the *Sublime* in *Writing* is no more than a Description of the *Sublime* in *Nature*, and as it were painting to the *Imagination* what *Nature* herself offers to the *Senses*'.[14] Throughout Baillie's short treatise it is the vastness of the objects perceived which produces the sublime effect (his 'vast' is Addison's 'great') and 'a *Consciousness* of her own *Vastness* is what pleases the soul' (p. 6). This consciousness is one which Hegel recognises: 'We often confess the *Sublime*', says Baillie, 'as we do the *Deity*; It fills and dilates our *Soul* without being able to penetrate into its *Nature*, and define its *Essence*' (p. 5), yet what this leads to is investigation and classification not of such an effect but of the sublime as it inheres in natural objects. So, in his final paragraph, Baillie says: 'the *Eyes* and *Ears* are the only *Inlets* to the Sublime. *Taste*, *Smell*, nor *Touch* convey nothing that is Great and Exalted; and this may be some farther Confirmation that large objects only constitute the *Sublime*' (p. 41).

Burke's *Philosophical Enquiry* formalises this gap between the senses and the mind by adducing astonishment (exciting terror, which is 'the common stock of every thing that is sublime' – p. 64 [II.v]) as a capacity inherent in the perceived object,

> and astonishment is that state of the soul, in which all its motions are suspended with some degree of horror. In this case the mind is so entirely filled with its object, that it cannot entertain any other, nor by consequence reason on that object which employs it. Hence arises the great power of the sublime, that far from being produced by them, it anticipates our

reasonings, and hurries us on by an irresistible force. (p. 57 [II.ii])

Burke's sublime then in anticipating and thus astonishing the reason remains sensationalist – the power of objects transmitting itself through the senses to a passive mind which registers only astonishment. His contention that all of the mind's 'motions are suspended' in the state of astonishment is consistent with Addison's 'Stillness and Amazement'. His distinction of the sublime from the beautiful affords the latter an insidiously seductive importance, but both are held within a relation of power: 'There is a wide difference between admiration and love. The sublime, which is the cause of the former, always dwells on great objects, and terrible; the latter on small ones, and pleasing; we submit to what we admire, but we love what submits to us.' While 'we are forced' by the sublime we are 'flattered into compliance' by the beautiful (p. 113 [III.13]). No third term is offered us. The extension of the sublime from a rhetorical quality to a quality also of natural objects comprehends throughout this effect of overmastering; an effect of which the pre-eminent vehicle is the eye.

Coleridge can write of a sky as a 'perfect union of the sublime with the beautiful . . . an aweful adorable omneity in unity . . . [in which] the eye itself feels that the limitation is in its own power not in the Object' (*CN*, II, 2346) – a use of the term recognisably within the prescriptions of, say, Burke. His own utterances on the sublime have been well studied[15] but they seem to me largely uninteresting, efforts at defining a received critical terminology which does not have much application in his poetic practice. Theories of the sublime more contemporary with Wordsworth and Coleridge – such as that of Payne Knight – do show a similar impulse towards the accommodation of a co-operating psychological or imaginative power. Archibald Alison, for instance, writes,

When we feel either the beauty or sublimity of natural scenery, they gay lustre of a morning in spring, or the wild radiance of a summer evening, the savage majesty of a wintry storm, or the wild magnificence of a tempestuous ocean, we are conscious of a variety of images in our minds, very different from those which the objects themselves can present to the eye.[16]

Thus, in a section on association, Alison makes 'imagination' a capacity for being affected by natural scenery 'embellished and made sacred by the memory of Theocritus and Virgil, and Milton and Tasso'. The sublime is increased 'by whatever tends to increase this exercise of imagination . . . [and] it seems reasonable to conclude, that the effect produced upon the mind, by objects of sublimity and beauty, consists in the production of this exercise of imagination'.[17] My point is only that by this stage the 'sublime' has been so extended (as in the lines from Wordsworth quoted above) as to have become unrecognisable, the 'overplus' having been assimilated to this 'production'. What is of greater importance, I think, is the way that theories of the sublime accept and extend an ocular metaphor for the activity of the mind, and the way in which Coleridge would turn the metaphor against itself by his dwelling on an 'inward eye'. Again writing of the sky, in Malta, he bursts out, 'O I could annihilate in a deep moment all possibility of the needlepoint pinhead system of the *Atomists* by one submissive Gaze!' (*CN*, ɪɪ, 3159). At the same time there is a danger of such a contrary, 'subjective' insight becoming subjectivism: Wordsworth's repeated 'gazing' discovers no significance in the instant of perceiving the daffodils, Coleridge none when repeatedly gazing, 'with how blank an eye' at moon, clouds and stars in the sky: 'I see them all so excellently fair, / I see, not feel how beautiful they are!' (*PW*, ɪ, 364).

Berkeley's *New Theory of Vision*, anticipating Kant in its stress on the distinction between perceptions and 'judgements', is a contingent underwriting of Coleridge's movement from sensationalism and the prescriptive rhetoric built upon it to a consciousness in which, ideally, mind and senses continually act upon each other. Berkeley makes his distinction in each of the three main divisions of his book:

> The judgement we make of the distance of an object . . . is entirely the result of experience . . .; the judgements we make of the magnitude of things . . . do not arise from any essential or necessary but only a customary tie . . .; the different situations of the eye naturally direct the mind to make a suitable judgement of the situation of objects intromitted by it.

Such judgement is necessary, he concludes, in a final polemic against positivism, because 'the perpetual objects of sight render them incapable of being managed after the manner of geometrical figures'.[18] Berkeley is not concerned with aesthetic judgement, but his claim for the eye is clearly congruent with Kant's for aesthetic judgment that 'instead of the object, it is rather the cast of the mind in appreciating it that we have to estimate as *sublime*'.[19] The 'egotistical sublime' is the 'cast of the mind' writ large as a mountain, but its perverse attraction is in alerting the soul to an infinitude which suggests divinity.

Hegel's recognition of a 'negative sublime' in Hebrew poetry is a reflex of the association of sublime feelings with an apprehension of the divine. Coleridge assumes that which Hegel will examine when he inquires: 'Could you ever discover anything sublime, in our sense of the term, in the classic Greek literature? I never could. Sublimity is Hebrew by birth' (*TT*, 25 July, 1832). Longinus himself cites the opening of Genesis in his treatise; and it is not surprising to find a close association of the sublime effect with the recognition and fear of God. Baillie's criterion of vastness as a prerequisite of sublime objects leads, logically for him, to the greatest of ideas, which are those of the divine. Such an effect is often referred to, not alway pejoratively, as 'Enthusiasm' – the Greek *en* (in) with *theos* (god). 'Inspiration' of course has a similar etymology, but Shaftesbury is careful to distinguish them: 'for inspiration is a real feeling of the Divine Presence, and enthusiasm a false one'. But, as he goes on, 'Something there will be of extravagance and fury when the ideas or images received are too big for the narrow human vessel to contain. So that inspiration may justly be called divine enthusiasm; for the word itself signifies divine presence.'[20] For John Dennis, early in the century, 'enthusiasm' is a feeling stimulated by the idea of an absent object, as opposed to those 'vulgar passions' excited by the objects themselves: 'the Enthusiastick Passions are chiefly six, Admiration, Terror, Horror, Joy, Sadness, Desire, caus'd by Ideas occurring to us in Meditation, and producing the same Passions that the Objects of those Ideas would raise in us, if they were set before us in the same light that those Ideas give us of them'. Dennis's 'Enthusiastick Passions' will be recognised as the sublime feelings. A greatness and capacity of soul in the writer (Dennis does not say the writing) will produce the same effect in the reader, mediated through Lockean 'Ideas'. Again, the greatest such are 'religious Ideas', 'which are not only great and wonderful, but which almost alone are great and wonderful to a great and wise Man; and which never fail to move very strongly, unless it is for want of due Reflection, or want of Capacity in the Subject'. The sublime is inherent in objects and therefore ought to be in Ideas. Thus Dennis posits *Paradise Lost* as a simple mimesis: speaking of himself, Adam's language is flat and prosaic, of God it is sublime, and there is a perceptible falling-off in the last books, where the archangel is describing the works of man, not of God. Dennis draws out what for him are the obvious implications of Longinus, but implications of which Longinus himself is unaware: 'the Spirit or the Passion in Poetry ought to be proportion'd to the Ideas, and the Ideas to the Object, and when it is not so, it is utterly false. . . . But nothing but God, and what relates to God, is worthy to move the Soul of a great and a wise Man.'[21] Kant too alludes to this tradition when he defines fanaticism (*Schwärmerei*) as 'a *delusion* that would *will some* VISION *beyond all the bounds of sensibility*; i.e. would dream according to principles'.[22]

Coleridge shares Kant's suspicion of the visionary claim for perpetual realisation of the vision, but this is in balance with his own suspicion of a 'sensible' determinacy. His visionary impulses could find affirmative authority in, for instance, his admired Jeremy Taylor:

> certain it is, that all that Truth which God hath made necessarie, he hath also made legible and plain, and if we will open our eyes, we shall see the Sun, and if *we will walk in the light, we shall rejoyce in the light*: only let us withdraw the Curtains, let us remove the *impediments and the sin that doth so easily beset us*; that's God's way. . . . In Heaven indeed we shall first see, and then love; but here on Earth we must first love, and love will open our eyes as well as our hearts, and we shall then see and perceive and understand.[23]

Coleridge can then make 'Reason' as a Kantian category accord with the 'discursive or intuitive' reason of the passage from Milton discussed above:

> Whatever is conscious *Self* knowledge is Reason; and in this sense it may be safely defined the organ of the Super-sensuous; even as the Understanding wherever it does not possess or use the Reason, as another and inward eye, may be defined the conception of the sensuous. (*Friend* [*CC*], i, 156).

Although he is privileging a 'Super-sensuous' over a 'Sensuous' eye, his very maintenance of the metaphor shows that he is alert to the 'delusion' of a wilful blindness against which Kant warns. Not all men can see as well, he continues, just as everyone can perceive straight lines, curves and geometric figures, but not everyone is Newton (I, 159–60). In a long note of 1808, which he thought important enough to return to ten years later, Coleridge discusses Paley's account of the Decalogue, and almost makes the categorical imperative into an eleventh commandment: 'Preserve the pure Reason pure – & debase it not by any mixture of <u>sensuality</u> – the sensuous Imagination. To consecrate & worship the eternal distinction between the Noumena & the Phaenomenon / and never to merge the former in the latter' (*CN*, III, 3293). 'Pure' is given a moral weight and empirical scepticism is denounced as immoral: Locke's system is productive of sense and sensuality. Following an anecdote about two blind men who fish, play cards, course, and are thought 'the best Beaters up of Game in the Country' (I, 572), a note of November 1799 recognises the pervasiveness of the Lockean view: 'How many blind men there are among us in metaphysics who talk the language of *Sight*, of the internal Sight, so glibly – playing sweet Tunes upon Hand Organs' (I, 573). However, dissatisfaction with the merely visual is rebuked by the material difficulty of the visionary, as a much later note records:

> One lifts up one's eyes to Heaven as if to seek
> there what one had lost on Earth / Eyes –
> Whose Half-beholdings thro' unsteady tears
> Gave shape, hue, distance, to the inward Dream /
> (III, 3649)

This will be the condition of the old man in 'Limbo'.

The late poem 'Limbo' (*PW*, I, 429–31) has its sole human protagonist repeatedly gazing upward; yet he is blind, 'his eyeless face all eye'. The 'sole true *Something*' in Limbo (an entirely noumenal realm) frightens even the frightening spectres, and the materialist 'moles' (also of course blind) 'See but to dread, and dread they know not why / The natural Alien of their negative Eye'. (This 'Alien' emerges as 'positive Negation', addressee of the poem immediately following in the notebook [*CN*, III, 4073–4], which is couched in the sublime form of a Pindaric ode.) The positivism of time and space is displaced:

> Time and weary Space
> Fettered from flight, with night-mare sense of fleeing,
> Strive for their last crepuscular half-being; –

The poem thus concerns indeterminacy and, dissatisfied with such indeterminacy, the reader might wish to parse the line 'Gazes the orb with moon-like countenance' as a simple inversion of subject and verb, followed by a prepositional phrase as adjunct. In this reading, however, the moon would be referred to as moon-like; yet with the line requiring 'the old man' as subject, his 'gazing' is oxymoronic, a foredoomed attempt at making an 'image' out of a 'thing'. Simile can only draw attention to the verbs, grammatically active, signifying inactivity: 'He seems to gaze on that which seems to gaze on him!'[24] Coleridge reprints the lines about the moles in the *Friend* when defending the Platonic 'Idea' against 'the partizans of a crass and sensual materialism, the advocates of the Nihil nisi ab extra' (*Friend* [*CC*], I, 494*), but what this 'Specimen of the Sublime' achieves then is recognition of a failure of the supersensuous. One syntactic ambiguity not exhibited by the poem is in fact closely analogous: it might be described as a double-negative sublime.

A glance at Coleridge's claims to have achieved a more sublime effect than those who would espouse the theory may help to explain the significance which 'gazing' can win. In a letter of 1809 he refers to Wordsworth's having 'condemned the Hymn [Before Sunrise] in toto . . . as a specimen of the Mock Sublime' and defends himself,

> the mood and Habit of mind out of which the Hymn rose . . . differs from Milton's and Thomson's and the Psalms, the source of all three, in the Author's addressing himself to *individual* Objects actually present to his Senses, while his great predecessors apostrophize *classes* of Things, presented by the Memory and generalized by the understanding.

He admits the result may be idiosyncratic but insists, as he had done in the letter to Poole quoted above, that 'from my very childhood I have been accustomed to *abstract* and as it were unrealize whatever of more than common interest my eyes dwelt on; and then by a sort of transfusion and transmission of my consciousness to identify my self with the Object' (*CL*, IV, 974–5). It is perhaps Coleridge's own peculiar psychology which leads him into a 'negative sublime' of abasement, but this process of 'unrealising' is a withdrawal from the sensory into the intuitive which returns us rather to Anna Seward than to Hegel. In a note already quoted (*CN*, III, 3293) Coleridge's technique is similar to that in the early political lectures discussed briefly above. Just as law must be negative, the individual must '*unlearn*' and '*de*habituate'. It may be that the only gesture to be made against the physical assertiveness of objects is a counter-assertion, such as that of the waking dream dubiously claimed as the condition in which 'Kubla Khan' was composed: a 'sleep . . . of the external senses . . . in which all the images rose up before him as *things*, with a parallel production of the correspondent expressions, without any sensation or consciousness of effort' (*PW*, I, 196).[25]

That 'sort of transfusion and transmission' which follows the 'unrealising' of the senses results from more labour than the effortlessness Coleridge remembers as bringing 'Kubla Khan' to birth. Two notes of 1805 help to construct a process between a laying asleep of the inner faculties and this sleep of the external senses. First:

> and I felt strongly, how apart from all concupiscence (unless perhaps that dying away or ever-subsisting vibration of it in the Heart & Chest & eyes (as it *seems* to us) which is the symbolical language of purest Love in our present Embodiment / for if mind acts on body, the purest feeling Impulse can introduce itself to our consciousness no otherwise than by *speaking to us* in some bodily feeling) – . . . .   (*CN*, II, 2495)

While the speculation ('if mind acts on body' – Coleridge imagining, or wishing himself physically punished for his desire for Sara) is one-way rather than a mutual interchange, a moral world affects the corporeal through the metaphor of language. It is still a process in which 'images' become 'things' and not vice versa, but in the second, more Kantian, note of the same month, the process is remarked as accommodating a life behind the eyes as well:

In looking at objects of nature while I am thinking, as at yonder moon dim-glimmering thro' the dewy window-pane, I seem rather to be seeking, as it were *asking*, a symbolical language for something within me that already and forever exists, than observing any thing new.   (II, 2546)

The subject has to seek and ask because these recalcitrant signifieds are *a priori* 'unrealised' and entirely self-originated. They must therefore be authorised by authorship. 'Transfusion and transmission' similarly relies on the acceptance and stability of a dichotomy of transmitter (giver) and receiver. Although Coleridge's diction here, together with what is said below, might suggest him as a proto-symbolist, it is this difficulty which distinguishes his writings from, for example, Arthur Symons's ecstatic claims for Verlaine:

I have never known anyone to whom the sight of the eyes was so intense and imaginative a thing. To him, physical sight and spiritual vision, by some strange alchemical operation of the brain, were one. . . . With Verlaine the sense of hearing and the sense of sight are almost interchangeable.[26]

The 'transfusion and transmission' of which Coleridge speaks is often accomplished rather by modulation and transposition, in which metaphor is drawn from aural perception, often of music. Of the 'music' of Shakespearean verse he says in the *Biographia*;

the sense of musical delight, with the power of producing it, is a gift of imagination; and this together with the power of reducing multitude into unity of effect, and modifying a series of thoughts by some one predominant thought or feeling, may be cultivated and improved, but can never be learned.   (*BL* [*CC*], II, 20)

The multitude of qualities here proposed are themselves reduced to rhetorical unity. This adjunctive 'power' is the ability to speak, and not merely to recognise, a symbolical language which, however, can 'never be learned'. Coleridge again proposes a 'realisation' outward rather than, as in Locke and the sublime, inward. While recognising dualism he also posits interlocution, communion, harmony. At the end of 'Kubla Khan', the 'symphony and song' of the damsel singing and playing her dulcimer are productive of that creative 'delight' which can cause the (positive) 'realisation' of the ideal in the poet figure of the 'flashing eyes'. The injunction 'Close your eyes with holy dread' allows the line 'All who *heard* should *see* them there' (emphasis added) to be read rather as prophecy of an achieved vision than as sensory displacement. In Wordsworth's 'Tintern Abbey' the 'wild eyes' of Dorothy certainly bespeak an excess, but it is *extra*- rather than *ir*rational. In her eyes the speaker reads 'gleams of past existence' as he anticipates her future memories of a present 'scene' now assimilated to a moral continuum and curtailed to 'these steep woods / And this green pastoral landscape'. Again, in Coleridge's 'The Nightingale' the child is as much protagonist in as recipient of the visionary experience. He is

> hushed at once,
> Suspends his sobs, and laughs most silently,
> While his fair eyes, that swam with undropped tears
> Did glitter in the yellow moon-beam!
>
> (*PW*, I, 264–7)

Each of these pairs of eyes is a kind of *locum tenens* for the speaker's. What is presented is a backward look, validating and authorising the process of the poem and, within it, also tending to prevent reader and speaker from meeting eye to eye. Conversely, the 'glittering eye' of the Ancient Mariner, and its occult connection with his 'strange power of speech', suggests the determining power of the physical eye when turned outward and fixed on an interlocutor.[27]

The ideal visual process is achieved in 'This Lime-tree Bower my Prison' (*PW*, I, 178–81) – ideal in both the superlative and the philosophic sense. The immobile Coleridge writes of a purely remembered 'dell' which is nevertheless, parenthetically, 'a most fantastic sight!', then wills on nature an intensification of its own energy, the significance of which is necessarily displaced, onto Charles Lamb:

> So my friend
> Struck with deep joy may stand, as I have stood,
> Silent with swimming sense; yea, gazing round
> On the wide landscape, gaze till all doth seem
> Less gross than bodily. . . .[28]

The tyranny of the eye is overthrown and the onlooker, speechless and sensorily adrift, becomes gazer. That last clause does not valorise the body over that which is gross but metaphor within that which is gross – too evident to the senses (*OED*, 8c) – and the repetition of 'gaze' insists on that verb being the carrier.

Wordsworth's 'Lines Left upon a Seat' (*WPW*, I, 92–4) have the same verbal insistence, but his narrative ends with the death of the proud 'lost man' as the 'emblem' for a sententious moral ('The man, whose eye / Is ever on himself, doth look on one, / The least of nature's works'), 'This Lime-tree Bower' with the turn to the absent 'gentle-hearted Charles'. This latter ending however reiterates the way Lamb has been addressed a few lines previously, with a suggestion of the significance which, at two removes, he wins:

> My gentle-hearted Charles! when the last rook
> Beat its straight path along the dusky air
> Homewards, I blest it! deeming its black wing
> (Now a dim speck, now vanishing in light)
> Had cross'd the mighty Orb's dilated glory
> While thou stood'st gazing.

This gazing is not acquisitive but acquiescent: so the speaker blesses a rook as the Mariner blesses snakes. The remembered and the imagined gazes are identified, and hence the gazers. The sublime has become a figure for a friendship and it is the sun rather than the eye which is dilated. Satan alights on the sun – 'Here matter new to gaze the devil met / Undazzled, far and wide his eye commands' (*Paradise Lost*, III, 613–14) – only to be 'admonished by the ear' (647), but Coleridge deems the transition a connection, a nightfall almost before the Fall. The 'ideal' at the end here, as at the end of 'Kubla Khan', is in the possible renascence of the speaker's former power, but in some other. Wordsworth's 'Tintern Abbey' has affinities with such an ideal, and I shall close this chapter with Coleridge's meditation on a pair of lines from that poem. They are quoted at the head of a reflection on the necessarily 'dim' consciousness of the subject as self. Here is the whole of the notebook entry from early 1801:

> – and the deep power of joy
> We see into the *Life* of Things –

i.e. – By deep feeling we make our *Ideas dim* – & this is what we mean by our life – ourselves. I think of the Wall – it is before me, a distinct Image here. I necessarily think of the *Idea* & the Thinking I as two distinct & opposite Things. Now (let me) think of *myself* – of the thinking Being – the Idea becomes dim whatever it be – so dim that I know not what it is – but the Feeling is deep & steady – and this I call *I* ~~the~~ identifying the Percipient and the Perceived – . . . .   (*CN*, I, 921)

If the passage did not offer itself as a gloss ('i.e. – ') on the lines from Wordsworth, its argument could be read as the dialectical opposite of its epigraph. In *The Prelude* Wordsworth comes hyperbolically close to Coleridge's example of the wall:

> To every natural form, rock, fruit, or flower,
> Even the loose stones that cover the highway,
> I gave a moral life
> > (1805, III.124–6)

but here the 'life of Things' seems to have become 'a distinct Image' which is in opposition to 'the Thinking I'. The argument of the passage, then, would be for a Cartesian 'I', kept in its place by the incontrovertible evidence of visual 'ideas'. Again Blake can be adduced as devil's advocate. Annotating Wordsworth's claim for the 'exquisite' and reciprocal 'fitting' of mind to the external world in *The Excursion*, Blake comments mischievously, 'You shall not bring me down to believe such fitting & fitted I know better & Please your Lordship.'[29] Yet even without the evidence of Coleridge's argument with Descartes, to read this passage as advocating an 'I' reminiscent of the *Cogito* would be to attribute to him an uncharacteristic decisiveness. In a letter to Clarkson of October 1806 he is still framing a question: 'first then, what is the difference or distinction between THING and THOUGHT?' (*CL*, II, 1194) and in the *Biographia* he is sure at least that the 'conjectures' of an empirical idealist such as Berkeley 'could not alter the natural difference of *things* and *thoughts*' (*BL* [*CC*], I, 90).

The passage does not criticise Wordsworth, as Anna Seward does, for an egotistical ascription of his own spirit to a lifeless nature, as though his more confident reconciliation of mind and nature might be achieved rhetorically by making claims which do not withstand questioning. What Coleridge suggests here is a gradual attenuation of sensory responsiveness (again, pre-eminently of the visual sense) so that 'deep feeling' renders even a wall as dim an idea as that of the self must be of necessity: so the film on the grate has 'dim sympathies' with the conscious mind of 'Frost at Midnight'.[30] Similarly, the capacity for 'deep feeling', here said to cause such a dimming, is very much a creative one: in a letter to Wordsworth of July 1803 Coleridge praises the former's poetry as 'Philosophy under the action of strong winds of Feeling' (*CL*, II, 957).

In the *Friend* he insists, *contra* the 'vivid and distinct ideas' of Descartes and Locke,[31] that the 'Ideas' of a truth which is not mere veracity are not correlative with clarity. On the contrary, 'deep feeling' is normally attached to 'obscure ideas'. He insists on the imperative.

> to reserve the deep feelings which belong, as by a natural right to those obscure ideas that are necessary to the moral perfection of the human being . . . for objects, which their very sublimity renders indefinite, no less than their indefiniteness renders them sublime: namely to the Ideas of Being, Form, Life, the Reason, the Law of Conscience, Freedom, Immortality, God!   (*Friend* [*CC*], I, 106)

However much he tries to make the 'I' or ego an object of consciousness, it remains pure or transcendental, the ground of consciousness, and can only be said to exist at all when activity is reflected upon. As Kant says, 'the subject of the categories cannot by thinking the categories acquire a concept of itself as the object of the categories' (*Critique of Pure Reason*, p. 377 [B422]). Nevertheless, the insistent 'Feeling', according to the note, leads to 'our life – ourselves', or at least to 'our' references to these processes.

I have tried to show Coleridge attempting to go beyond epistemology, but not (or at least not very successfully) into the embrace of a 'visionary' mode. Analysis of the sublime suggested that these options are not mutually opposed but are both available within, and comprehended by, its economy of representations. What I have often referred to as Coleridge's 'difficulty' in synthesising these two seeming options thus recalls that 'overplus' which Adam Smith identifies only to dismiss.

At the end of a remarkable book which argues that, historically, the visual metaphor dominated speculative philosophy to the extent of its being largely 'epistemology', and argues, less convincingly, for some contemporary alternatives, Richard Rorty distinguishes these two approaches as respectively 'systematic', the mode of which is inquiry, and 'edifying', the mode of which is the 'conversation':

> the difference between conversation and inquiry parallels Sartre's distinction between thinking of oneself as *pour-soi* and as *en-soi* . . . thus . . . the cultural role of the edifying philosopher is to help us avoid the self-deception which comes from believing that we know ourselves by knowing a set of objective facts.[32]

It is a felicitous coincidence that the term 'conversation' should have been generically applied to certain poems by Coleridge, but what I would draw attention to here is, first, a further parallel in that historical movement sketched in this chapter and, second, the way that Rorty himself replaces the metaphor of eyesight with one of self. That slippage certainly parallels what has been noticed in Coleridge. Inescapably, the Socratic injunction to 'know thyself', quoted more than once by Coleridge, enjoins *both* the 'systematic' inquiry associated with epistemological questions *and* the necessarily hazy intuition of responses to the question 'What am I?', which can lead, as in Werther, merely to narcissism. Before looking at Coleridge's 'conversation' poems it will be as well to discuss one system within which Coleridge unequivocally situates himself and one which, he would claim, is immune to the distortions egotism is able to effect within either of these philosophic modes: that is, a Christian account of history.

6   Blest Outstarting

To censure [egotism] in a Monody or Sonnet is almost as absurd as to dislike a circle for being round.   (Preface to *Poems on Various Subjects*, 1796)

> *To God*
> If you have formed a circle to go into
> Go into it yourself & see how you would do.
>   Blake, 'To God'

I have suggested that in aesthetics the sublime might be considered as an attempt to incorporate an 'overplus' of passion or of religious feeling, an attempt at enclosing the powers of the self. Thus resistance to the visual metaphor upon which it depends frees the self to take part in conversation rather than to partake of impressions. Whereas Lockean epistemology assumes a kind of linear interchange, the Christian scheme is often expressed metaphorically as a circle. Karsten Harries has demonstrated the transference of the metaphor of the sphere from theology to cosmology during the Renaissance.[1] In this chapter I shall argue for a transference or even a dissolution of the related metaphor of the circle during the eighteenth century. The metaphor is not itself immune to the problems associated with representation of the self. The language of reason is not a grid that can be fitted over the self's apodictic knowledge: there is no squaring of the circle.

M. H. Abrams's book *Natural Supernaturalism* proposes Romanticism as a 'secularization of inherited theological ideas and ways of thinking', a process not of the 'deletion and replacement of religious ideas but rather the assimilation and reinterpretation of religious ideas, as constitutive elements in a world view founded on secular premises'.[2] A governing metaphor of the ensuing cultural history is that of the circle. Abrams's book begins with and returns to Wordsworth's Prospectus to *The Recluse* in the manner of the 'circuitous journey' to reintegration it identifies. As a critic of Abrams has pointed out, it is therefore locally and ultimately consistent with his assumption that Romantic language is cheerfully mimetic:

> Abrams has identified exactly a basic paradigm of Occidental metaphysics – the picture of an original unity, lost in our present sad dispersal, to be regained at some point in the millennial future, or, in Lewis Carroll's cruel infantile parody: jam yesterday, jam tomorrow, but never jam today. Nietzsche and . . . others . . . do not so much reject this scheme (it cannot be rejected, for our languages repeat it to us interminably) as deconstruct it by turning it inside out, by reinterpreting it. They affirm that the situation of dispersal, separation, and unappeasable desire is the 'original' and perpetual human predicament. The dream of primal and final unity, always deferred, never present here and now, is generated by the original and originating differentiation. The beginning was diacritical.[3]

For Abrams the circle becomes a paradigm for literary structure. He treats Hegel's *Phenomenology* as a kind of *Bildungsroman*, both it and *The Prelude* as *Bildungsreisen* of 'a great circular journey'.[4] What is involved is the difficulty of assimilation and (narrative) reinterpretation, the problem for instance of temporality within process. Fichte speaks of the suspension of time in the sublime moment 'to the point . . . *where the presenting self is presented*' by the imagination (*Science of Knowledge*, pp. 194–5), but this presentation is of little help in that *re*presentation which Coleridge says is the business of the transcendental philosopher (*BL* [*CC*], I, 297). There remains that inherence of the merely temporal in the possibly transcendent which ensures that 'egotism' and 'meat & drink' will always be contiguous as subjects for poetry. As the close of Coleridge's 1818 lecture 'On Poesy or Art' makes clear, it need not be paradoxical to claim that a higher unity is to be found in an 'abridgement' of process: 'Remember that there is a difference between form as proceeding and shape as superinduced; – the latter is either the death or the imprisonment of the thing; – the former is its self-witnessing and self-effected sphere of agency.'[5]

One reason for the actual rather than ideal interest of Coleridge's forms, I shall argue, is his persistent sense of 'self' as

more than the reflexive particle it is here. I shall consider two
texts: the conclusion to the sixth lecture on the history of
philosophy, delivered in January 1819, and the long poem
'Religious Musings' from the volume of 1796. There Coleridge
designates 'Religious Musings' a 'desultory poem'. I shall try to
show the transformation of the 'desultory' into the potential
communion of 'conversation' within the hermeneutic circle of
Coleridge's poetry.

The actual poems of the volume of 1796 which the Preface
defends for their 'egotism' are the thirty-six which, 'in defiance of
Churchill's line "Effusion on Effusion pour away"' (*PW*, II, 1136),
Coleridge terms 'effusions'. For Blair, the origins of poetry itself
were in 'those rude effusions, which the enthusiasm of fancy or
passion suggested to untaught men'; the primitive bard 'sung
indeed in wild and disorderly strains; but they were the native
effusions of his heart'. (*Lectures on Rhetoric*, II, 315, 332–3 [Lecture
XXXVIII]).[6] Blair's are not terms to which the 'effusions' offer
themselves: their egotism is mainly at the level of the rhetorical
indecorum of reference to the self. Coleridge writes to Southey
praising a sonnet on the slave trade, yet deumurs,

> my Mind is weakened – and I turn with selfishness of Thought
> to those milder Songs that develop my lonely Feelings. Sonnets
> are scarcely picked for the hard Gaze of the Public – Manly yet
> gentle Egotism is perhaps the only conversation which pleases
> from these melancholy Children of the Muse.   (*CL*, I, 146)

The 'conversation' of egotism is a private one, but although it
takes place out of sight of the 'hard Gaze of the Public' it is
overseen by that gaze: its licence is analogous to that of pastoral.
For the purposes of the modern reader it is only in the penultimate
'effusion', called eventually 'The Eolian Harp', that Coleridge is
vindicated, but that poem, which in the volume of 1796 has its
composition ascribed to one specific day, is the product not of
spontaneous effusion but of a conscious, and self-conscious,
shaping.[7] Like the Preface, this is perhaps a justification as
'nature' of a tendency not obviously encouraged as art.

Blair's conjectures on the 'origin and progress of poetry' will be
recognised as a less sophisticated version of Schiller's 'naive'
poetry. The last chapter considered the development of two
discrete discourses: one physical, measurable (the visual

metaphor) and one immeasureable, transcendent (divine), with the sublime as a bridge between the two, an account of that 'overplus' which Adam Smith denies. Lowth's *Lectures* approach a collision of these discourses. Lowth considers the Old Testament as poetry, as a source of the sublime. He thus brings it within the realm of the aesthetic but wants to have his wafer and eat it, and must warn that caution is required 'lest while we wander too much at large in the ample field of Poetry, we should imprudently break in upon the sacred boundaries of Theology' (I, 53 [Lecture II]). Poetry has a religious origin, he says, in 'vehemence and passion':

> It is indeed most true, that sacred poetry, if we contemplate its origin alone, is far superior to both *nature* and *art*; but if we could rightly estimate its excellences, that is, if we wish to understand its power in exciting the human affections, we must have recourse to both. . . . (I, 44–5)[8]

Even the pagan Greek poets were 'accounted sacred' by the common people:

> they seemed to have retained some traces of an opinion impressed upon the minds of men in the very earliest ages concerning the true and ancient poetry, even after they had lost the reality itself, and when religion and poetry had, by the licentiousness of fiction reciprocally corrupted each other. (I, 50)

Poetry requires an originary validation as either 'nature' or 'religion'. Thus the interest in Ossian (or in 'Rowley' rather than in Chatterton) wanes when it is revealed as a fake, but what then is the status of Coleridge's 'effusions'? Although he refers to 'The Eolian Harp' as 'the most perfect poem I ever wrote' he invests his 'poetical credit' at the time in 'Religious Musings' (*PW*, I, 108–25).[9]

Any but the fullest reading of such a long and confessedly diffuse poem will be, in both senses, partial. The purpose here is to point out the suggestions that the fullest self-consciousness is a liberation from the self: a process I have called egotism. Like many poems in the volume, 'Religious Musings' specifies a time of composition (in others a place): here 'the Christmas Eve of 1794'.

(It begins with an allusion to Milton's Nativity Ode.) God is celebrated as 'th'ETERNAL MIND' while Christ is 'all of Self regardless' ('heedless of himself' in the volume of 1797), his identity exemplarily unselfish: his 'life was love', which is 'the most holy name' of the 'one omnipresent Mind'.

Coleridge's diagnosis of contemporary history as the result of a fall into anarchic separation (ll. 146–58) provides an antithesis: the human regression into savage egoism. Such egoism is, like idolatry or atheism, a species of superstition preventing the associationist progress towards the Godhead, and leaving the individual in a self-centred predicament much like Werther's, 'A sordid solitary thing . . . / Feeling himself, his own low Self the whole'. This is a dereliction of the will, for the individual self does possess the capacity for elision, for subsuming itself within the 'whole one Self' which is 'oblivious of its own / Yet all of all possessing'.

Christ's example is of the diffusion of the self, diffusing the one into the One, I am into I AM. The Soul is 'attracted and absorbed' by the 'perfect Love' of God 'Till by exclusive consciousness of God / All self-annihilated it shall make / God its identity'.[10] The end is the '*All in All*' of Hartley, 'We and our Father One!' (We are referred to Hartley by Coleridge's footnote, and he is praised as redemptive alongside Milton, Newton and Priestley in ll. 364–76.) For Hartley, the association of ideas leads to the 'pure Love of God, as our highest and ultimate Perfection, our End, Centre, and only Resting-place, to which yet we can never attain',[11] so that the progress towards God itself always entails a deferral, a continual becoming, but as sensation is ever more spiritualised the means of reconciling mind and nature is reasserted, for 'God' becomes 'mind'. He is the spirit which enlivens nature (ll. 97-113), 'Nature's Essence, Mind and Energy!' The power of this mind, and the means by which the individual participates in it is 'love':

> with the which
> Who feeds and saturates his constant soul,
> He from his small particular orbit flies
> With blest outstarting! From himself he flies,
> Stands in the sun and with no partial gaze
> Views all creation; and he loves it all
> And blesses it, and calls it very good!

Thus 'center'd', man too can see that it was good, and in this concurrence is godlike, but he does so by breaking from his 'small particular orbit' to stand in the light of the Son. The language of saturation and absorption is the language of a transcendent negative capability, a capability exemplified by Christ (cf. *LS* [*CC*], p. 71).

Christ's characterlessness is, like Shakespeare's, an absence of determined character, not a lack of character. (Interestingly, the young Hegel regarded Christ as locating his kingdom 'within', not in an outer world where the relationships of law and authority were already determined: 'He could find freedom only in the void'.[12]) Coleridge calls himself a Unitarian throughout this period and his own distrust of external authority is congruent with a dissenting tradition which, denying the Trinity, sees in Christ not authority but example, and takes his assurance that 'the kingdom of God is within you' (Luke 17:21) not as anodyne but as proof of equality.[13] Alternatively, this movement could be compared to the intellectual withdrawal from Jacobinism following events in France in the 1790s: that period in which Wordsworth says he 'once more did retire into' himself. Christopher Hill says of the period in which Milton 'retired' to write his epic,

> All roads in our period [1660–80] have led to individualism. More rooms in better-off peasant houses, use of glass in windows . . . use of coal in grates, replacement of benches by chairs – all this made possible greater comfort and privacy for at least the upper half of the population. Privacy contributed to the introspection and soul-searching of radical Puritanism, to the keeping of diaries and spiritual journals.[14]

With this context in mind Coleridge's praise of Milton's having given up 'his heart to the living spirit and light within him, and avenged himself on the world' in this period (*MiscCrit*, p. 165) begins to assume a relevance for the later poet. Whatever Milton's theology, the trajectory of his epic is a circular one, at least in Coleridge's reading. As man's proleptic substitute Satan journeys to Paradise 'alone thus wandering' (*Paradise Lost*, III.667), like Adam and Eve east of Eden at the end of the poem. The angel loses 'his former name' and becomes Satan (Hebrew, 'adversary') at the point when God announces he has 'begot' his 'only Son' as 'Head' and 'Lord' of the angelic host (v.42–61). Begetting is replaced by becoming. The linear imperatives of nonconformism – transgression and fall, conscience and guilt, cause and effect – become circular.

Even late in life, in *Aids to Reflection*, Coleridge is emphatic in his refusal of an external authority not assented to by the individual intelligence: 'He who begins by loving Christianity better than Truth, will proceed by loving his own Sect or Church better than Christianity, and end in loving himself better than all' (*AR*, p. 101). In the *Watchman* the biblical 'Truth' of the epigraph is the discovery of the actual circumstances of the present war, and within 'Religious Musings' the Christ who 'mourns for the oppressor' is appearing at a moment of crisis in 'the present state of society'. For Shelley, Christ is a prophet of revolution: if his teaching were to be acted upon, 'no political or religious institution could subsist a moment',[15] but Coleridge is closer to Keats, for whom Socrates and Christ are the prime examples of 'disinterestedness' (*KL*, ii, 80). In the second of the two texts by Coleridge under consideration, Christ is said to appear at a time primarily of moral crisis, in the epoch of Roman decadence, 'sensuality at home and ferocity abroad', when 'the eye which was the light of the body had become filmed and jaundiced' (*PL*, pp. 220–1). The characterless Christ is the embodiment of reconciliation. The philosophic and aesthetic desideratum is ultimately religious, and therefore more than etymologically a work of atonement: 'To *reconcile* therefore is truly the work of the Inspired! This is the true *Atonement* – i.e. to reconcile the struggle of the infinitely various Finite with the *Permanent*' (*CN*, ii, 208). The religious and the humanly creative terms are inextricably mixed.[16] Again, in the first Lay Sermon, the quality praised in Shakespeare's creation of characters is adduced in support of a late restatement of the 'one life' which must always be, ultimately, religious (*LS* [*CC*], p. 31). Everything follows the divine *fiat*. Even in the Argument of the poem, the Christian scheme brackets the political 'digressions'.

The 'mild laws' of Christ's love are 'unutterable'. Coleridge heavy-handedly attacks the invocation of God by the anti-French powers ('Religious Musings', ll. 173–211). Because only emblematically defined, the positives Christ represents are unexceptionably positive and are implicitly associated with those whom Coleridge supports. To be against them is to be against 'love'. This is that tendency of Coleridge's political language noted in Chapter 1. Christ's is the privileged discourse that Lowth enjoins and which is intended to function in relation to these 'digressions' only as ideal and by contrast. This is not to suggest that, as here, reading (Coleridge's reading of Christ's discourse) need necessarily be ideological appropriation, but to suggest that the reader's interest may rush to fill the distinterested vacuum which, for Coleridge, is the character of Christ.

The climax of the poem is in a vision of 'the Throne of the redeeming God', which 'Wraps in one blaze, earth, heaven and deepest hell', but this is not conflagration instead of reconciliation. 'Universal Redemption' inevitably follows 'Millennium', as it does in the Argument which prefixed the poem until 1803, but the vision of millennium is introduced with the line 'Life is a vision shadowy of Truth' (a footnote refers us to the 'sublime system of Berkley [*sic*]'); so that vision in turn is ideal rather than visual, a piece of conscious myth-making. Lowth must enter his *caveat* because in myth fiction and 'belief' are difficult of distinction. Within it Christ and Satan coexist as types as well as archetypes of character.[17]

God remains as the end towards which the self is willed, but this always presupposes self-consciousness: ''Tis the sublime of man, / Our noontide Majesty, to know ourselves'. We read that fallen man reaches his apotheosis in self-consciousness only for the enjambement to reveal that this apotheosis is reached in the self's being subsumed: 'to know ourselves / Parts and proportions of one wond'rous whole!' Thus, self-consciousness is an awareness not of separateness but of unity: 'This fraternises man. . . . But 'tis God / Diffused through all, that doth make all one whole'. At this point, however, we are close to the social philosophy propounded by Pope's *Essay on Man*.

Fallen man is said to lack that self-consciousness which will enable him to escape from the 'small particular orbit' of the self into the 'whole one Self' of the Godhead. Fall and redemption can thus be mythologised as the movement of consciousness within the self over history. This is Hegel's project in the *Phenomenology* and is the import of the project Coleridge outlines in the Prospectus to the *Philosophical Lectures*. He posits *Geist* as a fiction, proposing to 'consider Philosophy historically, as an essential part of the history of man, and as if it were the striving of a single mind' (*PL*, p. 67). The same month in which he delivers the lecture, Coleridge writes to Southey announcing his intention to publish transcripts of the whole series, 'because a History of *Philosophy*, as the gradual evolution of the instinct of Man to enquire into the *Origin* by the efforts of his own reason, is a desideratum in Literature' and a necessary propaedeutic to the 'system' of his own *magnum opus* which 'should be bona fide progressive, not in circulo – productive not barren' (*CL*, IV, 917).

In the sixth of those lectures Coleridge speaks of the Pythagorean transmutation of souls: 'after a thousand years were circled round, the souls, as if the bodies were to be by that time empty to receive them, were to come back and make up the same endless and objectless circle'. In his summary the survival of self not as a differentiated soul but as a kind of essential identity is the antithesis of Christian truth (despite his having suggested that this compound may become an oxymoron). What distinguishes the Christian God is that He is '*Our Father*'. It follows that

> immortality is only immortality for us as far as it carries on our consciousness, and with our consciousness our conscience; that it is truly the resurrection of our body, of our personal identity and with it all by which and for which we are to be responsible; that there is no metaphysical division . . . between the soul and body as two distinct or two heterogeneous things. No, we are taught that . . . there are bodies celestial as well as bodies terrestrial, and that only in the body, that is in that personal identity, that which constitutes every man's self and which as an intelligent being he has the power of communicating to another, <*is that*> which constitutes that body. (*PL*, pp. 223–4)

Coleridge's hesitations ('only . . . as far as', 'we are taught that') beg the question. This claim for verification by conversation will be relevant to the consideration of some of the poems; but, once the mechanical certainty of Hartley – for whom God was at the centre of the circle – is found untenable, the statement that *all* circles are 'endless and objectless' becomes provable merely by geometry. In a note of April 1805 Coleridge expresses the kind of *Entfremdung* that would be recognised by Werther in terms of a circle. Referring to the sense of 'duty' as a kind of helpless inactive conscience which increases in inverse relation to any actual 'Enthusiasm' for the moral or material amelioration of others, he notes that he

once wrote to W[ordsworth] in consequence of his Ode to Duty
& in that letter explained this [sense] as the effect of ~~Selfinterest~~
Selfness in a mind incapable of gross Self-interest – decreases of
Hope and Joy, the Soul in its round & round flight forming
narrower circles, till at every Gyre its wings beat against the
personal Self.   (*CN*, ɪɪ, 2531)

Indeed, as the lecture continues, it is 'the supplement of all
philosophy . . . to feel that philosophy itself can only point out a
good which by philosophy is unattainable' (*PL*, p. 226). Spirit, as
the 'intellectual Will', is therefore necessary, but the reader is left
in the position of the two men of Coleridge's parable. One whose
arms are paralysed is enjoined to 'Rub your arms against each
other!' As for the second: 'If I say to a man involved in habits of sin
who sees the misery of his vice, and yet still goes on from bad to
worse, "Exert your Will!" "Alas!" he would answer, "that is the
dreadful penalty of my crimes. I have lost my Will!"' (p. 224).'
All Coleridge can do, however, is assert the assertion of the will,
that it is possible to break out of the circle, to choose a point on its
diameter on which to begin. Unless the history which sees nature
as a circle is a reflexive one (unless, that is, it is believed in as a
fiction, produced by language) it *will* be a self-imprisonment. The
tripartite division of time is inscribed in syntax, a repeated
reminder of dislocation from an 'Original' state whether heathen
or Christian:

according to the Sacred Scriptures there is a threefold State, or
Order, of the Natural World, or *Heaven* and *Earth*; namely the
Past, the *Present*, and the *Future*. For so they are distinguished by
the Apostle St. *Peter*, [2 Peter 3: 5, 7] *The Heavens and Earth which
then were. The Heavens and the Earth which now are*, and in the 13th
ver. he says, *We look for new Heavens*, and *a new Earth.*[18]

Clearly we are not in that state of primal unity in which word and
thing are indissolubly connected, and Coleridge's claim to have
bridged this 'metaphysical division' by means of an intuited,
unexamined substitution of language is another manifestation of
that tendency noted in the last chapter. Lowth warns against the
'reciprocal corruption' of religion and poetry as he brings the two
discourses into contiguity. Coleridge increasingly tends to
collapse the barrier between the two discourses, as in a note
written in Italy in 1806:

The quiet circle in which Change and Permanence *co-exist*, not by combination or juxtaposition, but by an absolute annihilation of difference / column of smoke, the fountains before St Peter's, waterfalls / GOD! – Change without loss – change by a perpetual growth, that <once constitutes & annihilates change> the past, & the future included in the Present // oh! it is aweful.   (*CN*, II, 2832)

The final sublime vocative perhaps acknowledges the impossibility of representing at once the incarnational and devouring faces of the religious experience. This will be dealt with in discussing the projection of an interlocutor outside the poem, and it is a pair of opposites having a clear relationship to 'Kubla Khan'. The 'quiet circle' achieves its stillness by a process of 'annihilation'.

Self-consciousness can be, as for Werther, merely crippling, but a trust in individual intuition – which he carries to extremes – becomes crucial in the poems I discuss. A central paradox of 'Frost at Midnight', as of *The Prelude*, is the notion of self-consciously reappropriating a childhood self which unself-consciously occupied a place within nature but which can possess only now the significance of that place – perhaps a circular rather than a central paradox. For Geoffrey Hartman, predating Abrams, this is crucial to Romantic mythology, offering a parallel between the history of consciousness and the biblical history of man. As he summarises, 'Romantic art has a function analogous to that of religion. The traditional scheme of Eden, Fall, and Redemption, merges with the new triad of Nature, Self-Consciousness, and Imagination – the last term in both involving a kind of return to the first.'[19] For the Romantic artist, Hartman has implied, the Fall has occurred around the time of the epic which renders it (his diagram, seemingly, is drawn with the structure of *The Prelude* in mind), but his parallel can only offer 'a kind of return' because, just as redemption entails a prophecy, a deferral, his corollary 'Imagination' is not so easily reified by the Romantics as by this diagram. The very desire for a return to 'origins' in the attainment of ends suggests Schlegel's 'becoming'. (Coleridge himself speaks of nature as '*that which is about to be born that which is always becoming*' – *AR*, 244.) Hartman's indentification of anti-self-consciousness is a necessary reminder of the ambivalence attendant on the middle term of the secular scheme, though, taking the religious scheme as a grand fiction, he fails to take it with the overarching seriousness with which it would be taken by Coleridge. The problem, in other words, is not solved by the blithe acceptance of the analogy of 'religion' and 'fiction' as a synonym, by asserting the collapse of one scheme into the other, since the one scheme is 'true' and the other, precisely, fictional. For John Dennis, for instance, 'the great Design of Arts is to restore the Decays that hapen'd to human Nature by the Fall, by restoring Order'.[20] Much later for Coleridge the Fall is an inexplicable but explicative noumenal event – like the birth of the self, with which it is simultaneous, the most necessary of fictions:

> A Fall of some sort or other – the creation, as it were, of the nonabsolute – is the fundamental postulate of the moral history of Man. Without this hypothesis, Man is unintelligible; with it, every phenomenon is explicable. The mystery itself is too profound for human insight. (*TT*, p. 84)

Another of Coleridge's notes, this time from 1807, is pregnant in this respect:

> ?Every finite Being or only some that have the temptation to become intensely & wholly conscious of its distinctness, thence tempted to division – thence wretched / some so gross by it as not even to acquire that sense of distinctness wholly swallowed up in stupid instinct of Selfishness not even = self-love – to others Love the first step to re-union / (*CN*, ii, 3154)

The 'temptation' into wretched division is due to the inhibiting superfluity of self-consciousness identified by Hartman, and the terms suggest a kind of Fall, but it is noticeable that 'Selfishness' is the consequence rather of a deficiency of self-consciousness and that even egoistic 'self-love' is a step above this. However, the power of breaking out of what 'Religious Musings' called the 'small particular orbit' of the self remains not in thought but 'Love'. (As the remainder of this note, which I discuss below, makes clear, this 'Love' must be profane as well as sacred if the 'division' is not to be perpetuated.) The will which has chosen disunity, it is implied, can also choose to move towards reunification. Considering the Fall, Hegel was emphatic on this point: 'The principle of restoration is found in thought, and thought only, the hand that inflicts the wound is also the hand that heals it.'[21] Yet what Hegel's cure omits from the diagnosis implicit in Part I is the dynamism of nature. In its insistence on the mind alone it returns dangerously close to the very mechanism from which the giant's hand of Kant released Coleridge, that separation of mind and nature which was the penalty of the Fall.

To speak of 'process' is to extract from Coleridge's writings an alternative value to the 'systematic', to the making of systems.[22] This of course relates back to the problem of fragments, of the entailment in the word of some prior, lost unity. The system of Hegel, which is often described in terms of a circle,[23] is itself the Absolute which is its goal. Thus Spinoza's positing of the Absolute as infinite substance is, for Hegel, inadequate: 'In my view, which can be justified only by the exposition of the system itself, everything turns on grasping and expressing the True, not only as *Substance*, but equally as *Subject*' (*Phenomenology*, pp. 9–10 [Preface]).[24] Not only the history of philosophy but also the philosophy of history is a process of ultimate reflexiveness in which subject and object are complementary and the Absolute, as *Geist*, comes to think itself. Thus the image of a spiral may be more satisfactory for the process of Hegel's system: the circle completes itself at a higher level. This ascent, however, is dependent on assent. The validation of the process can only be in the self's recognising itself as at one with the state. Similarly, Hegel says that 'the universal need for art . . . is man's rational need to lift the inner and outer world into his spiritual consciousness as an object in which he recognises again his own self'.[25] In this century Martin Heidegger acknowledges, as he tries to distinguish the three nouns of his title, 'The Origin of the Work of Art', that

> we are compelled to follow the circle. This is neither a makeshift nor a defect. To enter upon this path is the strength of thought, to continue on it is the feast of thought, assuming that thinking is a craft. Not only is the main step to art a circle like the step from art to work, but every separate step that we attempt circles in this circle.[26]

This is a circularity which his own essay does not escape: 'art', he says at the end, 'is by nature an origin'.[27] The circularity of this argument is, to mix metaphors, its point.

The quest for 'origins' must therefore be an infinite regress, a dead end, and Lowth and others bar the road to the Infinite which lies in the opposite direction. Perhaps it is unjust to Lowth to cast him in the role of Abdiel, as defence counsel to the advocacy of Hegel, but the problem is precisely one of 'justice': of the appropriateness – and of the appropriation – of discourses. At another level, indeed, this will be the problem of the discourse of the poem considered in Part III.

Coleridge's writings cannot be made a composite text, but his positing of the problem in the two texts considered can be usefully juxtaposed with two near contemporary literary accounts. Consider first the brief dialogue 'Über das Marionettentheater' written by the German playwright Kleist in 1810, the year before his suicide. Surprised, on meeting an old friend, to find him preoccupied with the puppet theatre, the narrator inquires as to its attraction. The reply is that there is a non-human grace in the puppets, which are under the penalty only of gravity: 'Only a god can equal inanimate matter in this respect. This is the point where the two ends of the circular world meet.'[28] Then Herr C, the narrator's friend, goes on explicitly to cite the account of the Fall in the third chapter of Genesis, and to claim this apparent paradox as a consequence of the Fall: man lacks grace, in both senses of the word. The return to innocence must be through knowledge, to outrun the continual re-enactment of the Fall, and loss of grace, which is otherwise the lot of man. The narrator's final question is then rhetorical: 'Does that mean we must eat again of the tree of knowledge in order to return [*zurückzufallen*] to the state of innocence?'[29] Like Schiller, Kleist insists that the artist must begin in self-consciousness, but his taking the puppet theatre as the image of the artist's work ironically acknowledges the difficulty of that beginning. The puppets are at once determined and characterless, graceful and dead.

The Christian scheme guarantees both original unity and ultimate reunification, so that if the poem treats of a dialectic of mind and nature it also takes place (or, rather, is in process) within this scheme. Milton's epic has the advantage of direct association, taking that scheme for its subject, so that the literary work itself has 'original' status and itself becomes the unattainable origin of which it treats. Towards the end of his *Conjectures* Young criticises Pope's having rendered the *Iliad* in heroic couplets: '*Blank* is a term of diminution; what we mean by blank verse, is verse unfallen, uncurst; verse reclaim'd, reinthroned in the true *Language of the Gods*; who never thunder'd, nor suffered their *Homer* to thunder, in Rhime' (p. 60). If this claim for the 'language of the gods' is consonant with Lowth's claims for the poetry of the Bible, the great English exemplar of blank verse is also an irresistible inference. Milton too is an 'Original', an honorary Ancient. Young proceeds to an encomium of his own age as enlightened and providential, and says that a millennium of the intellectual world may also be hoped for, since, among other reasons, 'there has been no fall in man on this side *Adam*, who left no works, and the works of all other antients are our auxiliars against themselves, as being perpetual spurs to our ambition, and shining lamps in our path to fame' (p. 73). For Coleridge half a century later Milton's epic can be named as occupying such a place and as exemplifying such a process: 'It and it alone really possesses the Beginning, Middle and End – the totality of a Poem or circle as distinguished from the ab ovo birth, parentage, &c. or strait line of History' (*MiscCrit*, p. 161). Both irresistible force and immovable object, the poem, like the argument, is circular. What Coleridge will call the 'miniaturing' of the religious scheme – precisely a comparison of large things with small – is an imitation of this circle.

It was long ago noticed that Coleridge's 'conversation poems' too end with a 'return'[30] – a recapitulation of the time and place in which they began, now transfigured by a realisation of significance in the dislocations from that beginning. He cancelled the original closing lines of 'Frost at Midnight', he says later, because they destroyed 'the rondo, and return upon itself of the poem. Poems of this kind of length ought to be coiled with its' tail round its' [*sic*] head.'[31] Writing to Cottle in 1815 he is still more explicit: 'The common end of all *narrative*, nay, of *all* Poems is to convert a series into a Whole: to make those events, which in real or imagined History move on in a strait Line, assume to our Understandings a *circular* motion – the snake with it's Tail in it's Mouth.' Such a return is not a final closure but rather a re-embarkation on a circular orbit:

> Doubtless to *his* eye, which alone comprehends all Past and all Future in one eternal Present, what to our short sight appears strait is but a point of the great cycle. . . . Now what that Globe is in Geography, *miniaturing* in order to *manifest* that Truth, such is a Poem to that Image of God, which we were created into, and

which still seeks that Unity, or Revelation of the *One* in and by the *Many*, which reminds it, that tho' in order to be an individual Being it must go forth from God, yet as the *rec*eding from him it is to *pro*ceed towards Nothingness and Privation, it must still at every step turn backward toward him in order to *be* at all – Now a straight line, continuously retracted forms of necessity a circular orbit. (*CL*, IV, 545)[32]

'It' here is again the poem, overseen by the same law as the human, its process comprehended within the process of 'one eternal Present'. The necessary myopia of human sight makes its tyranny egotistical, causing, in its striving towards 'individual Being', a blindness to a process overseen by God. Though apparently deterministic, this process is like Hegel's formula for redemption in requiring the will for its apprehension. The return is a movement which at once closes and re-embarks on the circle, a movement 'towards' and not 'to' a God who, like Schlegel's Infinite or Kleist's grace, is apprehended not in 'being' but in a dynamic becoming, in which revelation is necessarily fragmentary and signification continually deferred. In the *Biographia* Coleridge writes that the poem should move 'like the motion of a serpent' (*BL* [*CC*], II, 14) and of course he describes Alph, the sacred river, as 'meandering with a mazy motion'. I shall suggest in Chapter 8 that the notion of a circular 'return' relates to more than the ancillary function of 'structure' to which Coleridge himself assigns it and that it functions rather as the kind of questioning Paul de Man proposes in Rilke:

The question is . . . whether Rilke's text turns back upon itself in a manner that puts the authority of its own affirmations in doubt, especially when these affirmations refer to the modes of writing that it advocates. At a time when the philosophical interest of Rilke's thought has perhaps somewhat declined, the present and future signification of his poetry depends upon the answer to this question.[33]

The actual process of that 'miniaturing in order to manifest' which is Coleridge's poetic practice will be the concern of Part III.

PART III

Sara, Hartley, Porlock

Preamble

If 'Religious Musings' and the other long visionary poems attempt the sublime and are a preparation for epic, then the shorter lyric poems are pathetic, a poetry of sensibility. The egotistical sublime and the egotistical pathos of the 'effusions' could be seen as reconciled within the 'conversation poems', which approach a domestication of the sublime. Stemming more directly from the 'effusions' than from 'Religious Musings' they attempt, among other things, a reconciliation of these discourses. The first 'Nehemiah Higginbottom' sonnet (*PW*, I, 209–210) 'had for its object to excite a good-natured laugh at the spirit of *doleful egotism*' (*BL* [*CC*], I, 27) but it is as much a parody of Coleridge's own effusive manner as of the early master Bowles. Coleridge recalls that, with Cowper, Bowles was 'to the best of my knowledge the first who combined natural thoughts with natural diction; the first to reconcile the heart with the head' (I, 25). In the case of Cowper the reconciliation is claimed as entirely formal, a 'divine Chit chat' (*CL*, I, 279), mediating between Miltonic sublimity and the trivial with a flexibility lacking from the 'swell and glitter' (*PW*, II, 1145; *BL* [*CC*], I, 7) of 'Religious Musings'.[1] The different terms of the salutation of Wordsworth as 'the only man who has effected a compleat and constant synthesis of Thought & Feeling and combined them with Poetic Forms' (*CL*, II, 1034) indicate Coleridge's belief that the problem is more than formal. The 'synthesis of Thought & Feeling' is prior to the poem, the discourse of which is merely a matter of appropriate 'combination'. What Coleridge found in Bowles in the mid 1790s was an enabling instrument for what he calls the reconciliation of subject and object in his own 'conversation poems'.

Chapter 8 will attempt a reading of 'Frost at Midnight' and then go on to examine the strategy that poem employs to effect such a reconciliation. It is a strategy, I shall suggest, of appeal to authentication outside the poem. Coleridge desires the authority

101

of speech: a language which is heard rather than eyed; a language which must be claimed to exist eventually even where its absence is acknowledged actually. The language of the self will be someone else's language. First some poems by these contemporaries which converge on 'Frost at Midnight' will be examined, along with the penultimate 'effusion', 'The Eolian Harp'.

7   A Mingled Charm

Part II tried to show that Coleridge's distrust of the 'despotism of the eye' is related to his 'suspicion, that any system built on the passiveness of the mind must be false, as a system' (*CL*, II, 709). Such a system would also fail, reciprocally, to give nature 'her proper interest' (II, 864) – a failure which Bowles exemplifies. The last phrase quoted occurs in a letter to Sotheby of September 1802. Bowles is deficient, says Coleridge, not in 'sensibility' but in 'Passion' and 'he has no native passion because he is not a Thinker'. The distinction he makes for Bowles parallels one made to explain the superiority of Hebrew over Greek poetry:

> It must occur to every Reader that the Greeks in their religious poems address always the Numina Loci, the Genii, the Dryads, the Naiads, &c &c – All natural Objects were *dead* – mere hollow Statues – but there was a Godkin or Goddessling *included* in each – In the Hebrew Poetry you find nothing of this poor Stuff – as poor in genuine Imagination, as it is mean in Intellect – / At best, it is but Fancy, or the aggregating Faculty of the mind – not *Imagination*, or the *modifying* and *co-adunating* Faculty. This the Hebrew Poets appear to me to have possessed beyond all others – & next to them the English. In the Hebrew Poets each Thing has a Life of its own, & yet they are all one Life.   (II, 865–6)

Despite this claim for coadunation the letter also reveals a sense of propriety akin more to Baillie then to Lowth: the sublime feeling of the 'Hymn before Sunrise' was occasioned not on Chamonix but on Scafell, and Coleridge 'transferred' himself to the Alps '& adapted my former feelings to these grander external objects' (II, 864–5).

The poems of Bowles that Coleridge specifies (*BL* [*CC*], I, 24) are 'Hope', the *Monody Written at Matlock* and the sonnets.[1] The model they provide is of a poetry which, situating meditation in

landscape, can seem to unify mind and nature, the ideal expressed
in Coleridge's introduction to a 'sheet of sonnets' by various
authors to be sent out with Bowles's 1794 sonnets:

> Those Sonnets appear to me the most exquisite, in which moral
> Sentiments, Affections, or Feelings, are deduced from, and
> associated with, the scenery of Nature. Such compositions
> generate a habit of thought highly favourable to a delicacy of
> character. They create a sweet and indissoluble union between
> the intellectual and the material world.   (*PW*, ii, 1139)

As in the *Poems on Various Subjects*, Bowles's poems generally
specify a place and time of composition. They frequently begin
with a river scene, as in Sonnet vi, 'To the River Tweed', where
the poet can 'with pensive peace . . . abide / Far from the stormy
worlds tumultuous roar'. He says of the passer-by in Sonnet v,
'To the River Wensbeck', 'whene'er of pleasures flown / His heart
some long-lost image would renew, / Delightful haunts: he will
remember you'. As in 'Tintern Abbey' the picturesque occasions
memories of significance, but for Bowles there is only nostalgia:
the childhood music of his 'native streams' is irrecoverable, 'the
sounds of joy, once heard, and heard no more' (Sonnet xiii,
'Written at Ostend, July 22, 1787').

The *Monody* is again concerned with the return to a scene of
remembered significance, of which a corollary is the revitalisation
of poetic powers ('Once more I meet the long-neglected Muse'),
but there is less a 'sweet and indissoluble union between the
intellectual and the material world' than an overmastering of the
one by the other, as in Sonnet xvii, 'In a Storm': 'Seek not in
nature's fairer scenes a charm, / But shroud thee in the mantle of
distress, / And tell thy poor heart "This is happiness."' So the
'scenes' of nature are yoked to the poet's state of mind with little
sense of interpenetration. At the end of the *Monody* the Derwent
lingers at the spot as the poet does, complaining 'like one forsaken
and unheard', and autumn leaves cause him to 'think of poor
Humanity's brief day / How fast its blossoms fade, its summers
speed away'.

As M. H. Abrams shows,[2] Bowles's poetry derives from the
loco-descriptive tradition of Sir John Denham's *Cooper's Hill*,
which finds in the picturesque a source of meditation (often
historical or political reflection, but also often 'moral' in the sense

in which Bowles moralises about 'Humanity'). The genre presupposes a point of temporal and spatial fixity from which to view the scene: temporally, the present; spatially, usually above it. (As Hazlitt says in his essay 'On Egotism', 'to *look down* upon any thing seemingly implies a greater elevation and enlargement of view than to *look up* to it' – *HW*, xii, 160.)[3] This then makes it possible for Bowles syntactically to connect his own present state of mind to the time and locale specified. Clearly, one of the striking features of 'Tintern Abbey', 'The Eolian Harp' or 'Frost at Midnight' is a disruption of this fixity, but Coleridge's own sonnet to Bowles is very like the manner of its addressee in its overemphatic alliteration and – more obviously in the first version (*PW*, i, 84) – the nervous tic of personification, which is another means of humanising the external (Bowles's Sonnet x features 'Poverty', 'Hope', 'Fortune', 'Pity', 'Patience', 'Piety', 'Content', 'Genius' and 'Sorrow'). Nature appears only as similes for this process, so that the final portentous simile is the intrusion rather than interfusion of nature: 'As the great SPIRIT erst with plastic sweep / Mov'd on the darkness of the unform'd deep'. The 'PLEASURE' of Bowles's poems is as a palliative to the troubled mind: 'Their mild and manliest melancholy lent / A mingled charm, such as the pang consign'd / To slumber'. Abrams's summary of the 'local-meditative formula' of the 'typical single poem' from Bowles's 1789 collection is just:

> [It] begins with a rapid sketch of the external scene – frequently . . . a river scene – then moves on to reminiscence and moral reflection. The transition is often managed by a connecting phrase which civilizes the shift from objects to concepts and indicates the nature of the relationship between them: 'So fares it with the children of the earth'; 'ev'n thus on sorrow's breath / A kindred stillness steals'; 'Bidding me many a tender thought recall / Of summer days'; 'I meditate / On this world's passing pageant'.[4]

The 'mingled charm' of Bowles's poetry is rather in its civilised mingling of 'objective' and 'conceptual' discourses than in any *a priori* 'union'. By 1802, in the letter to Sotheby, Coleridge complains of the poems in Bowles's second volume that this enabling-formula is, precisely, formulaic and mechanical – they are, in the phrase of his own 'conversation poems', '"Sermoni propiora" which I once translated – "*Properer for a Sermon*"' (*CL*, II, 864). Bowles is censured for failing in just that which Coleridge had regarded as his distinctive success: the 'reconciliation of the heart with the head' (*BL* [*CC*], I, 24):

> There reigns thro' all the blank verse poems such a perpetual trick of *moralizing* every thing – which is very well, occasionally – but never to see or describe any interesting appearance in nature, without connecting it by dim analogies with the moral world, proves faintness of Impression. Nature has her proper interest; and he will know what it is, who believes & feels, that every Thing has a Life of it's own, & that we are all *one Life*. A Poet's *Heart & Intellect* should be *combined*, *intimately* combined & *unified*, with the great appearances in Nature – & not merely held in solution & loose mixture with them, in the shape of formal Similies [*sic*]. . . .   (*CL*, II, 864)

Even here, however, the activities of to 'see or describe' are assumed as interchangeable, even as mutually complementary.

The passage of course prefigures the famous 'one Life' passage inserted into 'The Eolian Harp' (*PW*, I, 100–2) and its insertion in that poem suggests that Coleridge, considering it the 'favourite of *my* poems' (*CL*, I, 295) even in its earlier version, saw it as combining and unifying mind and nature in a way Bowles suggests but never achieves. However, the poem again begins in the manner of Bowles and the other 'effusions', having specified a time and place of composition. The particular objects of this location are then syntactically yoked to stated feelings – here, of marital contentment: 'merely held in solution with them, in the shape of formal Similies'. Jasmine and myrtle are 'meet emblems . . . of Innocence and Love', the brightness of a star occasions the remark 'such should Wisdom be'[5] and clouds are humanised, 'slow saddening round'. Thus the affinity of some lines from Cowper's *The Task* to the first part of 'Frost at Midnight', first noticed by Humphry House,[6] is rather to 'The Eolian Harp'. Assuredly, Cowper too is gazing idly into a hearth and recognises, as Coleridge does in the later poem, 'strangers' there. For Cowper, the 'faint illumination' of the 'glowing hearth' causing shadows to dance 'uncouthly to the quivering flame' is, in a proto-Wordsworthian locution, 'not undelightful'. The dramatic situation of the Cowper passage is one in which the passivity of nature is at once parallel to the passivity of the mind:

> such a gloom
> Suits well the thoughtful or unthinking mind,
> The mind contemplative, with some new theme
> Pregnant, or indispos'd alike to all. ·

Cowper does not present an internal drama, a process coinstantaneous with reading, but is recounting an habitual mood. It is also one which he distrusts, or can see only as an absence, 'an indolent vacuity of thought' – the phrase with which he undercuts his recognition of 'strangers' in the fire:

> Nor less amus'd have I quiescent watch'd
> The sooty films that play upon the bars,
> Pendulous, and foreboding in the view
> Of superstition, prophesying still,
> Though still deceiv'd, some stranger's near approach.

The recognition is qualified at once by the syntax through which it is won: the introductory locution again, 'nor less . . .'; two clauses of morally weighted diction modifying the visual recognition and two qualifying the intuited significance of this as a habitual ('still . . . still . . .') self-deception. The face of the gazer 'conceals the mood lethargic with a mask / Of deep deliberation'.

In Wordsworth's 'Tintern Abbey' (*WPW*, ii, 259–63) the moral sense connecting the present to past and future means that in the sleep of the body there is the capacity to 'become a living soul'

> While with an eye made quiet by the power
> Of harmony, and the deep power of joy,
> We see into the life of things.

Cowper's is a 'waking dream' of forms in the 'red cinders' on which 'with poring eye / I gaz'd, myself creating what I saw'. Distrustful of the unselectivity of the senses, he puts the senses to the service of the mind, yet when he recollects himself his 'gazing' is realised as fanciful. For all that it appeals to the authority of a misremembered line from Young's *Night Thoughts*, Wordsworth's lines for the coactivity of 'eye and ear' with mind upon nature, 'both what they half-create / And what perceive', are offered as the triumph of both where 'myself creating what I saw' may be only the creation of illusions.[7] Cowper goes on to snap himself out of a mood in which he 'lose[s] an hour', a nature which has remained external reconstituting its other: 'the freezing blast . . . restores me to myself'; 'It summons home / The recollected pow'rs'; 'snapping short / The glassy threads, with which the fancy weaves / Her brittle toys'. In the *Critique of Judgement* Kant adduces a flickering fire as a trivial example of the charm conveyed 'to the imagination because [it] sustain[s] its free play':[8] a 'toy of thought' in Coleridge's phrase, but unlike Coleridge Cowper does not go beyond his suspicion that such intuitions are merely the 'brittle toys' of the fancy.

In the opening lines of 'The Eolian Harp' the main verb in the half-line 'most soothing sweet it is' introduces a series of infinitives recording a soothed, inactive nature. Nature, however, is in the process of transition at twilight (ll. 34–53 are set 'at noon') although at first its very activity is confirmation of the inactive domestic contentment of the 'Cot' now projected into 'the world': 'The stilly murmur of the distant sea / Tells us of silence'. The stirrings of sound at the end of the second section are not, as at the end of the first, confirmation of a more pervasive silence, but of a continual potential in nature 'Where the breeze warbles, and the mute still air / Is Music slumbering on her instrument'. The parallel is marked by the phrases introducing the two intuitions of auditory significance: 'the world *so* hush'd!' has become 'a world so fill'd'. Mind is not yoked to nature but they are rhetorically interfused, the 'motion' of nature acquiring a 'soul' and the determinism of the senses overthrown in an energy understood at once as a 'life' not susceptible of sensory differentiation: 'A light in sound, a sound-like power in light / Rhythm in all thought, and joyance every where'.[9] This 'life' is again that of 'Kubla Khan' in the sensory displacement of 'All who heard should see them there'; in 'Tintern Abbey' it is an 'eye made quiet'.

Such a reading of 'The Eolian Harp', however, fails to take account of the 'frame' or the 'return' and, specifically, of the problem of Sara. For one critic she is 'a nuisance', while another calls her 'governessy'.[10] As an 'effusion', 'The Eolian Harp' is framed by an address to Sara with which it begins and ends. There is certainly a dialectic in the 'drama' of the poem, but it is a dialectic which is at first rhetorical. The speculation around the symbolic significance of the harp itself (ll. 43–8) is already modified by Coleridge's having acknowledged the possibility that his thoughts may be no more than 'idle flitting phantasies' before

Sara is said to reappear glancing her 'mild reproof'. The apparently more immediate experience, shared with Sara, of lines 34–43 is in fact a dislocation from the dramatic present of the poem, disguised by the fact that this other habitual activity, though introduced as an analogy ('thus . . . as . . .') is rendered, like the rest of the poem, in the present tense. Concurring with the 'holy dispraise' reported of Sara for other such 'phantasies', the poem dismisses them as 'Bubbles that glitter as they rise and break / On vain Philosophy's aye-babbling spring'.[11] The double negatives of Sara's imagined disparagement of the vision, 'nor such thoughts . . . dost thou not reject', evince the ambivalence in which both that vision and a possibly antithetical return are held. Coleridge enjoins on himself finally the silence of the first section. 'Shapings of the unregenerate mind' might also be the shapings of the imagination in its transactions with nature. The sublime praising God 'with awe' seems opposed to a 'faith that inly *feels*', and yet this feeling is ascribed not to the visionary but to the *dévot*, not to Coleridge but to Sara. His own sense of a residual ambivalence in the poem is demonstrated by his addition, from 1797, of a footnote to this line in which it is perhaps the 'pensive' Sara who is alluded to as, like the atheist, 'froid au spectacle le plus ravissant'.[12]

Coleridge's dubiety about his own speculative 'thoughts' is certainly akin to Cowper's. If the 'frame' is seen simply as the first and last paragraphs of the final text, the harp presents itself at the start of the poem proper. The perception is aural. The stirrings of the breeze on the harpstrings at once remove the poem from the moral and domestic aegis of the frame, Coleridge's imperative alerting us to a sensual as well as sensory awakening:

> hark!
> How by the desultory breeze caress'd,
> Like some coy maid half yielding to her lover,
> It pours such sweet upbraiding, as must needs
> Tempt to repeat the wrong!

The breeze, at first 'desultory' like the poet, is now the harbinger of an ecstatic displacement into a visionary world anticipating that of 'Kubla Khan', but dependent less on the visual than on the aural sense, the 'long sequacious notes' suggesting to the imagination a sensory voluptuousness in excess of the actual sensory stimuli. The 'long sequacious notes / Over delicious surges sink and rise', and the delicious surges of the verse movement already refer to a condition which is neither that of the external breeze nor of the poet's internal state alone. The second long simile for the sound of the harp (ll. 20–5) is the projection of an indeterminate 'Fairy-land', 'Where Melodies . . . like birds of Paradise / Nor pause, nor perch, hovering on untam'd wing'. The end of the following, interjected, passage is again 'love', which might accommodate the eroticism suggested by the breeze 'caressing' the 'clasped' lute to a love of 'all things in a world so fill'd'.

These erotic suggestions imply an incompatibility of the harp's significance with the social morality represented by Sara. The notebook entry quoted in Chapter 7 above goes on to define the 'Love' which is the 'first step to re-union'. Already here Coleridge has moved far from the Hartleian process of the 'Transformation of Sensuality into spirituality';[13] sacred love must accommodate profane love 'else Religion will not only partake of, instead of being partaken by & so co-adunated with, the summit of ~~real~~ Love, but necessary include the Nadir of Love, appetite / thence ~~the~~ dissensualize its nature into fantastic Passions, lewd Idolatry of Paphian Priestesses' (*CN*, ii, 3154). Reunification implies the reinstatement of the fallen 'lusts of the flesh [and] the eye' (*LS* [*CC*] p. 61) to their proper status within the human scheme.

The dialectic of the first and second sections is then explicated in the lines of the temporal displacement, which follow. Such an 'uncall'd' awareness is suspect and may be no more than the entertainment of 'idle flitting phantasies' by an 'indolent and passive brain'. Likening the mind to the 'subject-Lute' explicates a prior modification in which Coleridge worries over the 'indolent and passive' self's being prey to wild and various stimuli and therefore ultimately 'unregenerate'. The harp is perceived as creative in being stimulated by the breeze. It can be no more than intermediary, passive and, importantly, unselfconscious. The creative capacity of the self or subject in the transaction with nature is, however, recapitulated, for it can thus be enrolled within the energy of divine creativity:

> And what if all of animated nature
> Be but organic Harps diversely fram'd,
> That tremble into thought as o'er them sweeps
> Plastic and vast, one intellectual breeze,
> At once the Soul of each, and God of all?

In the Rugby School manuscript of the second (1797) draft of the poem (*PW,* II, 1022–3) recognition of the 'Soul of each' of the objects of dynamic nature is shown to be logically consistent with this egotistical climax:

> Thus *God* would be the universal Soul,
> Mechaniz'd matter as th'organic harps
> And each one's Tunes be that, which each calls I.

The lines of the final version may be 'an example of pure Neoplatonic Spinozism'[14] but the pantheist vision is a speculation and the reappearance of Sara is thus the reassertion of a dialectic.

Coleridge himself insists that the vital personal experience is rather in understanding the token emblems of 'Innocence', 'Love' and 'Wisdom' as the possession of 'Peace, and this Cot, and thee, heart-honour'd Maid'. The reader recalls a tension between Sara and the 'coy maid' of the simile, who is most unlike her. As William Empson points out, in successive revisions of the 1796 text Coleridge 'twice added further heretical or profane thoughts for his bride to have reproved'.[15] Two kinds of discourse clash, and Sara's reproof might be Lowth's *caveat.* Generally, Bowles, Cowper and pre-eminently Wordsworth are valued for the synthetic capabilities of their language. Locally, such a synthesis takes the form of a symbol – from the Greek *sumballein,* to bring together, as in two sides of a coin, teutonicised as *Sinnbild,* picture of sense. What the pat similes of the opening give way to is the symbol of the harp itself, which is prismatic: not a receptacle for the accretion of significance but a point at which the process towards significance is intensely visible and yet most diffuse. My authority for this description of symbol is De Quincey's essay 'Style':

> In very many subjective exercises of the mind, as, for instance, in that class of poetry which has been formally designated by this epithet (meditative poetry, we mean, in opposition to the Homeric, which is intensely objective), the problem before the writer is to project his own inner mind; to bring out consciously what yet lurks by involution in many unanalysed feelings; in short, to pass through a prism and radiate into distinct elements what previously had been even to himself but dim and confused ideas intermixed with each other.   (*QCW,* x, 226)[16]

(Against this could be set Empson's brusque comment, after explaining the ascription of a 'spirit' to inanimate objects as 'Animism, the condensation of the universal spirit into local centres of experience', that 'modern readers are familiar with such talk in poetry but regard it as admittedly nonsense ("imagery") or at best a device for hinting at some truth which it leaves obscure ("symbolism")'.[17]) Neither the visual nor the aural terms are adequate to the indeterminate, continually questionable character of an intuited significance. It is a vexed question whether the symbol merely represents or also participates – vexed enough in regard to the communion for this to constitute a fundamental difference between Protestantism and Catholicism. Coleridge's comment that the symbols of the Bible narratives are 'consubstantial with the truths of which they are the conductors' (*LS* [*CC*], p. 30) rather suggests the latter, particularly in its context ('symbol' is privileged over 'metaphor' and 'allegory') and not least by the transubstantiation of verb into noun.[18]

It is for this reason perhaps that Sara appears as a character in the poem. (This is not to say that she exists as a 'character' but to suggest that she does embody that ambivalence traced through the poem.) Wordsworth is at once more confident in his egotism, discernible in the way the painfully won synaesthesia of 'The Eolian Harp' is present throughout 'Tintern Abbey'. In 'Tintern Abbey', similarly, the process of the poem can demonstrate the assertion of 'something far more deeply interfused' without the mediation of the indeterminate symbols of 'The Eolian Harp' or 'Frost at Midnight'. Wordsworth's poem shares with 'Frost at Midnight' and 'The Eolian Harp' an initial temporal and spatial location, with the solitary speaker turning finally to a companion. While this location will encourage Coleridge's 'abstruser musings' the 'wild secluded scene' by the Wye impresses Wordsworth with 'thoughts of more deep seclusion'. His turning to Dorothy is towards confirmation of that which the self has already won: she appears only at the end. Already validated by 'nature', the mediation of sensory into moral both in the past and from past to present in the poem is projected onto Dorothy and into the future. The gift is that mediation:

> thy mind
> Shall be a mansion for all lovely forms
> Thy memory be as a dwelling-place
> For all sweet sounds and harmonies.

In Wordsworth's account, the 'meditation' which follows his ascent of Snowdon recognises a reciprocal dynamism in the mind of man:

> This is the very spirit in which they deal
> With all the objects of the universe:
> They from their native selves can send abroad
> Like transformation, for themselves create
> A like existence, and where'er it is
> Created for them, catch it by an instinct.
>
> (*Prelude*, 1805, xiii. 91–6)

Coleridge is dubious as to whether he is one of those who can both respond adequately to that 'flash' of a vision of nature 'for themselves' and 'combine' that responsiveness with poetic form; this dubiety is also a rhetorical tendency. The desire for external validation these of his poems express is not a final failure of confidence but the embodiment of an inherent ambivalence as to the status of the self, Coleridge differing from Wordsworth in the extent to which this is problematic. This tendency is crucial to that wavering before and assertion of the self in 'egotism'. Let us now trace that process.

8 The Frost Performs

> For all that meets the bodily sense I deem
> Symbolical, one mighty alphabet
> For infant minds.
>> ('The Destiny of Nations')

> Then said I, Ah, Lord GOD! behold, I cannot speak: for I am a
> child.   (Jeremiah 1:6)

At the end of the first volume of the *Biographia* Coleridge takes up a
suggestion of the epistolary 'friend' to answer himself by
promising for volume II 'a detailed prospectus' of his 'great book
on the CONSTRUCTIVE PHILOSOPHY' (*BL* [*CC*], I, 304, 302). 'There
is', as Paul Hamilton notes, 'no poetic content in this broken
promise, yet if we read *Biographia* as the ironic gambit within a
larger philosophical solution we must take the promise
seriously.'[1] Promise piles upon promise, each one apparently
infelicitous, each performative in the sense that the process of the
text continually disrupts any systematised 'philosophic solution'.
I want to look at a poem by Coleridge in terms of the problems
raised by its attempted solution. Specifically, I want to consider
the last thirty lines, the last two verse paragraphs, of 'Frost at
Midnight' (*PW*, I, 240–2) as a speech act.[2]
  In its way, the passage reduces to a matrix which is both
transitive and a classic performative: 'I bless you.' It follows lines
in which you can recognise at least three distinct temporal axes –
Coleridge remembering himself as a schoolboy, who both
remembers the past and looks forward. So I think that what
grammatically has the structure of a continuous present held
within a future construction (the last lines) is also a local
illocutionary act. Or we might say that it acknowledges the force
of a performative versus a constative mode throughout the poem.
Furthermore, this is in J. L. Austin's terms a perlocutionary act.

114

Coleridge is not saying simply 'thou shalt' – a *fiat* like that of Kubla Khan, or indeed God. What he says is 'it thrills my heart / . . . to think that thou shalt' (ll. 47–9), implying something like 'I hope that you will.' To come near an understanding of this act we need to consider the whole process of the poem.

Like 'The Eolian Harp' the poem assumes four parts, the last of which is in a sense a 'return' to the dramatic situation of the first, ostensibly inhabited by the poet in the act of writing. Again significance is won not by external action (which may serve, as it does in 'The Eolian Harp', to question the significance claimed) but by the claim for coalescence of external nature and the first-person consciousness, both of which are in process through the 'companionable form' of an indeterminate, prismatic symbol.

Gray's lines 'Now fades the glimmering landscape on the sight / And all the air a solemn stillness holds' dramatically situate his 'Elegy' in the stillness necessary to a meditation which becomes overtly elegiac only at the end. 'Frost at Midnight' begins with natural process: 'The Frost performs its secret ministry / Unhelped by any wind.' The active verb already suggests comparisons with the dormant human creativity of the lines that follow. Unperceived, the natural 'ministry' is like that of the Holy Spirit, though Coleridge would still be a Unitarian at this time: this is in contrast to the public 'ministeries' which are the vocation of the young poet of 'Religious Musings'. (Natural processes employ a 'ministry' for Wordsworth too).[3] With the introduction of the human protagonists in the fourth and fifth lines there is, then, a trinity proposed of mind, nature and an absolutely other 'ministry', unmediated.[4] The possibility of a kind of crude Hegelian reading emerges – in the way that Daniel Stempel proposes the Snowdon episode from *The Prelude* as an exact imitation of the Fichtean model of the mind.[5] However, as any reading of Fichte or Hegel would show, the ego expands into the world sequentially, dramatising the relationship between consciousness and self-consciousness. The problem becomes one of representations, of textuality. Coleridge could even have the earlier poem in mind when he insists that the frost's 'performance', unlike that of the eolian harp, is 'unhelped by any wind'. The stillness is, at once, potential. All noise and motion is at first external. In the 'Elegy' the 'complaint' of an owl is the only real disturbance of the stillness: here 'The owlet's cry / Came loud – and hark again! loud as before'. The change into the past tense, with a repetition stressing the immediacy of a present moment evoked in the rest of this first section, presents those opposites which are to be reconciled: a jarring presence of the external together with a natural process which continues just beyond perception. Nature is as yet unreconciled. Inside, the 'sole unquiet thing' becomes the symbol of remembered and potential significance, but, outside, this repeated staccato cry is potentially malignant, in contrast to the 'secret' benignity of the frost. In 'Fears in Solitude' the 'owlet Atheism' represents wilful human blindness which 'hooting at the glorious sun in Heaven / Cries out, "Where is it?"' (In a notebook entry of 1796 'men anxious for this world' are likened to 'owls that wake all night to catch mice' – *CN*, i, 178.) Even in the opening lines, then, the potential exists for both Christian benignity and the Satanic perversion of the self.

It cannot be said that it is at this point that the self *enters*, because the introduction of the first person contrasts this active nature with an internal stasis:

> The inmates of my cottage, all at rest,
> Have left me to that solitude which suits
> Abstruser musings: save that at my side
> My cradled infant slumbers peacefully.

It is only the dim perceptions of the opening lines which can be the element differentiated by the comparative 'Abstruser'.[6] At the end of 'The Eolian Harp' there was a compensation in the Christian gift of 'possession' of 'Peace, and this Cot, and thee, heart-honour'd Maid'. The sequence of possessives in the lines above is an act of enclosure which establishes a mental as well as physical space: in the self's possessing it there is self-possession. The exception to its solitude is important. The presence of Coleridge's child provides him with an interlocutor who is silent and passive, unlike Sara, and can become the agent of the significance discovered.

While there are noise and motion outside, within the cottage silence and stillness are emphasised: 'peacefully', a 'strange / And extreme silentness', 'Inaudible', a 'hush', a repeated 'calm' all connote not lifelessness but life 'at rest', a dormant activity and potential creativity. The cry of the owl here, like the sea's 'murmur' at the end of the first part of 'The Eolian Harp', serves to intensify silence. The repetition of 'loud' in the third line, like the repetition of 'Sea, hill, and wood', is accommodated to the 'silentness' within the cottage. Yet the syntax betrays unease. Only in the last sentence of this first part, as the speaker discovers externally in the 'sole unquiet thing' an image for himself in relation to the 'inmates of my cottage, all at rest', are the clauses conterminous with the lines. Here 'all the numberless goings-on of life' are too many to fix on and are 'Inaudible as dreams'. The 'hush of nature' is by this point that *inside* the cottage, and the very calmness produces the unease:

> so calm, that it disturbs
> And vexes meditation with its strange
> And extreme silentness.

The process of self-consciousness is not that of 'meditation'. The 'strange / And extreme silentness' is itself a strange locution, 'silentness' seeming more than a metrically convenient synonym for the 'silence' of 'The Eolian Harp'.[7] While the possible destruction of calm and solitude serve only to confirm them, what disturb are the 'Abstruser musings' themselves. A movement from religious to abstruser musings is itself circular.

Now the consciousness fixes on the sooty film on the grate which has 'motion' and is 'unquiet'. Thus it suggests itself at once as a 'companionable form' for the self's own just lucent creativity. The noun phrase 'dim sympathies' perhaps comments on the quality as it makes the connection. What is criticised is not the connection but the barely perceptible activity of the referents of the simile which makes the similitude possible: the 'puny flaps and freaks' of the fire are seen to be easily reconcilable with the 'idling Spirit' and it is this very ease which is susceptible to criticism. The repetition of the verb 'flutter' before the connection between mind and film is made (the word is applied to the film again in l. 26) can apply to either, and in the movement from 'fluttered' to 'Still flutters' there is a suggestion of the significant continuity claimed for the frost in the first line and a half.

The readiness to find such connections, which is the capacity Wordsworth posits in the passage discussed at the end of the last chapter, is one about which Coleridge is more uneasy. The 'companionable form' is one which 'By its own moods interprets, every where / Echo or mirror seeking of itself', and the explanation is immediately qualified by criticism of this egotistical act which 'makes a toy of Thought'. In a note of 1796 Coleridge writes, 'Our quaint metaphysical opinions in an hour of anguish like playthings by the bedside of a child deadly sick' (*CN*, I, 182). The harp is, literally, a toy, teasing the mind with an aural significance as the shadows on the hearth tease the mind with the flutterings of visual significance. The intuition is stirred by the memory (in a footnote added in 1802) that 'in all parts of the kingdom these films are called *strangers* and supposed to portend the arrival of some absent friend'.

A transition, signalled by the interjection 'But O!', displaces the reader from the present dramatic situation of the first part into that of the memory. Similarly, in 'Tintern Abbey' the moment of intense insight is set against the memory of an habitual deprivation of such insight, the transition marked by 'yet, oh! how oft. . . .' Again, in 'Kubla Khan' the interjection 'But oh!' after the first part is the marker not of an antithesis, but of a displacement from the transfigured landscape of *Purchas, his Pilgrimage* into a 'savage place' correlative, perhaps, of the mind in a 'sleep . . . of the external senses' (*PW*, I, 296), a descent into 'that deep romantic chasm'. The access of energy here is, of course, syntactic, but rather than being accomplished by that 'But' the contrast is implicit in the length of the sentences, the way clauses are relative to the lines. The syntactic hinge was in the representation of the symbol. The new energy renders a memory of schooldays which is introduced as an habitual way of life ('how oft . . . how oft . . .'); in which the 'bars' of the grate suggest too, in this context, the shades of the prison house; and in which signification is not retrieved but was even there deferred.

The memory is at once of the schoolboy Coleridge reaching forward into a future which has become the present in which the poet writes and of the schoolboy's reaching further backward still. His recognition of 'strangers' in the fire is a recognition of potential significance, a deferral 'with most believing mind / Presageful', but 'as oft' a habitual experience is the visionary, dreaming with 'unclosed lids' of the still younger self. This is marked again, as in 'This Lime-tree Bower', by the repetition of the verb 'gaze' and the 'swimming' of the visual sense. There is a further spatial and temporal displacement of the dramatic situation to the primal significance of 'my sweet birth-place'. Wordsworth quotes this phrase in a passage of his own on beginnings (*Prelude*, 1799, I. 8; 1805, I. 276) and, like

Wordsworth's, the primal significance in Coleridge's poem is figured as aural. Unlike Wordsworth's, the significance is not there to be retrieved: Coleridge remembers how the egotistical child was father to the man. The sound of church bells, 'the poor man's only music', is itself 'Presageful', 'Most like articulate sounds of things to come'. Even here the child defers the significance of sensuous experience – this is a more self-conscious child than Wordsworth's – and in sleep there is only an extension of the waking dream.

What began as habitual experience is now narrative, 'And so I brooded all the following morn', not of a paradisal and unselfconscious state, but of one in which the tyrannical eye was itself tyrannised, 'Awed by the stern preceptor's face', while it sought rather the '*stranger*'s face' at the door. Again the significance is not retrievable from the past but is deferred within it, the half-open door a fair analogue for the intermittent access of creative energy. When significance is projected onto Coleridge's own child, the 'Great universal teacher' in place of his 'stern preceptor', is manifestly not drawn from the remembered experience of his own childhood. The 'absent friends' prefigured by the strangers in the fire, the concrete referents of the symbol, cast an ambivalence backward on the solitude of the first part, the presence of the sleeping child gradually revealing itself as more than a parenthetic detail of the dramatic situation. Thus, the next part of the poem displaces significance backwards onto the child and displaces the dramatic present into a potential future denied to the child of this part. The last of the hoped-for visitors displaces us again – although rather than being a third stage back in memory this seems to recapitulate the spatial and temporal displacement into 'my sweet birth-place'. Here, finally, it does seem to be offered as a prelapsarian state in which sex was undifferentiated ('sister more belov'd / My play-mate when we both were cloth'd alike!') and in which she is therefore most nearly like himself.[8]

Now Coleridge, reminded of his continuing presence, turns to his 'Dear Babe'. In the 'deep calm' established from the start, the child's 'gentle breathings . . . Fill up the interspersed vacancies / And momentary pauses of the thought' – a background rhythm which, like the frost's performance of its 'secret ministry', carries a sustained significance to be apprehended beneath such sporadic breaks in the calm as the owlet's cry forcing itself upon the passive consciousness. The return to the dramatic present is signalled by the transition from 'thought' to sight, but this only facilitates a transition from the senses to the 'heart' and thence back from sight to thought in the present. When he was a child the speaker's heart 'leaped up' at the momentary glimpse of the known community outside the schoolroom door; now he is an adult it 'thrills' his heart that in the child's future life nature will be readily available. Significance is displaced first, most obviously, from the speaker to his child, but second from human society to nature. Though he says he 'saw nought lovely but the sky and stars' as a child, what he has remembered is the hope of human society promised by the portent of the 'arrival of some absent friend' in the film on the bars and the hope of such an arrival projected through the half-open door of the schoolroom. Similarly, in the 'Letter to Sara Hutchinson', Coleridge remembers of a younger self 'the Sky was all, I knew, of beautiful' but goes on to record the 'Fancy's' vision of the ideal maiden, 'linking on sweet Dreams by dim Connections / To moon, or Evening Star, or glorious western Skies'.[9] The potential for achieved human relationship is already achieved, the child forming part of a self-possession subverted by these 'abstruser musings'.

Thus the 'but' here is the hinge of an antithesis ('For I . . . But *thou*') making explicit the implied comparison of the speaker's remembered childhood to the potential of the child. The child is, however, sleeping and, as in the near-contemporary 'The Nightingale' (*PW*, I, 264–6), capable of 'no articulate sound'. The 'articulate sounds' may even be metonymic of poetry. Dennis writes of poetry as 'harmony': 'Numbers are nothing but articulate Sounds. . . . And the periods of Prosaick Diction are articulate Sounds . . . .'[10] In the dream of the stone and the shell in *The Prelude* what Wordsworth hears in the Arab's shell are 'articulate sounds' (1805, v.95). Furthermore, that the 'prophetic blast of harmony' he then hears is succeeded by a 'glittering light' presaging inundation suggests affinities with 'Kubla Khan'. The ideal and uncomplicatedly significant 'language' which will be wished on the child is, then, at least partly the ideal language of the poem. The potential projected onto him in 'Frost at Midnight' can then only be defined against the memories of the father. It is the child who will 'learn far other lore / And in far other scenes'. Thus the contrast here is, in effect, between the possession of immediate surroundings and relationships and the memory of being possessed, 'pent'. This is, by extension, the true contrast afforded by that between the 'stern preceptor' and the 'Great universal Teacher', yet the pupils, the beneficiaries of this teaching are different. The internal claim is validated by projection onto some other; the poem moves to an address to the still-sleeping child. In 'The Nightingale', the function of this other is supplied both by the 'maid' and by the Wordsworths, 'My Friend, and thou, our Sister', who can testify to his having learnt the 'far other lore' then wished on the child. They are called on for support – ostensibly – against the artificialities of a pseudo-Miltonic poeticising:

> we have learnt
> A different lore: we may not thus profane
> Nature's sweet voices, always full of love
> And joyance!

In 'Frost at Midnight' it is given to the child to hear these voices, but the potential for 'love and joyance' is the other side of the antithesis, the 'but': 'for I was reared / In the great city, pent 'mid cloisters dim'. (The phrase echoes Milton's line 'As one who long in populous city pent', which begins the epic simile for Satan's response to Eve in the Garden: the sensory 'delight' at a pastoral landscape is supplanted by the exploitative 'delight' of the eye at the 'fair virgin' – *Paradise Lost*, ix. 444–54.[11]) In 'This Lime-tree Bower', it is Lamb who escapes this rearing, wandering like a breeze, having 'pined / And hunger'd after Nature, many a year / In the great City pent'.

Wordsworth's almost verbatim quotation of the lines from 'Frost at Midnight' in the address to Coleridge which closes the two-part *Prelude* of 1799 (1805, ii.466–7) leads to the affirmation that in spite of Coleridge's rearing 'in the great city' he joins Wordsworth at the 'self-same bourne'.[12] In the 1850 version, Coleridge's search for the 'truth in solitude' makes him not 'The most intense of Nature's worshippers' but 'The most assiduous of her ministers' (ii.464): his 'ministry', like that of the frost, is a facility in 'that eternal language' Coleridge's child will be privileged to know. It is set by Wordsworth against the 'silent language' intervening 'betwixt man and man' and between man and the 'beauty' and 'love' of nature. For Wordsworth, however, Dorothy is no more than a text over which he claims authority and in which he can read the 'language of my former heart'. In 'The Eolian Harp' the symbol yields itself as the eventual title for the process. Here, the even less tangible symbol will necessitate finally a different 'language'.

This facility, painfully won by the father, will be the child's gift in the vision of the achieved potential (ll. 54–64). The child, unselfconsciously and pre-linguistically creative, 'like a breeze', will not require the mediation of, for instance, the eolian harp. His perceptions will be attuned to the image-making capacity of nature. The reconciliation of mind and nature is rhetorically achieved in the lines in which the clouds form an echo or mirror of nature itself. The process leads beyond the dramatic present constituted by the poem to an ideal interchange of mind and nature; what the child will 'see and hear' is the 'eternal language' of God.

The attentive reader may recall Coleridge's satire of the inattentive reader of his own writings (*Friend* [*CC*], I, 26) in the realisation that energy and attentiveness are also required on the part of the reader of this language: 'and by giving, make it ask'. Like the gift, its reception should be dynamic, and the process remains one of continual becoming. This at least is the conventional reading, one which could be supported by a passage from the second Lay Sermon (in which the metaphorical language of the second sentence again replaces the hierarchical superiority of the visual over the reason with their interfusion):

> it is impossible that the affections should be kept constant to an object which gives no employment to the understanding. The energies of the intellect, increase of insight, and enlarging views, are necessary to keep alive the substantial faith in the heart.   (*LS* [*CC*], p. 180)

This seems consistent with the precision of the final clause in this section of the poem. The poem seems to insist in conceptual terms, as it does structurally, on the openness of 'becoming', but the insistence is a rhetorical one. (We shall see the problems attendant on constancy to an ideal object in Part IV.) The 'Therefore' which introduces the final paragraph of the poem is, like the earlier 'but', less the marker of a logically validated process than of a process of consciousness which is self-validating in the fully ambiguous sense of the compound term. 'Therefore' requires the burden of the mystery to have been the burden of proof, and the use of the future tense rather than of a subjunctive assumes itself proven.

This ending is, however, the product of second thought. The original printed version contains a further six lines. The 'secret ministery' there is that of a less active and more abstract 'cold' and the potential projected beyond the poem is much more specifically that of the child. The icicles' transient 'novelty [will] / Suspend thy little soul', making the child 'stretch and flutter from thy mother's arms' – a reductively particular explication in which the recurrence of 'flutter' was presumably a distracting reminder of a creativity then only potential. The final version ends with the line 'Quietly shining to the quiet moon'. Adverb and adjective refer to different objects (icicles and moon), which are thereby 'held in solution' not by 'formal simile' but by the suggestive identity in difference of metaphor. The parataxis of the final paragraph ('Whether . . . whether . . . Or'), the second last line's echoing of the opening line and the repetition of 'quiet' in the final line suggest an attempted closure thwarted by the participle. The precedence of a performative over a constative mode is acknowledged at the end.

This mode, however, is the cause of the reader's problems with the poem. At this point, it seems to me, there are three: this 'language', the benediction itself and its recipient. The actual language proposed is conventional enough. What God and the schoolmaster share is that they teach us to read. In both Christian and Platonic tradition the material script is devalued in favour of a spiritual writing imprinted directly on the soul. This 'language', then, is that of the text of nature, the signature of God. Coleridge speaks in an early theological lecture of 'the Volume of the World' in which we apprehend 'the Transcript of Himself . . . the bright Impressions of the eternal Mind' (*Lectures 1795* [*CC*], p. 94). Again, he writes that 'We see our God everywhere – the Universe in the most literal Sense is his written Language' (p. 339). More than twenty years later he explicates the education of the 'materialist' into the 'philosopher' in an allegory of the missionary bringing words and hence the Word to the 'unlettered African': 'Then will the other great Bible of God, the Book of Nature, become transparent to us, when we regard the forms of matter as words, as symbols, valuable only as being the expression, an unrolled but yet a glorious fragment, of the wisdom of the

Supreme Being' (*PL*, pp. 366–7). The difference is the acknowledgement of the opacity, of difficulty in the interpretation, of such a 'glorious fragment'. The ideal 'language' gifted to the child as it is framed by the language of the poem can then be considered as a product of an older 'atomist' theory of language, in transition throughout the eighteenth century to a formalist theory: a transition which Stephen Land has characterised as 'from signs to propositions'.[13] Coleridge certainly seems aware of this. In a passage quoted in Chapter 7 above he privileges 'symbol' over 'allegory' describing the latter as 'but a translation of abstract notions into a picture-language which is itself nothing but an abstaction from objects of the senses; the principle being even more worthless than the proxy, both alike unsubstantial, and the former shapeless to boot' (*LS* [*CC*], p. 30). A consequence of the juxtaposition of the two languages here is that, since the reader too is susceptible to the interpretative confusion allegory may imply, symbol cannot be naively accepted as ideal. Like Coleridge, the reader cannot complete the circle alone. I agree with Michael Cooke that 'the relation between purposive acts and meandering actuality in *The Prelude*, while it pivots around the self, is less and less devoted to the ego. . . . For the self comes to operate as a medium or principle in the text and not as an idol or goal'.[14] The real 'goal' can only be, as has been said, the achievement of that growth of a poet's mind in relation to nature 'which fits him to receive it, *when unsought*' (1805, XII.14 – emphasis added). Before turning to 'Books' in book v of *The Prelude* Wordsworth reiterates that his 'mind hath looked / Upon the speaking face of earth and heaven / As her prime teacher' (v.11–13). The characteristic slippage from visual to aural is here a desire for an unmediated *Bildung* more easily decipherable as speech than text. As Hegel says, 'the real issue is not exhausted by stating it as an aim, but by carrying it out, nor is the result the actual whole, but rather the result together with the process through which it came about' (Preface to *Phenomenology*, p. 2). The problem then is one of the status of the act (perlocutionary, in Austin's terms) of benediction.

　　Coleridge, then, wishes for what Hegel says is impossible. He wants the performative also to be transformative, to carry with it the 'truth' or 'falsehood' which Austin said it annulled. He wants *an* interpretation (product) without interpretation (process). The responsibility for interpretation is handed on to the child. Clearly it is a projection of Coleridge's own ideal self, but the process of projection extends to the child: 'by giving, make it ask'. Dr John Barrell once told me in a seminar that I seemed 'to regard the verb "make" as extraordinarily innocent'. Perhaps the projection is deterministic, even authoritarian, not the reflexive process of 'Religious Musings' by which the soul can 'make / GOD its identity' (ll. 49–50). The direct transmission of an unfallen language will by-pass the imagination, by which, it is clear even from 'Religious Musings', man can make himself godlike. Dr Barrell suggests that a passage from 'This Lime-tree Bower' might be read as rationalising the necessity for that other, the interlocutor in the poems:

> sometimes
> 'Tis well to be bereft of promised good
> That we may lift the soul, and contemplate
> With lively joy the joys we cannot share.

It is an ambiguity which again is Miltonic, like the 'chosen laws controlling choice' of the poem to Wordsworth. Elsewhere 'becoming' is quite explicitly such an act of the will. In Appendix C of *The Statesman's Manual* Coleridge insists that 'what the plant *is*, by an act not its own and unconsciously – *that* must thou *make* thyself to *become*' (*LS* [*CC*], p. 71). The alternative can be gauged from Coleridge's utterances on childhood.

Other scattered comments on childhood and the child as 'literary' and moral archetypes make clear that the ambivalence with which 'Frost at Midnight' seems charged is not due to particular paternal worries. In the *Friend* Coleridge finds the existence of free will entailed by that of conscience and says that his 'arguments were not suggested to me by Books, but forced on me by reflection on my own Being, and Observation of the Ways of those about me, especially of little Children' (*Friend* [*CC*], II, 8). The child may be an ideal of undivided being: in the essay 'On Poesy or Art' he speaks of the 'seeming identity of body and mind in infants'.[15]

This ideal must of course be the privileged perspective of the adult – an irony dramatised by many poems in the *Lyrical Ballads*. There is an association of the pre-visionary life with childhood but it must be superseded; 'The child is father of the man'. Coleridge's early comments on Shakespeare as child and Milton as responsible adult – of which Hazlitt's report quoted in Chapter 3 is an example – are within an eighteenth-century tradition coming from Milton himself (in 'L'Allegro'): 'Or sweetest Shakespeare, Fancy's child, / Warble his native wood-notes wild'. Childhood therefore functions as a metaphor. As Schiller says, for example, 'the naive is *childlikeness where it is no longer expected*, and precisely on this account cannot be attributed to actual childhood in the most rigorous sense' (*Naive and Sentimental Poetry*, p. 90). The metaphor would be unacceptable had not the (albeit tacit) acceptance of the Fall as metaphor enabled the diffusion of Rousseauist theories of childhood. The metaphor functions within the imperative to unlearn and dehabituate discussed in Chapter 5, an imperative

> to carry on the feelings of childhood into the powers of manhood, to combine the child's sense of wonder and novelty with the appearances which every day for perhaps forty years had rendered familiar . . . this is the character and privilege of genius, and one of the marks which distinguish genius from talents.   (*Friend* [*CC*], I, 109–10)

The child is father of the man (even the preposition signifies rather a state or condition than a process: the reader might expect 'to'). In the *Friend* Coleridge quotes the lines from that fragment in which Wordsworth's 'heart leaps up' (*WPW*, I, 226). He has been attacking the notion that a good cause may be served by lies:

> Every parent possesses the opportunity of observing, how deeply children resent the injury of a delusion; and if men laugh at the falsehoods that were imposed on themselves during their childhood, it is because they are not good and wise enough to contemplate the Past in the Present, and so to produce by a virtuous and thoughtful sensibility that continuity in their self-consciousness, which Nature has made the law of their animal life.   (*Friend* [*CC*], II, 41)

By quoting Wordsworth's lines in this context Coleridge returns to the problem explored earlier by the two poems: the possible unification of process with moral responsibility. (It may also be true, as the case of Sara suggests, that there is an *un*natural piety.) In a notebook entry dated 17 March 1801, he remarks of the young Hartley trying to distinguish a prospect of mountains from its mirror image: 'I ~~think~~ never before saw such an Abstract of *Thinking* as a pure act & energy, of *Thinking* as distinguished from *Thoughts*' (*CN*, I, 923). Such an activity is not dissimilar from that for which the speaker is chastised in the two poems discussed: consciousness may be at the expense of the conscience to which it is etymologically related.[16] In October 1820 Coleridge again writes of Hartley, after his Oxford fellowship had not been confirmed after the probationary year,

> From his earliest childhood he had an absence of any contra-distinguishing Self, any conscious 'I' . . . there was . . . no semblance produced by accident of language, or the more than usually prolonged habit of speaking in the third person . . . but a seemingly constitutional insensibility to the immediate impressions on the senses, & the necessity of having them generalised into *thoughts*, before they had an interest, or even a distinct place, in his Consciousness. (*CL*, v, 110)

Coleridge opposes this characterlessness to a rigidity of personality which, in his wife, is also frigidity in 'all that forms *real Self*'. Rather than that self-possession which is a 'true' moral being 'she creates her own self in a field of Vision and Hearing, at a distance, by her own Ears & eyes – & hence becomes the willing Slave of the Ears & Eyes of others' (*CN*, I 979). Hartley's characterlessness is a cause for paternal alarm but, as Coleridge writes to John Dawes, headmaster of the school at Ambleside where Hartley had been found a position,

> hard it is for me to determine which is the worse, *morally* considered, I mean: the selfishness from the want or defect of a manly Self-love, or the selfishness that springs out of the excess of a worldly self-interest. In the eye of a Christian and a Philosopher, it is difficult to say, which of the two appears the greater deformity, the relationless, unconjugated, and intransitive Verb Impersonal with neither Subject nor Object, neither governed or governing, or the narrow proud Egotism, with neither Thou or They except as it's [*sic*] Instruments or Involutes. (*CL*, v, 232)[17]

The former, although rarer, is the case with Hartley. In 1826 Coleridge writes to his second son, Derwent,

O if I could but promise myself five or six years of practical
health, and Hartley could but promise himself to be a *Self* and to
construct a circle by the circumvolving line – what a comfort
and delight it would be to have him with me, as a Literary
Partner!   (vi, 551)

In addition to syntactic parallelism in 'Frost at Midnight' I
might have adduced the mutual reflectivity of clouds and lake,
icicles and moon, and the reification of 'eave-drops' into 'ice' to
demonstrate the attempt at containing spatial and temporal
displacement within a formal unity. Clearly, what I have
described as the displacement of significance onto Hartley in
'Frost at Midnight', while it does not break the (formal) circle,
does have the effect of making him, etymologically, eccentric. The
problem of the fictionality of first-person narration ('egotism' as
conceived in the 1796 Preface) and of naming existent characters
within that narration is by no means a trivial one. Compare
Coleridge's summary of Fouqué's *Undine* in the letter quoted
above: 'Before she had a Soul [Undine was] beloved by all
whether they would or no, & [was] as indifferent to all, herself
included, as a blossom whirling in a May-gale' (*CL*, v, 110). This
reminds Coleridge of Hartley and he goes on to quote the passage
of benediction to the child in 'Frost at Midnight' (11.44–58 –
which is to say everything *but* the speculation on language). The
current desires of the adult may be projected backwards, perhaps
onto the poet's representation of his own, or his own child's,
childhood. To say that childhood is always viewed from the
perspective of the adult is to state the obvious, but even without
Austin's help it is clear that 'to state' is not itself unproblematic.
To imagine other perspectives will again be to become involved in
a circular argument. The former, after all, is what Coleridge does
in 'Frost at Midnight'. Declension in awareness of the fissure of
'THING and THOUGHT' (*CL*, ii, 1194) may lead to a continual
becoming, this 'pure act & energy of Thinking', yet, as is clear
from the letters above, what is admired in the child would be an
abrogation of responsibility in the adult.
A notebook entry begun before Coleridge went to Germany
contains a draft of lines used in 'Frost at Midnight'. Below it is a
list headed 'Infancy & Infants' which he subsequently added to
more than once. I quote, out of sequence, two numbered items:

14. The wisdom & graciousness of God in the infancy of the human species – its beauty, long continuance &c &c. <Children in the wind – hair floating, tossing, a miniature of the agitated trees, below which they play'd – the elder whirling for joy, the one in petticoats, a fat Baby, eddying half willingly, half by the force of the Gust – driven backward, struggling forward – both drunk with the pleasure, both shouting their hymn of Joy.> (*CN*, ɪ, 330).

The interpolation seems to come from observation of the sons, Hartley and Derwent, since the same wording occurs in a letter to Sotheby of 1802 (*CL*, ɪɪ, 872); but 'whirling' and 'shouting' for joy hardly recalls the child in the poem. Rather, the notes offer an empirical parallel to the unproblematic interpretability of nature there projected both onto the child and into the future:

5. Sports of infants – their incessant activity, the *means* being the end. – Nature how lovely a school-mistress – A blank-verse, moral poem – . . .

If 'Frost at Midnight' is not exactly that poem, the moral ambivalence which will be seen in Part IV to actuate some of Coleridge's moral-political comments also centres on the problem of ends and means. An analogy between spatial and self-possession was noted above; but by this point the satisfying 'return upon itself' of the poem has revealed itself as continuation rather than closure of the circle. In a double sense the process of the poem *takes place*. The spatial displacement represented by the benediction (to a nature that confessedly does not exist upon any of the – past – temporal axes of the poem) is matched by the performative utterance which represents it. The act of enclosure at the point where the 'I' of the speaker makes an entrance must then be revalued as the enclosure of an absence and of a desire: an act, perhaps, of squaring the circle. I have called the transference or projection as it occurs in several poems 'displacement of significance'. The problems this causes for the reader of them (and, apparently, for Coleridge himself) are amplified by Coleridge's attitude to childhood as it surfaces elsewhere. Coleridge's 'cradled infant' subtly desynonymises the roots of the word 'infant' – a conflation of Latin *infans* ('unable to speak') and Old French *enfant* ('child'). The child of 'Frost at Midnight', then, is a kind of voiceless voice. To realise the implications of the poem will then require consideration not only of the recipient of this process but also of the process itself.

9 Communion

Coleridge's sense of some of the early sonnets and blank-verse poems as egotistical 'effusions' certainly indicates his own suspicion that they may be conterminous with the empirical self, a closed circle, but, even without Fichte's projection of nature as the non-ego, it follows from the investigation of the status of both sensory and of religious experience in Chapters 5 and 6 that to speak of a solipsistic language would be oxymoronic. In the crucial seventh thesis of Chapter 12 of the *Biographia* Coleridge deduces that 'the spirit in all the objects which it views, views only itself' but then at once makes this deduction conditional: 'If this could be proved, the immediate reality of all intuitive knowledge would be assured'. What satisfies this condition is the implication of 'an act' of the will, but such an act presupposes a prior 'identity' unknowable except through that activity (*BL* [*CC*], I, 276–80).

The displacements I have identified in some of Coleridge's poems are not, then, a continuing attempt to validate consciousness by reference to memories of the self, as Locke implies, but rather the reverse: forays which validate the existence of self to the consciousness. The criticism of concepts – in Kant's sense by which the self is the 'vehicle of all concepts' – also involves a self-criticism, and returns to a sense of instability of the self. If the self is a state towards which the process tends, rather than its mere point of departure, this is to equate it with an infinite which Coleridge knows as 'God'. Not wholly accepting a thoroughgoing idealist theory of perception such as Berkeley advances in the *Principles*, he is aware of his vulnerability to both the trivial and the metaphysical stricture of 'egotism'. The former is the static selfishness or egocentrism identified in Gray's 'Elegy'[1] and in Goethe's *Werther*; the latter is chiefly within the bounds of the German idealism which 'possessed [his] soul' in the years following the period under discussion – though the earlier interest in Berkeley is clearly relevant. That the climax of the process that I have outlined in 'Frost at Midnight' should be an appeal to some

131

other self – elsewhere, usually named – is the phenomenon to be dealt with. I call this phenomenon 'displacement' rather than 'transference' to indicate an analogy with the temporal and spatial shifts imposed by the poem which necessitate that 'position'.

Wordsworth quotes 'Frost at Midnight' at the beginning and end of the two-part *Prelude* (1799, I.6; II.496–7) and the second address to Coleridge in the 1805 version, its 'appointed close', is the 'discipline / And consummation of the poet's mind' (1805, XIII. 270–1), in which the redemptive language (the echo of Christ's *consummatum est*) occurs within a partial displacement of the potential for achieved significance onto the poet's interlocutor. The very process towards that achievement gathers a confident momentum which renders the interlocutor progressively less important, as in 'Tintern Abbey', despite the earlier avowal that *The Prelude* was always a 'story destined for thy ear' (x. 946). Nevertheless, the displacement of the significance of a work of men's 'redemption' (XIII.439–41) is more than the convenience of an 'indulgent Friend'(1850, IV.275) saving Wordsworth from the charge of (trivial) egotism. Wordsworth first enters a plea of deferral, that the work to which *The Prelude* was but a 'sort of portico'[2] will vindicate his 'having given this record' of himself (1805, XIII.389); then recalls the personal and aesthetic closeness of Coleridge and himself at Alfoxden in 1798, before appealing to Coleridge's 'feeling' if not his 'knowledge' for the justification of this work – fit audience though fewer than the 'men' to whom God's ways are to be justified through the medium of Milton's epic:

> To thee, in memory of that happiness,
> It will be known – by thee at least my friend,
> Felt – that the history of a poet's mind
> Is labour not unworthy of regard:
> To thee the work shall justify itself.
>
> (1805, XIII. 406)

The apparent dedication proceeds through the doubt of 'at least', 'not unworthy' and the justificatory weight borne by the verb 'feel' to the final resolutely iambic line.

A distinction must be made between the reader and those fictional constructs which may, I have suggested, function as his or her surrogate. These are named as friends and family: Coleridge ought to be certain of their responses outside his text, as Wordsworth can rely 'at least' on his friend's feelings. However, this also prevents such projected characters from being regarded negatively as the necessary 'other' of the self in Fichte or Schelling. The child's inability to speak in 'Frost at Midnight' is in this sense a retreat from the problem of Sara in 'The Eolian Harp'. (She is self-subsistent if not 'articulate'.) As the cases of the child image and of Sara have shown, this strategy encounters as many difficulties as it escapes.

Since the total process approximates to a metaphysic, and perhaps to a Christian *schema*, the fiction of Sara (or of the child) is made to bear an unbearable significance. Empson's insight, if not his terminology, is relevant here, though he is writing of *Paradise Lost*: 'Milton . . . could not have made God automatically good in the epic; God is on trial . . . and the reason is that all the characters are on trial in any civilized narrative.'[3] This is not merely a late example of what C. S. Lewis would call Romantic 'satanism' but an account of the conditions which make such readings possible. The problem of those characters onto whom significance is displaced in the conversation poems is analogous to the problem of the 'Abyssinian Maid' in 'Kubla Khan', or the more complex trialogue between Mariner, Wedding-Guest and reader: a moral problem by virtue of its being a fictional problem. Thus the effect of the poems' egotism is to expose the reader to the doubts concerning and contiguous to egotism which animate their process. The turning to the child in 'Frost at Midnight' is not a vicarious fulfilment, but a turning towards a fulfilment which is necessarily potential. At the end of 'Kubla Khan' narrative in the simple past switches to the modals of possibility: 'could', 'would' and 'should' – a series of conditionals to represent a potential revival.[4]

To summarise, then. Coleridge remembers himself as a 'Presageful' child, the bells of his local church as 'Most like articulate sounds of things to come', but the childhood memory's significance is displaced not into the present of the poem but into the future, and not, therefore, onto the adult but onto the sleeping child incapable of 'articulate sounds'. There is a similar displacement in 'This Lime-tree Bower', onto 'my gentle-hearted Charles'; in 'The Nightingale', onto both the Maid and the Wordsworths; and perhaps too in 'Dejection', onto the Lady. Even in 'Kubla Khan', the speaker's power is in the past, and in 'The Ancient Mariner', within the dramatic present of the poem, it is the Wedding-Guest who is taught a lesson, not the Mariner. It is the former who wakes up next day 'A sadder and a wiser man'. In Chapter 7 such instances were referred to as examples of a desire for external validation. Clearly, where what is to be validated is personal feeling which is merely self-referential, as in many of the 1796 effusions, the desire is more easily satisfied and is therefore less urgent. The poem can rest on the desire, as in the Bowlesian 'Lines on Climbing Brockley Coombe': 'Deep sighs my lonely heart: I drop the tear: / Enchanting spot! O were my Sara here!' (*PW*, I, 94). Wordsworth's 'She dwelt among the untrodden ways', on the other hand, presents the reader with a final ambiguity. The narrative of the first quatrain is balanced against the symbol of the second, and if the third does not merely pass into an acknowledgement of the impossibility of referentiality it relies, egotistically, on authorisation by the speaker outside the poem:

> She lived unknown, and few could know
>   When Lucy ceased to be;
> But she is in her grave, and, oh,
>   The difference to me!
>
> > (*WPW*, II, 30)

In the turn from the indifferent 'few' to the querulous lyric 'I', any ambivalence will be on the part of the reader, but Coleridge, unable to take himself as a fiction, cannot achieve such a resolution.

If 'The Eolian Harp' and 'Frost at Midnight' are accepted as performative utterances (with all the difficulties inherent in such a description), then 'The Ancient Mariner' (*PW*, I, 186–209), a longer poem and one not couched in the first person, might seem to represent a generic problem – more obviously 'fictional' problems of structure and 'character'. Yet what happens in 'The Ancient Mariner' cannot be reduced to what happens to the Ancient Mariner, however much the reader might want to wish away its 'too much moral' (*TT*, 31 May 1830). Assuredly, at the level of apparent 'plot' the moral is *about* 'too much': about an egotistical act of the Mariner, 'finding in self the sole motive for action'. To pursue such an interpretation would itself result in too much of a domestication, as though the Mariner merely behaves socially *de trop* and shooting the albatross were like passing the port in the wrong direction or, indeed, using the pronoun 'I' too much. The Mariner acts, and is thereafter acted upon. By his action, it seems to me, the Mariner invokes, willy-nilly, an arbitrary punishment – what punishment could be more arbitrary than one which depends on the throw of a dice (ll. 195–8)? At the same time, he is henceforth cursed, or gifted, with a visionary capacity and with his 'strange power of speech'. The indictment of egotism is far more damning. Despite his long repentance, and his being shriven, the Mariner's confession never releases him from the curse of repetition. All that is left is for him continually to repeat his story.

Therefore, it is not crudely to posit 'The Ancient Mariner' as spiritual autobiography to say that one way of reading it is as showing the consequences of such a self-inaugural act. The act is the transgression of an unwritten law of which, as in the letter of the law, ignorance is no excuse. The consequences are, on the one hand, the punishing isolation of the Mariner, voyaging, as it were, east of Eden, and, on the other, direct contact with that parallel visionary order suggested in the epigraph from Burnet; with the daemonic forms which are objects of that punishment. For such loss, perhaps, abundant recompense. Two simple declarative sentences at the end of the first and of the fourth sections neatly represent this paradox. 'I shot the ALBATROSS', recounts the Mariner; then, of the water snakes, 'I blessed them unaware'. The first sentence apparently signifies a wilful intervention which itself inaugurates that process culminating in the 'unaware' speech act of the second. (He receives the vision 'when unsought'.) The first sentence signifies an arbitrary cause for such excessive effects. The second is hardly less arbitrary. (If this is an allegory of the Fall, what can it mean that he blesses *snakes*?) This 'blessing', unlike that in 'Frost at Midnight', but like all the Mariner's speech acts, is overly successful in that it unwittingly calls into existence forces which can then be seen teleologically as effects. The 1798 'Argument', even though it apparently imposes the least in the way of an interpretative 'frame', signals an arbitrary trans-gression: 'How a Ship having passed the Line was driven . . .'.

The objectification of desire there is essentially similar to that in the conversation poems. Indeed, the problems the reader has with 'The Ancient Mariner' are again to do with the complexities of interlocution, only more apparent because there is no first-person

narrative voice. It is the Wedding-Guest's interruption, delivered
with the naivety of the comedy straight man, which alerts the
reader:

> 'God save thee, ancient mariner!
> From the fiends that plague thee thus! –
> Why look'st thou so?' – With my cross-bow
> I shot the ALBATROSS.
>
> (ll. 79–82)

The addition of the epigraph (which justifies a 'frame') and of the
argument and gloss (which provide such a frame), the *narrative*
frame (the wedding, dry land) and the relative authority of the
voices of Wedding-Guest and Mariner all seem to me such
problems. In fact it is only in telling the story that 'The Mariner
hath his will'. All these instances of displacement have the effect of
denying closure and thereby conferring responsibility on the
unknown other who is the reader. In 'The Ancient Mariner' the
onus of response is on the Wedding-Guest, who, forced to attend
to the Mariner's story, functions in some respects as the reader's
surrogate.

   Unfortunately, in turning 'from the bridegroom's door' he
becomes the kind of naive reader who would merely retail the line
of the gloss, of Coleridge's later 'explanations', and of the
apparent import of the Mariner's own last words. He is caught
within the fiction. For example, 'real' space and time are
obviously suspended in the Mariner's story:

> The Sun's rim dips; the stars rush out:
> At one stride comes the dark;
> With far-heard whisper o'er the sea,
> Off shot the spectre-bark.
>
> (ll. 199–202)

Yet it's less obvious that this confusion of tenses occurs too within
the narrative 'frame':

> The Wedding-Guest he beat his breast,
> Yet he cannot choose but hear;
> And thus spake on that ancient man,
> The bright-eyed Mariner.
>
> (ll. 37–40)

The Wedding-Guest too is in a temporal no-man's-land. One additional vantage point the reader indubitably has is that which enables him or her to witness the buttonholing of the Wedding-Guest by the Mariner. The point may be that it is unsafe to assume that we as readers are in a superior position. We cannot come after something which is of no time. All there is after language is more language, so that even the notorious moral which the Mariner 'tells' in lines 612–17 takes for its highest term not 'love' but 'prayer'. It is the gloss – not the Mariner – which offers a cause for the effects which follow shooting the albatross. (Neither offer a cause for the shooting itself.) It is the Mariner's shipmates who offer blame (ll, 95–6) or praise (ll. 101–2) for his action. He is a better reader than the Wedding-Guest in that he never offers such rationalisations. As someone once wrote, those who do not understand their own histories are condemned to repeat them. Despite the gloss's efforts at domestication the Mariner's fate is a circular one. He is a story-teller ('till my ghastly tale is told / This heart within me burns') whose one story is about 'agony' and is agony to tell, but whose only release is to tell the story.

The addition of the gloss to the final text of 'The Ancient Mariner' does not furnish us with another interlocutor but provides a juxtaposition. (At ll. 263–71, for example, the gloss is clearly providing supernumary action.) The text proper piles on the agony but the gloss piles on explanation – most notably at the lines (79–82) quoted above. Where the Mariner relates merely 'I shot the ALBATROSS', the gloss provides the first term of a moral cause and effect: 'The Ancient Mariner inhospitably killeth the pious bird of good omen.' This comes as it were *ex cathedra*. Though we may prefer the Ancient Mariner's account of his own experiences, the gloss insists on a different interpretation. The normative force of the gloss cannot be ignored. Just as we cannot live by what we can only *see*, we cannot live by what we can only *speak*. Living is not speaking. There is an absolute which literally goes without saying. In effect then there are two Gods – one which can be comprehended (and criticised) within our categories, and one which we simply apprehend.[5] Double vision. It is a source of unease for Coleridge that he should feel it necessary to accommodate both. Much of the pathos of 'Kubla Khan', for example, stems from this unease.

In a passage considered in Chapter 2 above, Burke endeavours to explain 'How Words influence the Passions'. One means is the representation of things which have no correspondent 'reality'. Their power is in verbal 'combination', so that, 'by the contagion of our passions we catch a fire already kindled in another, which probably might never have been struck out by the object described. Words, by strongly conveying the passions . . . fully compensate for their weakness in other respects' (*Philosophical Enquiry*, p. 176 [v.viii]). In the *Friend* this 'contagion' or mutual 'kindling' is explained as a faculty in the reader approximating to a faculty in the writer (Coleridge), although the actual objects of their attention may be different. This faculty is the reason, which is the essential source of moral being, and therefore creative:

> the Writer wishes . . . not so much to shew my Reader this or that fact, as to kindle his own torch for him, and leave it to himself to chuse the particular objects, which he might wish to examine by its light . . . the elements of Geometry require attention only; but the analysis of our primary faculties, and the investigation of all the absolute grounds of Religion and Morals, are impossible without energies of Thought in addition to the effort of Attention.   (*Friend* [*CC*], I, 16)

The objects presenting themselves to the writer's consciousness and being represented by him (lute, flames and frost) are less important than the process in the consciousness of both writer and reader. (The ideal reading, then, would be like Hegel's Absolute Knowing). A similar imperative is sketched in a note to a copy of *The Statesman's Manual* given to Gillman, in which Coleridge's object, he says, is to

> rouse and stimulate the mind – to set the reader a thinking – and at least to obtain entrance for the question whether the <truth of the > Opinions in fashion ~~are~~ is quite so certain as he had hitherto taken for granted – rather than to establish the contrary by a connected chain of proofs and arguments.   (*LS*, [*CC*], p. 114n2)

This active questioning demanded of the reader should not be confused with a kind of cosy mutual congratulation. I spoke in Chapter 7 of a possibly antithetical return. I had in mind the superficial or 'dramatic' level upon which Coleridge's wife confirms his dubiety and upon which the Ancient Mariner becomes a kind of evangelist who admonishes the Wedding-Guest and 'teaches' him to repent. This problem of the return, of the completion of the circle, has a long theological history. ('Secret ministry' is itself a phrase from book III of Calvin's *Institutes*.) The final swerve in 'Frost at Midnight' links it to the religious lyric of the seventeenth century, and to what has been called the Protestant poetic. A conversion poem can't go on beyond its recognition scene, because the poet is rewriting the past in terms of the new, privileged perspective – rewriting it, almost, in his own image. To go on would be to imply that he shares God's vision, that he can mediate what is immediate.[6] This, as I shall suggest, is no trivial worry, particularly because Coleridge's poem *begins* in the present. It ends with the eternal 'now' of the sublime projected into a future when Babel could be rebuilt (as, perhaps, a 'dome in air').

Spatial and temporal displacement, then, relates to the displacement of significance in that each undermines a grounding authority to replace it with another. Thus Coleridge's endings are provisional, as that ground too will register the tremors of newer, or potential, landings. As in the Protestant narratives, the reader too must go through the self-deceiving stages which preceded the writer's conversion. However we may choose to read his text, Coleridge enjoins us to question and not to come and play. It is an injunction which as a reader himself, he claims to obey. In the tenth lecture of the 1818 series, speaking of Donne's 'The Canonisation', he posits a greater readerly 'delight' in the protean immersion of the self in the process of the writing:

> As late as ten years ago, I used to seek and find out grand lines and fine stanzas; but my delight has been far greater since it has consisted more in tracing the leading thought thro' out the whole. The former is too much like coveting your neighbour's goods; in the latter you merge yourself in the author, you *become he*. (*MiscCrit*, p. 137)

The change in reading-habits described is the change from the trivially egotistical to the protean, and the obvious contrast of such a sympathetic process with the forms offering a '*conjunction disjunctive*, of epigrams' (*BL [CC]*, I, 19; cf. *CN*, II, 2112) belongs rather to the former level. In spite of the disavowal of 'coveting

your neighbour's goods', the reading-process Coleridge claims to
have won later is similar to that in which the reader is encouraged
in the 'conversation poems'.

The passage quoted above can be compared with the young
Hegel writing, at about the time of composition of 'Frost at
Midnight', of the sacramental consumption (which is also
destruction) of bread and wine:

> the love made objective, this subjective element become a *thing*,
> reverts once more to its nature, becomes subjective again in the
> eating. This return may perhaps in this respect be compared
> with the thought which in the written word becomes a thing and
> which recaptures its subjectivity out of an object, out of
> something lifeless, when we read.[7]

Hegel identifies a confusion rather than 'reconciliation' of object
and subject. This is a confusion still more evident in the case of
reading, which he takes only as an example. There consumption is
of a different kind: the sacramental object remains intact, pristine,
and there follows a re-embarkation on the circle in which the
reader can only claim the memory of communion. There may be
the possibility of the transubstantiation of the written word.
Taken out of context, the benediction to the child might be read as
claiming such a status, but in the context of 'Frost at Midnight' it
is clear that there has occurred a desacralisation of that (existent)
world in which Coleridge might have located the 'language'
projected onto his child: a locus of meanings in relation to which
the self could be defined. That this correspondent order has
broken down – that, in Hegel's terms, the division (*Entzweiung*) of
'subjective' and 'objective' knowledge necessitates an act of
communion – is indicative of the problems with that actual
language which are the concern here. It remains a communion
devoutly to be wished. Certainly Sara functions, in 'The Eolian
Harp', as a point of fixity, as part of the 'frame'. What 'set[s] the
reader a thinking' is the undermining of the frame by the
intervening process. What, to continue in his own terms, are the
limits to what the reader should be 'a thinking'? For instance, he
or she, struck by the consonants in the opening line of 'Frost at
Midnight', might find in it an acrostic: 'the fro*S*t *P*erforms *I*ts
sec*R*et m*I*nis*T*ry'.[8] If significance is to be entirely displaced
outside his text, Coleridge would have to accept such

interpretations, yet retention of his authority within the text would associate him with the magisterial egotism of Milton. Again the argument is circular in that these effects themselves can only be interpretations. There is, then, more than a hint of exasperation or pleading in what Coleridge avers of the 'work of true genius': 'As it must not, so neither can it be lawless, for it is even this that constitutes it genius – the power of acting creatively under laws of its own origination' (*ShakCrit*, I, 223).

In a sense, then, the process I have described is a *via media* – a recasting of the 'mingled charm' of the synthetic language of Bowles or Cowper as a synthesising 'tertium aliquid' (*BL* [*CC*], I, 300). It would be possible (it is still often done) to trace this 'one life' concept through Coleridge's life and writings, perhaps to its hardening into the refusal of process in the late poem 'Self-Knowledge', which ends 'Ignore thyself, and strive to know thy God!' This in Coleridge's 'own' voice, is the voice of Sara in 'The Eolian Harp'. In examining the vision, she interrupts it; questioning it, she is implicitly questioned by it, revealing the limitations of the unexamined social morality she represents. As a fictional construct, she is indeed like the famous 'person from Porlock' (*PW*, I, 296); but, as Leslie Brisman realises, 'if we think of the original pre-interruption poet as inspired, and the interruptor as the natural man, we can say that Coleridge is his own person from Porlock'.[9] The process comprehends its own interruption, and as such must be in part a process of equivocation. Escape from the imprisonment of system into the openness of becoming (of which 'This Lime-tree Bower' would be the structural paradigm) cannot always be achieved in the certainty of Lamb's approbation. Indeed, 'becoming' itself may become the will to overcome. If the characterlessness of Christ and Shakespeare is one ideal of egotism, the means of a more radical displacement, the other is the Satanic 'mind not to be changed by place or time' (*Paradise Lost*, 1.253), which is its opposite. The intentional aspect of perception that was considered in Chapter 7 enforces a 'contemplative' or 'philosophic' distance –

I think Wordsworth possessed more of the genius of a great philosophic poet than any man I ever knew, or, as I believe, has existed in England since Milton; but it seems to me that he ought never to have abandoned the contemplative position, which is peculiarly – perhaps I might say exclusively – fitted for him. His proper title is *Spectator ab extra*   (*TT*, 21 July 1832)

– and the analogy noted there between perceptual and spatial distance renders such a position not far from that of Milton, who is 'the deity of prescience; he stands *ab extra*, and drives a fiery chariot and four, making the horses feel the iron curb which holds them in'   (12 May 1830). His egotism is a linguistic presence, a rhetorical sublimity against which self-consciousness must apply its own curbs. 'Prescience' implies a certitude impelling a linear rather than circular process, and the 'iron curb' a will capable of detachedly attaining ends to which the means are instrumental.[10] Paradoxically, in other words, Coleridge suggests the energy of Satan quite as much as the mastery of Milton – such a free creative will correlates with those of the amoral characters of its fictions. To give them their head is to risk incriminating the self. Regarded in others, the freedom of 'becoming' may be both personally and socially subversive. Responsibility and responsiveness, conscience and consciousness – like the words, those states they signify are so close that the second term almost annuls the first. Hence, Coleridge examines them within forms emphasising, rather than the temporal process, spatiality and causality: the forms, that is, of drama, and the language of power.

PART IV
The Language of Power

Preamble

'Egotism' as conceived in the 1796 Preface represents not a programme for poetry but a problem for it. The problem of the self in political, moral and metaphysical discourse emerged in Part I alongside the recurrent problem of the representation of the self in poetic language. In this final part I propose to sketch the confusion or reconciliation of these discourses in comparative attitudes to Napoleon. Thus its argument will be from analogy.

As I. A. Richards points out, the 'new moon overspread with phantom light' at the beginning of 'Dejection' refers to light from the earth: 'when we perceive that light we are having returned to us what we have given'.[1] All I would quarrel with in this fine remark is the pronouns chosen. This is more than a quibble: it is to instance once more that ambivalence towards 'egotism' which has been noted throughout. Wordsworth and nature have an authority for Coleridge that he is reluctant to arrogate to himself. His poem addressed to Wordsworth recalls *The Prelude's* evocation of

> moments awful
> Now in thy inner life, and now abroad,
> When power streamed from thee, and thy soul received
> The light reflected, as a light bestowed – . . . .
>
> (*PW*, 1, 404–5)

This triumph of the egotistical sublime is analogous to the power worshipped by the 'enamoured rustic' on the Brocken in 'Constancy to an Ideal Object' (*PW*, 1, 455–6): his shadow is enveloped by a 'glory'. In 'Dejection', of course, the recognition that 'we receive but what we give' is a recognition of incapacity, dullness – an inability to 'give' to, and therefore to receive a reciprocal energy from nature. (Taking this with the poem to Wordsworth the implication is that if we bestow a wedding-garment on nature it is up to us to wear the trousers.)

145

Many of Coleridge's later poems make an appeal to absolutes in the allegory or drama (the 'content') they present. 'Constancy to an Ideal Object', which switches from first- to third-person address through the medium of a famous symbol, is such a poem. Coleridge presents himself as standing outside the experience presented finally, as in 'He seems to gaze on that which seems to gaze on him!' ('Limbo') The final image of the Brocken spectre is the projection of an absolute:

> An image with a glory round its head;
> The enamoured rustic worships its fair hues
> Nor knows he makes the shadow he pursues!

The image with a glory round its head is thrown by the perceiver but he is, we are told, an 'enamoured rustic'. The problem is similar to that I elaborated in Gray: where in these lines written in the third person are we to situate Coleridge? There is, as I have said, a disjunction between the two parts of the poem. This 'image' is itself an image, a simile for the 'yearning Thought' of the opening lines, which rewrites 'to yearn' with a more tangible predicate as 'to pursue'.[2] It may be that the use of the image is strategic, a means of incorporating within the poem the kind of criticism Anna Seward made of 'Daffodils', but Coleridge is not, even *faute de mieux*, constant to a limbo of indeterminacy.

In a letter of 1829 he appears to gloss his own *sum quia sum* (see Chapter 2 above) as 'the identity or co-inherence of Act and Being of which there is and there can be but one perfect Instance – viz. the Eternal I AM, who *is* by his own *act* – who affirms himself to *be* in that he is; and who *is*, in that he *affirms* himself to be' (*CL*, VI, 816–17). This recalls both J. L. Austin's notion of 'performative' utterance and Fichte's self-positing of self in the second introduction to his *Wissenschaftslehre*: 'It *is* so because I *make* it so' (*Science of Knowledge*, p. 36). It is this problematic analogy that I shall pursue in this concluding part. It is a problem the Romantics invoke for themselves by their arrogation of divine creativity to poetic power. The problem is, then, one of authority. I want to approach it by way of analogy, through some responses to those actual figures who would arrogate divine power to themselves. While there is nothing absolute about Coleridge's language, there is continual reference to absolutes. The claim in the poem to Wordsworth that 'The truly great / Have all one age' refers to an

ideal age, to no time, to the time of the fulfilled potential of the
child in 'Frost at Midnight'. The 'ideal' of 'Constancy to an Ideal
Object' is one that cannot or should not be embodied in the
person, presumably, of Sara Hutchinson: 'She is not thou, and
only thou art she'. The response to seeming embodiments of the
absolute who may be far from ideal will be the concern of this part.

My concern with the concept of 'egotism' is with its
consequences for Coleridge's language, yet in this part I shall deal
with 'history'. Again this may seem a category mistake, yet, in the
nature of the case, we deal almost exclusively with interpretations
of history. I shall argue first that the sublime response to certain
'literary' characters is essentially similar to that to certain
'historical' characters. (They are associated by their 'egotism'.)
The sublime, it was suggested in Chapter 5, was the codification of
linguistic responses to those apprehensions which were felt to lie
beyond language: in Adam Smith's term, an 'overplus'. If my
argument there is accepted, it will be difficult to claim that a
discourse of 'history' has privileges not afforded to one of 'religion'
or 'morality' or those 'subjective' accounts of history (the
eighteenth-century term is 'conjectural'[3]) considered there.

The argument about the relative authority of history and poetry
goes back at least as far as chapter 9 of Aristotle's *Poetics*. In his
Essay on Pope Joseph Warton attempts a distinction in Aristotelian
terms: 'a minute and particular enumeration of circumstances
judiciously selected, is what chiefly discriminates poetry from
history, and renders the former, for that reason, a more close and
faithful representation of nature than the latter'.[4] Poetry is
privileged by a principle of selection, while history may select *us*.
The poet's 'enumeration' of his own 'selection' from nature is,
then, the means of achieving clear representational ends in which
there is a consonance of the poet's intentions and the effect upon
the reader. History and poetry are said to be enfolded within the
common process of nature not of history. Similarly, 'history' is an
object and not a discourse, debarred from 'judicious selection'
presumably by its aspirations to objectivity.

Clearly it would be ridiculous to claim that history can be
reduced to textuality, but the reverse claim, while not as clearly
ridiculous, would be as dangerous: and the danger would be of
misinterpretation. Probably this is a danger felt more acutely by
the critic than by the historian, but Hayden White is an exception.
He calls the introduction to his *Metahistory*, a study of nineteenth-

century historiography, 'The Poetics of History', and recognises that the status of his chosen writers on history 'depends, ultimately, on the preconceptual and specifically poetic nature of their perspective on history and its processes'. He studies them therefore through their employment of 'literary' modes of 'emplotment', of argument and of style. As he recognises also, 'Historiographical disputes on the level of "interpretation" are in reality disputes over the "true" nature of the historian's enterprise'[5] – disputes also over the nature of the 'true' and the 'good'. Coleridge's circumscription of genius, 'as it must not, so neither can it be lawless', might be compared with Young's unproblematic analogy of 'Genius' and 'Conscience': 'Genius can set us right in Composition, without the Rules of the Learned; as Conscience sets us right in Life, without the Laws of the Land: *This*, singly, can make us Good, as Men; *That*, singly, as Writers, can, sometimes, make us Great' (*Conjectures*, p. 31). If, as Coleridge suggests, the 'one life' can be represented in the language of poetry, it ought to follow that Young's terms could be reversed: that conscience could set us right in composition as genius sets us right in life. However, as terms of moral and aesthetic evaluation, 'Good' and 'Great' may be at odds with each other. We read Hume not as definitive but as consciously paradoxical when he writes, 'it is no wonder, that languages should not be very precise in marking the boundaries between virtues and talents, vices and defects; since there is so little distinction made in our internal estimate of them'.[6]

Perhaps we enjoy (or presume) a superior vantage point over that space of history which is Coleridge's own times, but the qualification expressed in Chapter 7 – that there are distortions attendant on that 'superiority' – should be remembered. What we are afforded is (usually) some prior interpretation of that historical space or those historical characters and thus we rely less completely on the prior, experiential (and unique) authority of the poet: at least it is to be hoped that a willing suspension of disbelief is more readily granted to the poet than to the journalist. This does not necessarily mean that Coleridge's journalistic language will be less problematic than the poetic language which is my continuing concern, but it does mean that we shall at least be aware of our own interpretative culpability – with this *caveat*, for instance, I can return to address an imaginary 'reader' – and the reader, whose attitude even to those imperatives to co-operation in the process of poems may be somewhat patronising, will enter these texts as participant in a dialectic. The encounter of language with the apparently 'objective' facts of history is obviously a terrain for the metaphysical encounter of subject and object (witness Hegel) but it will also be a testing-ground for my claims for Coleridge's language.

10　Great Bad Men

> Not to know me argues your selves unknown.
> (Satan, speaking in *Paradise Lost*, IV)

> The beautiful is valuable only with reference to the *human being*, but the sublime with reference to the *pure daemon* in him.　(Schiller, *On the Sublime*)

In 1795 Coleridge praises Brissot, the French Girondin leader guillotined in October 1793, as 'rather a sublime visionary' than a quick-eyed politician. Perhaps the dichotomy suggested in Chapter 5 above will be recognised. Coleridge says that Brissot proved 'unfit for the helm in the stormy hour of Revolution', and contrasts him with Robespierre, for whom ends justified means:

> What that *end* was, is not known: that it was a wicked one, has by no means been proved. I rather think, that the distant prospect to which he was travelling, appeared to him grand and beautiful; but that he fixed his eye on it with such intense eagerness as to neglect the foulness of the road.　(*Lectures 1795* [*CC*], I, 35)

The correlation of the despotism of the eye with Jacobin despotism is clear. What is not clear is the nature of the correlation. The rhetoric here is careful, despite its apparent extravagance, the imagery and syntax contributing rather to obfuscate than to pronounce judgement. In his first editorial for the *Morning Post*, in January 1798, Coleridge attributes to himself 'the eye of a calm observer' (*EOT* [*CC*], I, 37), and in this earlier passage – the 'Introductory Address' to *Conciones ad Populem* – his 'endeavour' is 'not so much to excite the torpid, as to regulate the feelings of the ardent' (*Lectures 1795* [*CC*], p. 33). While admitting the possibility of Robespierre's tyranny, Coleridge places the burden of proof on those who charge it, before positing, in justification, the presence of the visionary within the tyrannical egotist. Coleridge goes on to describe Robespierre's character as 'enthusiasm . . . blended with gloom, and suspiciousness, and inordinate vanity', before moving to a further justifying generalisation: 'The ardor of undisciplined benevolence seduces us into malignity: and whenever our hearts are warm, and our objects great and excellent, intolerance is the sin that does most easily beset us.' So the accusation, when it comes, is modified: 'to prevent tyranny he became a Tyrant' (*Lectures 1795* [*CC*], p. 35). What Coleridge claims as clear-eyed judiciousness might be said to be a kind of double vision.

This early text is characteristic of the difficulties inherent in applying aesthetic 'principles' outside the aesthetic realm. A version of his own acknowledgement of the incongruity of doctrine and form 'chiefly' in 'Religious Musings' might be invoked more generally against Coleridge's writings: 'Satisfied that the thoughts, such as they were, could not have been expressed otherwise . . . I forgot to inquire whether the thoughts themselves did not demand a degree of attention unsuitable to the nature and objects of poetry' (*BL* [*CC*], I, 7). The compounding of aesthetic and political, the presence of which in Coleridge's writings I shall go on to argue for, is not the 'ghost of reading' by which Shelley's line 'An old, mad, blind, despised, and dying king' refers not to King Lear but to King George III.[1] Rather, it is the way in which, in the passage quoted, Coleridge projects Robespierre and Brissot as types of a personal and aesthetic dichotomy already noticed: they stand in a similar ratio to one another as does Milton to Shakespeare, or Wordsworth to Coleridge himself. Here I wish to discuss Coleridge's confounding of a literary character, Milton's Satan, both with his own creator and with a historical figure, Napoleon Bonaparte.

Both are archetypes rather than types of the egotist, and yet neither shares the narcissistic introversion of a Werther. Their egotism is of the kind which – perhaps having both in mind – Coleridge defines as 'commanding genius' (*BL* [*CC*], I, 31–2). The secularising eighteenth-century readings of *Paradise Lost* produce a more psychologically complex Satan, a rebel himself, and Coleridge's references to the satanism of Napoleon always imply the Miltonic rather than the biblical character. That is, the imperative for moral condemnation of Napoleon is at odds with an admiration for his vigour, daring and activity. The ambivalence, even equivocation, before such a figure which can be traced through Coleridge's political journalism will clearly have consequences for a reading of 'The Ancient Mariner' or 'Kubla Khan', but a literal-minded pursuit of the analogy may also provide the grounds for assessing Harold Bloom's claim that Milton's Satan is the modern poet 'while God is his dead but still embarrassingly potent and present ancestor, or rather ancestral poet'.[2]

Coleridge, who thought himself to have 'a smack of Hamlet', necessarily identifies himself more with those characters against whom the figure of 'commanding genius' is set off. He calls the Girondins as a whole 'men of enlarged views and great literary attainments; but they seem to have been deficient in that vigour and daring activity, which circumstances made necessary' (*Lectures 1795* [*CC*], p. 34). The attraction of Jacques-Pierre Brissot is that of the humane artistic temperament in a man who yet wielded political power: one of the 'eloquent men' who are 'stung to rage by Pity' (*PW*, I, 118). Both Priestley and Brissot stood, unsuccessfully, against the candidates of the Commune in the French elections of 1792.[3] Both appear in a roll call of Girondin heroes from whose company the anti-revolutionary Burke is not excluded but within which he must be relegated (*Watchman* [*CC*], p. 39).

Coleridge's respect for the leaders of the Commonwealth in the English revolution – they were, he says, 'the stars of that narrow interspace of blue sky between the black clouds of the first and second Charles's reigns' (*Church and State* [*CC*], p. 96) – is often replicated by the Girondin leaders, beneath the commoner comparison of revolutionary France with Augustan Rome, in their references to the libertarian writings of Milton and James Harrington; and to the martyrs of a later English revolution, Lord William Russell and Algernon Sidney, who were invoked by Brissot in anticipating his own execution.[4] The distinction Coleridge makes between Robespierre and Brissot is thus reinforced by Robespierre's emphatic defence of his own principles against contemporary charges both of royalism and republicanism: 'I care no more for Cromwell than for Charles I. The yoke of the Decemvirs is as intolerable to me as that of Tarquin.'[5]

Coleridge has Robespierre express respect for 'Brissot's

thoughtful soul unbribed and bold' even as he refers to Brissot's being a victim of his power (*PW*, II, 497). Robespierre as a dramatic character, in the play Coleridge and Southey coauthored, is the Robespierre of that prose passage. Coleridge's ambivalence is in stark contrast to the emotions Wordsworth recollects in book x of *The Prelude*. The perversion of revolutionary ideals in practice into tyranny and institutionalised atheism diminishes all who had participated in that idealism – Wordsworth is left with 'a sense / Of treachery and desertion in the place / The holiest that I knew of – my own soul' (1805; x.378–80). Wordsworth had walked through Arras, Robespierre's birthplace, four years before, and now, in the year of the Terror, he finds that 'Tyrants strong before / In devilish pleas, were ten times stronger now' (x.309). 'Devilish' here refers us to Milton's Satan, who 'with necessity, / The tyrant's plea, excused his devilish deeds' (*Paradise Lost*, IV.393). The allusion associates the tyranny of Robespierre with that of Satan newly landed in Paradise: for Wordsworth, no ends can justify these means. Yet in terms of what I shall argue below it is significant that in recording his 'exultation' on hearing the news of Robespierre's execution Wordsworth compares him not to Milton's Satan but to his Moloch:

> O friend, few happier moments have been mine
> Through my whole life than that when first I heard
> That this foul tribe of Moloch was o'erthrown
> And their chief regent levelled with the dust.
> (*Prelude*, 1805, x.466)

The confident syntax and monosyllabic diction of these lines make them convincingly emphatic, while Coleridge's immediate response is at once ambivalent: 'Fallen is the Oppressor, friendless, ghastly, low, / And my heart aches, though Mercy struck the blow' (*PW*, I, 65). In the dedicatory letter to *The Fall of Robespierre* he promises to detail 'the fall of a man whose great bad actions have cast a disastrous lustre on his name' (*PW*, II, 495). The paradox of 'great bad actions' admits the force of both sides of the ends-and-means debate as does Shakespeare's purported 'Caesar never did wrong but with just cause'.

On the manuscript of *Osorio*, the play written three years later, Coleridge describes Osorio as

> A man who, from constitutional calmness of appetites, is
> seduced into pride and the love of power, by these into
> misanthropism, or rather a contempt of mankind, and from
> thence by envy . . . into a most atrocious guilt. A man who is in
> truth a weak man, yet always duping himself into the belief that
> he has a soul of iron.   (*PW*, II, 1114)

Within the play Albert makes much the same judgement (II, 543,
553), but in the single act of *The Fall of Robespierre* written by
Coleridge there is less an attempt to account for the psychology of
power than a kind of awe in face of it. The time-serving Barrere's
first soliloquy on the 'tyrant' acknowledges a power not ascribable
to the external force at Robespierre's command: 'I feel, I hate
him – / Yet there is in him that which makes me tremble!' (*PW*, II,
496). The pairing of a petty with an overreaching egotist is
apparent both in Schiller's *Die Räuber* (Spiegelberg and Karl
Moor) and his *Wallenstein* (Butler and Wallenstein): wickedness
can be impressive. We are encouraged to feel the justice of
Robespierre's retort after Barrere has accused him of being too
fond of slaughter: Robespierre taunts his '*Self-centering Fear!*' (*PW*,
II, 500). His brother Augustin ('Robespierre Junior' in the play)
quotes the 'sections' of the people, who recognise the same
paradox as in the dedicatory letter, calling Robespierre 'the *tyrant
guardian* of the country's *freedom!*' (II, 498). In terms of the drama
Robespierre has softened, but his reply suggests the satanic
'necessity' which privileges him as the sole arbitrator of ends and
means, asserting that if all others fail him he will be left 'Myself!
the steel-strong Rectitude of soul / And poverty sublime 'mid
circling virtues' (II, 499). While this is from an almost journalistic
work – it was in fact written largely from newspaper accounts[6] –
the assertion both of a dispossessed sublimity and of a
self-sufficient certitude are characteristic of Romantic readings of
Milton's Satan, just as Coleridge later anatomises the corollary
dejection attendant on the mind's being its own place.
   The eighteenth-century's appropriation of Milton as the great
exemplar of the Longinian 'sublime' has less to do with the later
appropriation of him as a great republican than with an impulse
to instal him, along with Shakespeare and the Bible, as bulwarks
of a national identity. In his translation of *On the Sublime* Leonard
Welsted concedes that Homer's description of the goddess
Discord is

undoubtedly very great; but to any one who has read the prodigious Description *Milton* gives us of *Satan*, as when he rises from the fiery surge, when he views the Host of fallen Angels, and particularly when he is apprehended in Paradise, this perhaps will seem but moderately Sublime.[7]

Also early in the century, John Dennis says, 'Milton is to be admired above . . . all [the Ancients] for one thing, and that is for having carried away the Prize of Sublimity from both Ancients and Moderns.'[8] Satan satisfies the demand of the neoclassical rules that the hero of epic be active, but his conjunction with a recognition of the 'sublime' effect – Addison singles out the first, second and sixth books of *Paradise Lost* for their 'sublimity' (*Spectator*, II, 585–90 [no. 279]) – is significant. The sublime emotion is a kind of secularisation of the awe felt before the divine – we remember that, for Burke, terror is 'the common stock of every thing that is sublime' – and by the time of Blair's *Lectures on Rhetoric* the thin line between pleasurable terror and admiration for its object is perceptibly being crossed. Blair speaks of the 'daring sublimity' of Milton's genius and says that in the characterisation of Satan

> concur a variety of sources of the sublime; the principal object eminently great, a high superior nature, fallen indeed but erecting itself against distress; the grandeur of the principal object heightened by associating with it so noble an idea as that of the sun suffering an eclipse; this picture shaded with all those images of change and trouble, of darkness and terror, which coincide so finely with the sublime emotion. . . .   (*Lectures on Rhetoric*, II, 471–4)

So, for Blair, although 'Adam is undoubtedly [Milton's] hero', Satan 'in particular makes a striking figure, and is indeed the best drawn character in the poem' (II, 422, 472). Not until Blake and Shelley is there a positive assertion of Satan's being the 'hero' of Milton's poem with a consciousness of the revolutionary consequences entailed by it, but in his 'Illustrations on Sublimity' (published the same year as Blair's *Lectures*) James Beattie must equivocate, detaching moral judgement from the sublime emotion:

When great qualities prevail in any person, they form what is called a sublime character. Every good man is a personage of this order: but a character may be sublime which is not completely good, nay, which is upon the whole very bad; for the test of sublimity is not moral approbation but that pleasurable astonishment wherewith certain things strike the beholder.[9]

Then, after a series of classical examples, he adduces Milton's Satan, who, though self-evidently 'evil', possesses 'grandeur', 'boldness' and 'force' which 'are astonishing: and though we always detest his malignity, we are often compelled to admire that very greatness by which we are confounded and terrified'.[10] This admiration must then be accounted for as akin to that with which a natural force is responded to. At the same time Beattie reminds us that Satan is partly imaginary: 'So far, therefore, as we admire him for sublimity of character, we consider him, not as the great enemy of our souls, but as a fictitious being, and a mere poetical hero.'[11] The first of the '*Affections* unexceptionally Sublime' in Baillie's *Essay* is '*Heroism*, or Desire of *Conquest*, such as in an *Alexander* or a *Caesar*' (*Essay on the Sublime*, p. 19). The objects of such a desire are power and fame: the greater the power the greater the sublime, hence 'it is in the *Almighty* that this Sublime is compleated, who with a *Nod* can shatter to Pieces the *Foundations* of a *Universe*, as with a *Word* he called it into *Being*' (p. 21). Kames calls sublimity 'the most delightful of all emotions':

the reader, engrossed by a sublime effect, feels himself raised as it were to a higher rank. Considering that effect, it is not wonderful, that the history of conquerors and heroes should be universally the favourite entertainment. And this fairly accounts for what I once erroneously suspected to be a wrong bias originally in human nature; which is, that the grossest acts of oppression and injustice scarce blemish the character of a great conqueror: we, nevertheless, warmly espouse his interest, accompany him in his exploits, and are anxious for his success: the splendor and enthusiasm of the hero transfused into the readers, elevate their minds far above the rules of justice, and render them in a great measure insensible of the wrongs that are committed.[12]

The problem here is again one of the authority of discourse. In

Kames's account the effect of the poem is a sublime elevation of the mind, an experience of a different order from that in which 'rules of justice' are a standard. This is less of a problem for Kames than for Coleridge. Such a bias towards mere 'success' gives the latter more cause for anxiety. As with the character of Christ, the character of Satan is then open to appropriation. Godwin's argument in *Political Justice* recalls Coleridge on Robespierre: 'it seems to appear that men of talents, even when they are erroneous, are not destitute of virtue, and that there is a fullness of guilt of which they are incapable. . . . Can great intellectual power exist without a strong sense of justice?' In such terms, Godwin writes, 'we shall find that even Caesar and Alexander had their virtues' and can cite a Satan revalued as a rebel in support of his claim:

> poetical readers have commonly remarked Milton's devil to be a being of considerable virtue. It must be admitted that his energies centred too much in personal regards. But why did he rebel against his maker? It was, as he himself informs us, because he saw no sufficient reason for that extreme inequality of rank and power which the creator assumed. It was because prescription and precedent form no adequate ground for implicit faith.

Satan 'disdained to be subdued by despotic power' and rebelled against injustice done him; is taken, that is, much at his own valuation within the poem.[13]

Coleridge's first, ecstatic response to his reading of Schiller's *Robbers*, in a letter to Southey dated 3 November 1794, indicates the connection between satanic characters and the idea of 'sublimity':

> My God! Southey! Who is this Schiller? This Convulser of the Heart? Did he write his Tragedy amid the yelling of Fiends? – I should not like to [be] able to describe such Characters – I tremble like an Aspen leaf – Upon my Soul, I write to you because I am frightened – I had better go to Bed. Why have we ever called Milton sublime? That Count de Moor – horrible Wielder of heart-withering Virtues – ! Satan is scarcely qualified to attend his execution as Gallows Chaplain –. . . . (*CL*, I, 122)

Looking back, Hazlitt connects this sublime *frisson* with the 'dawn' of political hope. In 'On the Feeling of Immortality in Youth' he quotes Coleridge's sonnet (*PW*, I, 72–3) on the Gothic appeal of *The Robbers*: such pleasurable terror, he says, 'could be borne only amidst the fulness of hope, the crash of the fall of the strong holds of power, and the exulting sounds of the march of human freedom' (*HW*, xvII, 196–7). Elsewhere he claims that Goethe and Schiller among others 'have made the only incorrigible Jacobins, and their school of poetry is the only real school of Radical Reform' ('On the German Drama', *HW*, vII, 362). The association of *The Robbers* with Jacobinism was close enough for it to be parodied (as *The Rovers*) in Canning's *Anti-Jacobin* in 1798, and Schiller himself had been proclaimed an honorary citizen of the French Republic on 26 August 1792: the 'Bard tremendous in sublimity' (*PW*, I, 72) is also (at this stage) a supporter of the Revolution, so Coleridge's response to Karl Moor as the 'horrible Wielder of heart-withering Virtues' anticipates what he is to say, equivocally, of Robespierre in the preface to his play ('great bad actions') and in the prose passage with which I began. Although he deprecates both, the fact that Coleridge feels the propinquity of Milton's sublimity and of his Satan to a play so concerned with the morality of freedom and revenge suggests not only that his own reading of Satan would be recognised by Godwin but that he will suspect the political consequences entailed by the exercise of such satanic 'Virtues' even as he is drawn to them.

However, it should be clear from the relation of the metaphor of the circle to that of the Fall considered in Chapter 6 that all of human history will lose something in the translation to the local and temporal action of the dramatic image – even laying aside the problem of the dramatic representation of politics.[14] Hegel speaks of Goethe and Schiller's 'attempt to win back again within the circumstances existing in modern times the lost independence of the [heroic] figures', but this pathetic turning against civil society is 'tiny and isolated'. Karl Moor's crime 'incorporates the wrong which it intends to destroy' so, of his fall, 'even if this is tragic, it is still only boys who can be seduced by this robber ideal'.[15] Satan's heroism begins not in the justice or injustice of his treatment but in his resistance: chained on the burning lake and hailing its horrors he brings with him

A mind not to be changed by place or time.
The mind is its own place, and in itself
Can make a heaven of hell, a hell of heaven.
                    (*Paradise Lost*, i.253–5)

While this seems to assert that coadunation which for the
Romantic mind is to be striven for and celebrated – we might
substitute 'self' and 'world' or 'nature' for 'mind' and 'place' –
Milton is emphatic that the 'paradise within' promised to the
fallen Adam at the end of *Paradise Lost* is dependent not just on
wisdom but on answerable deeds and Christian virtues, and that
there are more than constraints upon the imaginative autonomy
Satan claims for himself. *En route* for Eden he is troubled by

The hell within him, for within him hell
He brings, and round about him, nor from hell
One step no more than from himself can fly
By change of place.
                    (iv.20–3)

The translator of *Die Räuber*, in the version probably read by
Coleridge, clearly sees the similarity of Karl Moor and his band of
robbers to Satan and the fallen angels – dismissing his men at the
end, Karl alludes to Kozinski as a kind of Abdiel: 'Young man!
. . . Thou art yet unspotted – amongst the guilty, only guiltless!'[16]
– yet the dialectic of the rebel's heroic self-sufficiency with his
self-condemnable conscience, latent in *Paradise Lost*, is the whole
impulse of Schiller's play. In the opening scene, to effect the
disinheritance of Karl from which the plot follows, Franz von
Moor must persuade their father that Karl's promise of becoming
'the hero, the great man!' has all along depended on his setting
consciousness over conduct, on his satanic 'ambition', and Karl's
career follows the logic of this unjust dispossession. Finally
he submits to a morality from which he has exiled himself but to
which he has always subscribed.
    Once outlawry is forced on him Karl's actions are existential,
acts of the will, but, never having resolved 'Evil be thou my good',
his activity is always tempered by a more than residual moral
sense, the function of which can be seen in the great moral
set-piece preceding a battle in which the eighty robbers defeat a
force of 1700 Bohemian cavalry come to arrest them. The robbers

are exhilarated, having just rescued one of their number, Roller, from hanging, yet in so doing they boast of having killed women and children, at which Moor is outraged. He does not, however, have to apologise to the Commissary (Priest) who comes to treat for their surrender:

> I am none of those banditti who are in compact with sleep, and with the midnight hour – I scale no walls in the dark, and force no locks to plunder. – What I have done shall be engraven in that book where all the actions of mankind are recorded – in heaven's eternal register: – But with you poor ministers of earthly justice, I hold no further communing. – Tell your master, that my trade is the *lex talionis*; like for like: – Vengenace is my trade![17]

Yet vengeance is *mine*, saith the Lord, *I* will repay. Roller is killed in the ensuing fight, but Karl's appropriation of the Satanic role implies his gradual forfeiture of natural as of institutional justice: Karl may be a prodigal son, but after the battle, as after the Fall, there can be no return to innocence.

All the same, we can regard Karl as the hero of *The Robbers* with nothing of the conscious heresy by which Blake can call Satan the 'real hero' of *Paradise Lost*. Coleridge defines sin as 'an Evil which has its ground or origin in the Agent, and not in the Circumstances' (*AR*, pp. 245–7). He does so in the course of a meditation on a passage from Jeremy Taylor about Original Sin ('Aphorisms on Spiritual Religion', x), in which what appears to be merely a verbal quibble culminates in the assertion that the phrase 'Original Sin' is a pleonasm, and that 'a State or Act, that has its origin in the will, may be calamity, deformity, disease, or mischief; but a *Sin* it cannot be' (*AR*, p. 261). Some choose evil – there is such a thing as 'an Evil in human nature which is not wholly grounded in the limitation of our understandings' (*Friend* [*CC*], II, 9) – but some have evil thrust upon them; and Karl is finally regenerate.

Thus it seems to me mistaken to see Werther and Karl Moor as, effectively, interchangeable, as Marilyn Butler does in her recent book.[18] Certainly the introspection of both is recognisably that of Satan. Werther's 'I look into myself and find a world' only confirms to him the incapacity for action he finds in the outer world, and on the face of it Karl Moor's version is little different:

'Be what thou wilt, thou dread Unknown, so but this Self remains: – this Self within. – For all that is external, what has it of reality beyond that form and colour which the mind itself bestows? – I am myself my heaven or my hell.'[19] Karl is here at his psychological nadir, but in what follows that development from the Werther-like hero of sensibility to the hero as satanic victim and/or rebel which has been traced by Peter L. Thorslev[20] can be seen taking place. Karl shoots his lover, Amalia, because he realises the impossibility of redeeming all he has done since his initial wronging, and rather than kill himself he will give himself up to a labourer with eleven children who would have need of the bounty offered on him. Werther's suicide is the final, narcissistic expression of the alienation from man and nature in which he is entrapped, an implicit acquiescence to the values of the society from which he is alienated. Karl's act is wasteful, tragic but, as the robbers say, he wants to be admired, finally free, and his self-sacrifice is a final assertion of free will: Schiller suggests that redemption through action is not untenable as a possibility.

In his preface to the first published version of the play Schiller takes Karl Moor much at the character's own evaluation of himself within the text – as, increasingly, Milton's Satan was read in the same period in England – disturbing settled order in celebration of his own power: 'A strangely momentous human being, equipped with all power [*Kraft*], in pursuit of what these may get him, necessarily becoming either a Brutus or a Catiline.'[21] Satan, 'following us with shuddering astonishment through trackless chaos', is one of the characters with whom Karl Moor is held up to comparison. The applicability Coleridge, Hazlitt and others might see in such a hero, to the decade culminating in the fall of the Bastille, is clear, yet the literary culture Schiller ironically addresses in his preface is, with little extension, that society which is pacified by its acceptance of Karl as a sacrificial victim. This is to suggest that, as in the case of Coleridge, the disenchantment with or default of revolutionary 'hope' is implicit in its original manifestation, bound up as it is with admiration (even, in Carlyle's terms, 'hero-worship') for individual actors. In the abstract, certitude can be admirable – 'A noble soul endures as few lasting moral disharmonies [*Dissonanzen*] as the ear the screaming of a knife on glass'[22] – and even ideal: 'Every individual human being, one may say, carries within him, potentially and prescriptively, an ideal man, the archetype of a human being, and it is his life's task to be, through all his changing manifestations, in harmony with the unchanging unity of this ideal.'[23] Yet this near-deification of the individual will can, as Schiller has realised, validate a Brutus *or* a Catiline, a rebel or a tyrant. The tendency of Coleridge's comments on Napoleon is to the conclusion that the former grows inevitably into the latter (he might, speaking of Satan, paraphrase Wordsworth as 'the rebel is father of the Father'[24]). As Walter Benjamin says of the *Trauerspiel* (German drama of the seventeenth century), 'in the baroque the tyrant and the martyr are but the two faces of the monarch'.[25] Coleridge's movement to this conclusion is neatly comprehended in the contrast between his response to *The Robbers* and his own translation of the last two parts of Schiller's *Wallenstein* trilogy.

Wallenstein himself begins in a self-delighting power in which, as Octavio says, 'the soldier's boldness constitu[t]es his freedom' (*PW*, ii, 607) and in which dispossession has turned the victim into the commander 'indignant at my destiny' (ii, 622), but his very activity and certainty in his own actions come to condemn him in terms of a morality situated outside any of the factions within the play. In agreeing with the Countess Tertsky's assertion of the moral weakness of the Emperor – that acts of conquest and pillage are to the Emperor only relatively immoral – prior to defecting from him, Wallenstein is subscribing to an absolute morality as though such an action were relativist, to a morality that must condemn him:

> What at that time was right, because thou didst it
> For him, to-day is all at once become
> Opprobious, foul, because it is directed
> Against him.
>
> (ii, 704)

The plays' moral absolutist is in fact Max Piccolomini. When he says to his father, refusing to flee with him, '*Thy way is crooked – it is not my way*' (ii, 721) he is displaying a consistency admirable as Wallenstein's (at least as the latter appears against, for example, the time-serving of Isolani) but recognising a principle wholly other than the will, which becomes mere expediency. He is loyal to Wallenstein but when for the first time he questions his General's actions it becomes an irrevocable judgement – 'he who once hath acted infamy, / Does nothing more in this world' (II, 708) – whereas Wallenstein has now said, 'Evil be thou my good' (II, 709), and Max in turn becomes a victim. Hegel points out that Wallenstein's officers desert him because they owe an absolute loyalty rather to their oath of duty to the 'universally recognised power and government. . . . Thus in the end he finds himself alone; he is not so much fought and conquered by an opposing external power as denuded of all means of achieving his end'.[26]

'Great bad actions' are here those of a tyrant, but the very investigation of the tyrant's personal power which is, for Coleridge, among the flaws which weaken Schiller's plays as drama (in a note reproduced by E. H. Coleridge), will serve as ammunition as the critic turns to the drama of contemporary tyranny. Wallenstein is, he writes,

> a finer psychological than dramatic, and a more dramatic than a tragic character. Shakespere draws *strength* as in Richard the Third, and even when he blends weakness as in Macbeth – yet it is weakness of a specific kind that leaves the strength in full and fearful energy – but Schiller has drawn weakness imposing on itself the love of power for the sense of strength. . . .   (II, 599n)

Dubiety is possible as a critical reaction to the recognition, by characters within the play, of an unaffected 'power'. As quoted to him by Wrangel, the Swedish king's opinion of Wallenstein is one that will be reiterated seriously by Carlyle: 'always the commanding Intellect, / He said, should have command, and be the King' (II, 693), and Max acknowledges a personal power in Wallenstein separable from that with which he is (at this point) entrusted: Wallenstein is 'possessed by a commanding spirit. / And his too is the station of command' (II, 612).

In Shaftesbury's 'Advice to an Author' 'commanding genius' is a moral faculty similar to the 'conscience' of Coleridge or Butler, commanding the 'natural' man. Readers of the Socratic dialogues

> would acquire a peculiar speculative habit, so as virtually to carry about with them a sort of pocket-mirror, always ready and in use. In this, there were two faces which would naturally present themselves to our view: one of them, like the commanding genius, the leader and chief . . . the other like that rude, undisciplined, and head-strong creature whom we

ourselves in our natural capacity most exactly resembled.[27]

Coleridge's sense of 'commanding genius' is almost directly opposite. The phrase reappears in contradistinction to 'absolute genius' at the beginning of Chapter 2 of the *Biographia*. The man of 'commanding genius' will be more original and creative than he of 'mere talent' yet fall short of the 'creative and self-sufficing power of absolute Genius' (*BL* [*CC*], i, 31) by which man becomes godlike. Therefore he will need continually to confirm his own self-image as creator by the evidence of what, by an act of the will, he is able to effect in the external world. (Ostensibly Coleridge is writing, as he goes on to write, of poetic genius, but from the way in which he comes to illustrate the contention its validity must be intended as general.) 'In tranquil times' creativity can be realised in the subjection and moulding of nature, as in the *fiat* of Kubla Khan, commanding, metaphorically, 'a perfect poem', yet dependence on the external world also leaves such a man, despite his apparent success in then subjecting people and events to his will, at the mercy of temporal events. 'In times of tumult' such 'are the men destined to come forth as the shaping spirit of Ruin, to destroy the wisdom of ages in order to substitute the fancies of a day, and to change kings and kingdoms, as the wind shifts and shapes the clouds' (*BL* [*CC*], i, 33). The 'shaping spirit of Imagination ('Dejection') as embodied in these men is perverted into that of 'Ruin'. The recognition of a repressed creativity finally expressing itself in destruction is one thread running through some Romantic discussions of such men. Another is that they do actively embody a *Zeitgeist*.[28] (Even Hazlitt's 'Spirits of the Age' in the *New Monthly Magazine* become *The Spirit of the Age*.) In 1817 as in 1795, Coleridge is quite prepared to give the devil his due.

11   The General Will

> ... the *moral egoist* is a man who limits all ends to himself,
> sees no use in anything except what is useful to him and, as
> a eudaemonist, locates the supreme determining ground of
> his will merely in utility and his own happiness, not in the
> thought of duty.   (Kant, *Anthropology*)

Before looking at some presentations of the 'hero' it is as well to
consider Rousseau, not simply as intellectual progenitor of the
Revolution throwing up those figures of 'commanding genius',
but as such a figure himself, or at least as an irresponsible creator
whose own presence within such presentations is more
commanding even than his own sentimental heroes. Perhaps
remembering the reburial of Rousseau's remains in the Pantheon
(along with those of Voltaire) by the revolutionary Convention in
1794, Carlyle says that 'the French Revolution found its
Evangelist in Rousseau'.[1] Indeed, like the fallen angel, the
evangelist seems to furnish an example of the conflation of an
actual and a literary character. The depiction of the self as a given
in the *Reveries* and the *Confessions*, and of a socially alienated hero,
is at least logically consistent with the ideal that liberty in the state
should be that which allows every man to be himself; that with the
state expressing the *volonté générale* – as distinct from the *volonté de
tous*, which is merely the aggregate of individual egoisms – each
citizen obeys himself when he obeys the dictates of society.[2]

Rousseau's *Confessions*, completed in 1770 but not published
until 1781, posthumously, begin with a claim, like Wordsworth's
for *The Prelude*, that 'it is a thing unprecedented in literary history
that a man should talk so much about himself': 'I have resolved
on an enterprise without precedent, and which, once executed,
will have no imitator. I wish to portray to my fellow beings in a
way true to nature, a man, and this man will be myself.'[3]
Rousseau's early awareness of a special temperament and claim

165

for his uniqueness, the tendency to introspection and melancholy and the desire to identify with fictional characters all associate him with the sentimental hero we looked at in *Werther* and which include the heroes of his own novels.

Those heroes and the government of Reason proposed by *The Social Contract* do not share merely the coincidence of publication (all within two years in England). Hazlitt co-opts Rousseau as a Romantic hero in his essay 'On the Character of Rousseau' in the *Round Table*. The dominant quality of Rousseau's mind, for Hazlitt, is 'the most intense consciousness of his own existence', and he 'filled all objects with himself' (*HW*, IV, 88). By now, what such a claim involves should be clear, so it is no surprise to find Hazlitt also invoking Wordsworth. Rousseau 'interests you in certain objects by interesting you in himself', while 'Mr. Wordsworth would persuade you that the most insignificant objects are interesting in themselves, because he is interested in them' (IV, 92). Hazlitt does not mean to imply that this is merely an unintended defect of Wordsworth's character – indeed the last stanza of 'She dwelt among the untrodden ways' is a clear example of the defect being deployed – but his definition of 'egotism' certainly seems confused by the fact of his chosen trio all having written autobiographies of a kind: 'The three greatest egotists that we know of, that is, the three writers who felt their own being, most powerfully and exclusively, are Rousseau, Wordsworth, and Benvenuto Cellini. As Swift somewhere says, we defy the world to furnish out a fourth' (IV, 92–3). There is a distinction, not acknowledged by Hazlitt, between mere braggadoccio and the epistemological act he has described, an act of self-authentication. (The same distinction can be perceived in his essay 'On Egotism' [XII, 157–68] and Addison cites as examples of 'egotists' both the 'Authors of Memoirs' and 'our modern Prefaces' [*Spectator*, IV, 520, 521].)

Hazlitt's view of Rousseau is affected by that coming down from Burke which would discredit the social morality the Revolution would have installed by reference to the 'immorality' of the author of *The Confessions*. Burke attacks Rousseau for offences against the 'little platoon' which is the touchstone of his morality. In its place the *Confessions* seem to offer an 'ethics of vanity'. In his *Letter to a Member of the National Assembly* Burke says that, seeking for new governing principles, the Revolution settled on Vanity, and thus on Rousseau, 'because in him that peculiar vice which they wished to erect into ruling virtue, was by far the most conspicuous'. The inconsistency of private and professed morality which Burke perceives makes this 'vanity' a damning judgement: 'Thousands admire the sentimental writer; the affectionate father is hardly known in his parish.'[4]

In admitting Rousseau to his own pantheon of Great Men, Carlyle too accepts a challenge posited by the opening of *The Confessions*:

> The fault and misery of Rousseau was what we easily name by a single word, *Egoism*; which is indeed the source and summary of all faults and miseries whatsoever. He had not perfected himself into victory over mere Desire; a mean Hunger, in many sorts, was still the motive principle of him.   (*On Heroes*, p. 185)

Disingenuously, Carlyle's characterisation of Rousseau implies not just the responsibility *for*, but the irresponsible intention *of*, what Carlyle regards as the democratic disaster of the French Revolution. The product of the 'effete', sceptical and anti-heroic eighteenth century, Rousseau sits 'kindling French Revolutions by his paradoxes' (pp. 167–8).

I suggest that here we have returned to that sense of 'ego[t]ism' which was designated 'trivial' in Chapter 1 above and that to break this circle we need to consider the Hegelian spiral. In the section on the 'Unhappy Consciousness' in the *Phenomenology*, consciousness begins in the trivially egotistical state: 'Self-will is the freedom which entrenches itself in some particularity and is still in bondage'; while it ends in a new 'identity': 'The surrender of one's own will is only from one aspect negative; in principle, however, or in itself, it is at the same time positive, viz. the positing of will as the will of an "other", and specifically of will, not as a particular, but as a universal will' (pp. 121, 138). In the preceding section, on *Herrschaft* (lordship, mastery), the existence of an 'other' as a necessary condition of self-consciousness is elucidated in the parable of the master and slave. Even the slave sees his own true self in terms of another, and objectifies himself through labour, through the transformation of material things, while the Unhappy Consciousness can only lose itself in work, which confirms its essential division. The confirmation of self-consciousness achieved in 'mastery' is of less value than the slave's self-consciousness of ability and may be mere egoism:

A consciousness that opens up a subject-matter soon learns that others hurry along like flies to freshly poured-out milk, and want to busy themselves with it; and they learn about that individual that he, too, is concerned with the subject-matter, not as an *object*, but as his *own* affair.   (p. 251)

In the process from 'pure subject' to 'absolute spirit' which Hegel plots, showing thereby that the being of self is also its becoming, he does not attempt to name his protagonist. This anonymity facilitates appropriation of his dialectic by both 'left' and 'right'. The self can be named 'class', 'citizen' or 'child', with consequential differences in interpreting the form taken by the articulation of Spirit in the state, where self and other are atoned. This is the enactment of that desire broached as a problem in Chapter 1 above. The process towards 'Reason' in Hegel's next chapter, the realisation of the Hegelian *Begriff* (notion, concept), emerges in this absolute. As an 'actualization of self-consciousness', it is a process different in kind from Schelling's *Identitätsphilosophie*, that night in which all cats are grey.

For Hegel, 'to begin with, this active Reason is aware of itself merely as an individual and as such must demand and produce its unity in an "other"' (p. 211). That self-consciousness should be activity rather than observation and that it implies a negativity of the other is something we have already looked at in Fichte, but this for Hegel is only a point of departure. This 'becoming' will be a movement from mere 'independence' to 'freedom', the first in a series of displacements which includes, for example, an ethical displacement from 'commandments' to 'laws'. In being conscious of an 'individuality', a 'mere being of himself in Spirit', separated from the nation and the *real* ethical order, this pleasure-seeking '*individual* consciousness' characterised by 'levity' 'takes hold of life much as a ripe fruit is plucked, which readily offers itself to the hand that takes it'. The end is not this fulfillment of 'desire', 'for it is not as *this particular* individual that it becomes an object to itself, but rather as the *unity* of itself and the other self-consciousness, hence as an individual that is only a moment, or a *universal*' (pp. 217–18). This being-for-self is opposed to being-in-itself, in which 'the individual has simply perished, and the absolute unyieldingness of individual existence is pulverized on the equally unrelenting but continuous world of actuality'. Thus the consciousness is thrown back on itself as 'essence' before acceding to the state as 'substance' in which it is conscious of itself as a 'thing'. In only being cognisant of this absolute, 'what contradicts itself in its consciousness has for it in each case the form of essence and of its own reality', and it is therefore 'deranged', aware of itself as 'unreal' (pp. 220, 225).

The escape from this derangement, which is Werther's, is in the divestment of 'individuality'. The consciousness which 'knows it must sacrifice' individuality is virtue, which takes as its antagonist 'the way of the world': it is the 'virtuous knight' of romance, striving for a grail in which 'end and essence are for [self-consciousness] henceforth the spontaneous interfusion of the universal . . . and individuality'. The latter is thereby superseded: 'its account with its previous shapes is thereby closed; they lie forgotten behind it, and no longer confront it as a world given to it, but are developed solely within itself as transparent moments'. The need for opposition to an other (a limitation) is now cast away and consciousness occupies itself with itself: 'Action has, therefore, the appearance of the movement of a circle which moves freely within itself in a void, which, unimpeded, now expands, now contracts, and is perfectly content to operate in and with its own self' (pp. 236–7). The 'actualization' demanded, then, is a sensuous or concrete rather than abstract universal, the form of art in the *Aesthetics*. In terms of the individual consciousness such an actualisation is in action, which is 'simply the coming-to-be of Spirit as consciousness'. But this necessity must be attended with the acceptance of being caught in a circle:

> The individual who is going to act seems . . . to find himself in a circle in which each moment already presupposes the other, and thus he seems unable to find a beginning, because he only gets to know his original nature, which must be his End, *from the deed*, while, in order to act, he must have that End beforehand. (*Phenomenology*, p. 240)

This is the predicament Coleridge identifies as Hamlet's. Hegel's answer is simple: begin to act 'without further scruples'. He abolishes the problem of 'ends and means' and even of 'good' and 'bad'. 'The individual, therefore, knowing that in his actual world he can find nothing else but its unity with himself, or only the certainty of himself in the truth of that world, *can experience only joy in himself*' (p. 242). Ethics are to be replaced by 'knowledge'. So, even an ethical imperative such as 'love thy neighbour as thyself' reaches its 'richest and most important form' in the 'intelligent' love of the state, while 'the only significance left for beneficence, which is a *sentiment*, is that of an action which is quite single and isolated, of help in [a situation of] need, which is as contingent as it is transitory' (p. 255). The goal of 'Reason' is reached in Reason's becoming the giver of laws, not merely their arbitrator. It is therefore a universal reason of a different (Hegel would say, a higher) order from the 'practical' reason of Kant. 'Law' is absolute and essential, as opposed to 'commandments', which can only express an 'ought':

> The law is . . . an eternal law which is grounded not in the will of a particular individual, but is valid in and for itself; it is the absolute *pure will of all* which has the form of immediate being. Also, it is not a *commandment*, which only *ought* to be: it *is* and is *valid*; it is the universal 'I' of the category, the 'I' which is immediately a reality, and the world *is* only this reality. (p. 261)[5]

So Hegel ushers in the return of 'identity' and the actualisation of self-consciousness in performance. This is one way out of that fix described in Chapter 9. What Kant thought he had remade as science on a new, firm bedrock has become historical and textual. Any satisfaction the self may feel at having reached the Celestial City, at having dominion over reason, is sure evidence that the self is halted at the Mountain of Error. Only in knowing objects as itself can the consciousness be free of alienation. Yet this process, this endless supersession, depends on a sleight of hand. By exercising self-consciousness man is aware of his selfhood,[6] and Hegel therefore blurs the division between 'man' and 'self'. The *schöne Seele* 'is not only the intuition of the Divine but the Divine's intuition of itself' (p. 483). Our suspicion that the relative weight of the two terms may be the converse of this formulation is fed by what follows. The drive towards 'universalization' is Nietzschean: a ravenous *Wille zur Macht*. By virtue of that circular movement to which Hegel appeals here, 'it is only when the "I" communes with itself in its otherness that the content [object] is comprehended' (p. 486). In so doing the 'I' is trapped within serial time, awaiting completion as the World Spirit. Finally, Absolute Knowledge is a blockage against knowing: it is to be known by an Absolute. We

are in a further fix. Stanley Cavell puts it nicely in a summary of
Kant's achievement: 'In discovering this limitation of reason,
reason proves its power to itself, over itself.'[7] Yet Coleridge wants
to affirm that 'the free will [is] our only absolute self' that 'to
know is in its very essence a verb active' (*BL* [*CC*], ɪ, 114, 264). He
is wandering between two worlds, one dead, the other
inconscionable.

12 Whatever They Do is Right

Coleridge's discussion of Rousseau at least deals overtly with Rousseau's ideas, but coming to a theory of the 'government of Reason' from Kant's explication of categorical reason enables him to paraphrase the former as an absurd utopianism (*Friend* [*CC*] I, 192). The *volonté générale* leads to an immoral confusion of a thing ('Reason') with a person. Following Rousseau, the 'physiocratic philosophers' and the French legislators

> by these high-sounding phrases led on the vain, ignorant, and intoxicated populace to wild excesses and wilder expectations, which entailing on them the bitterness of disappointment cleared the way for military despotism, for the satanic Government of Horror under the Jacobins, and of Terror under the Corsican. (*Friend* [*CC*], I, 194)

There is, then, a direct relationship between the influence of *The Social Contract* and the acquiescence to despotism: 'the influence of these writings contributed greatly, not indeed to raise the present emperor, but certainly to reconcile a numerous class of politicians to his unlimited authority' (*Friend* [*CC*], I, 197). Coleridge is, then, less committed to the unlimited authority of a hero in the abstract than is Carlyle (and therefore to the backtracking in which Carlyle will involve himself in the consideration of Rousseau and Napoleon); but in his fascination for the individuals who act upon history his attitude to the authority by which they do so necessarily becomes problematic. He would recognise what Hazlitt has to say in the essay 'On Thought and Action' as commensurate with what he had written of 'commanding genius': 'To accomplish great things argues, I imagine, great resolution: to design great things implies no common mind. Ambition is in some sort genius' (*HW*, VIII, 108). Ambition is the Satanic sin, yet the very activity it presumes can blur moral judgements, or even questions. As late as 1800 Coleridge can refer to Napoleon as 'the first military genius of the modern world' (*EOT* [*CC*], I, 71) and two years later he acknowledges that rivalry with France is rivalry with a nation 'guided by the greatest genius in the world, who is as restless, ambitious, and artful, as he is superior in ability' (I, 310). The necessary caveat Hazlitt goes on to enter can only rename the diagnosis:

> But still I conceive that a genius for action depends essentially on the strength of the will rather than on that of the understanding; that the long-headed calculation of causes and consequences arises from the energy of the first cause, which is the will, setting others in motion and prepared to anticipate the results; that its sagacity is actively delighting in meeting difficulties and adventures more than half way, and its wisdom courage not to shrink from danger, but to redouble its efforts with opposition.   (*HW*, VIII, 108)

There is more of a vicarious 'active delight' in Hazlitt than we meet in Coleridge, but even as the latter suspects the activity of mere will he is attracted to it.

Coleridge's recognition of the dependence of virtue on talent (a version of the problem of ends and means) 'is one proof. . . among many, that there is a natural affinity between Despotism and modern Philosophy' (*EOT* [*CC*], II, 81). In the article from which this is quoted (in the *Courier*, 22 Dec 1809) Coleridge quotes himself from the sixth number of the *Friend*, arguing that it might be a sign of comfort if the devastation of war *were* the sign of a truly general will. Yet there is a consistency possible in wickedness, where virtue must be inconsistent. The admiration felt by the literary man for purposefulness in a man of action must therefore always be morally ambivalent:

> It is not vice, as vice, which is thus mighty; but *systematic* vice. . . . The abandonment of all *principle* of right enables the soul to chuse and act upon a *principle* of wrong, and to subordinate to this one principle all the various vices of human nature. . . . He, who has once said with his whole heart, Evil be thou my Good! has removed a world of obstacles by the very decision, that he will have no obstacles but those of force and brute matter.   (*Friend* [*CC*], II, 84)

In the later *Courier* article such a totalising 'consistency' in evil is explicitly stated as 'the main power of a remorseless tyrant, such as Bonaparte' (*EOT* [*CC*], II, 83) – thus refuting the hero spirit suggested even in the tyrants of the plays. In the essay from the *Friend*, quoting from his own version of Schiller's *The Piccolomini*, Coleridge suggests the dichotomy as being between a human uncertainty and a superhuman certainty. 'The road of Justice / Curves round the corn-field and the hill of vines, / Honouring the holy bounds of property!', [1] but 'straight the fearful path / Of the cannon-ball. Direct it flies and rapid, / Shattering that it may reach, and shattering what it reaches' (*PW*, II, 613).

The later theorisation of 'absolute' and 'commanding genius', although offered as generally applicable, offers in turn only generic examples. It is itself an absolute concept. The emblematic importance of the similar dichotomy Coleridge finds in Schiller – that Justice can always be recognised by its respect for the 'holy bounds of Property' – is another such absolute. The later *Friend* essay proposing a simply causal relation between the influence of the *philosophes* and the French Revolution still acknowledges inability to account for the rise to power of a particular individual – or for his authority as opposed to the acquiescence to it. In Fichte, Hegel and Carlyle we can see attempts at such an account which, finding in individuals a basis for and example of an ideal conception of the hero, progressively accede to his authority. Immanuel Hermann Fichte contrasts his father with a predecessor in the chair at Jena: 'Reinhold wanted to make good men; Fichte wants to make great men. . . . Through his philosophy he aims at directing the spirit of the age; he knows its weak side, and thus tackles it from the angle of politics.' [2] But in the lectures delivered at the Berlin Academy and published as *Addresses to the German Nation* it is rather Fichte's own idealism which is restrained by political pressure. The lectures were delivered in 1807–8 with Berlin still occupied by Napoleonic troops, so the ideal vision is modified both by an insistence on its unthreatening idealism and by cunning flattery:

> We are pointing the way to a regeneration of the human race, a way to turn earthly and sensuous creatures into pure and noble spirits. Does anyone think that such a proposal could be felt as an insult by mind that is itself pure and noble and great, or by anyone who forms himself after that pattern?   (p. 187)

A test of the greatness of the individual then, for Fichte, will be his ability to recognise the greatness of the 'Self' of the nation; both are emanations of the 'eternal and spontaneous spirit world':

> Is not greatness based on the fact that to one person a new and individual view of the universe has dawned, and that this person has the firm will and the iron strength to impose his view on the actual world? But it is quite impossible for such a soul not to honour in peoples and individuals external to himself that in which his own internal greatness consists, viz., independence, constancy, and individuality of existence.   (p. 186)

The new national identity (and, therefore, national will) which the *Addresses* posit is, then, much like that the conqueror might recognise in himself; but the parallel of a national with a particular, individual 'self' is not merely pragmatic.

Fichte claims that Germany has entered a new epoch in its history. In the interval between his *Characteristics of the Present Age* (1804–5) and the *Addresses*, which continue them, history has progressed from the third to the fourth stage of the 'world-plan' laid down in the earlier lectures, from an 'age of completed sinfulness' characterised by liberation from external authority and indifference to truth to an age in which Reason will be grasped as 'Knowledge'. The German national education which the book proposes is an education not of the senses but 'in the world of thought': it will produce, correlative with the construction of 'a universal and national self', a whole race of heroes. Fichte could here be speaking nationalistically, or only psychologically:

> only according to the needs of noble-minded men is the world to be regarded and arranged; as they are, so all men ought to be, and for their sake alone does a world exist. They are its kernel, and those of other mind exist only for their sake, being themselves a part of the transitory world so long as they are of that mind. Such men must conform to the wishes of the noble-minded until they have become like them.   (p. 114)

In the end the satanic virtues which associate the national and the rare – as yet – individual self continue to appertain to them both, taking them out of the 'transitory world'. In proposing an education away from the sensory towards the ideal, Fichte's difference from Hegel is only terminological, his identification of a *Zeitgeist* with 'the wishes of the noble-minded' fraught with the same difficulties.

The first draft of Hegel's *Introduction* to the *Philosophy of History* survives as notes on lectures perhaps delivered only fifteen years after Fichte's. Already in Hegel pragmatism tempers not the ideal, which is absolute, but morality, which is not. Certainly history teaches moral 'lessons':

> But the destinies of nations, the convulsions of states and their interests, predicaments, and involvements are of a different order from that of morality. . . . Each age and each nation finds itself in such peculiar circumstances, in such a unique situation, that it can and must make decisions with reference to itself alone (and only the great individual can decide what the right course is).[3]

The difficulty is the same as in Fichte's formulation: only the great individual is, at present, in touch with the *Zeitgeist* and it is realised in him alone. In the process from the 'particular' to the 'general' (analogous to that in Fichte from 'sensory' to 'ideal') morality will be displaced. But the 'different light' in which the actions of such a man are to be viewed is, perhaps, only that afforded retrospectively:

> such world-historical individuals [as Caesar], in furthering their own momentous interests, did indeed treat other intrinsically admirable interests and sacred rights in a carefree, cursory, hasty, and heedless manner, thereby exposing themselves to moral censure. But their position should be seen in an altogether different light. A mighty figure must trample many an innocent flower underfoot, and destroy much that lies in its path.   (p. 89)

Clearly even this explanation cannot absolve all such an individual's actions from 'moral censure' until the explanation is formulated abstractly: 'The particular is as a rule inadequate in relation to the universal, and individuals are sacrificed and abandoned as a result' (p. 89). Hegel's 'universal', however, is not merely a set of the ends willed by any individual and to which other individuals are means to be forfeited. The importance of 'world-historical individuals' is that, in both senses of the verb, they *realise* the *Geist*. The individual will is at the service of, and subservient to, a spirit in which the borders between 'national', 'universal' and 'divine' or 'absolute' are blurred:

> Only those who know the spirit of the nation and shape their actions in accordance with it can be described as truly inspired. . . . Individuals fade into insignificance beside the universal substance, and it creates for itself the individuals it requires to carry out its ends.   (p. 52)[4]

So even 'world-historical individuals' may be sacrificed and abandoned to the pursuit of these ends, and to the extent that they 'realise the end appropriate to the higher concept of the spirit . . . they may be called *heroes*. . . . For this spirit, the present world is but a shell which contains the wrong kind of kernel' (p. 83). Yet the argument remains circular: all we know of these 'ends' still is that they are those identified by such individuals (and therefore identified *with* them):

> The only true ends are those whose content has been produced by the absolute power of the inner spirit itself in the course of its development; and world-historical individuals are those who have willed and accomplished not just the ends of their own imagination or personal opinions, but only those which were appropriate and necessary. Such individuals know what is necessary and timely, and have an inner vision of what it is.   (Ibid.)

Fichte was able to read transcendental liberty out of French Revolutionary liberty, a national state from one which could, for him, still be seen as the embodiment of the ideals of Rousseau. In Hegel, the historical advance he posits is conterminous with the advance of the state, which, as the vehicle of the 'Idea', is the embodiment of the ends of spirit for those not privileged with an 'inner vision' of them:

> Only in the state does man have a rational existence. The aim of all education is to ensure that the individual does not remain purely subjective but attains an objective existence within the state. . . . The subjective will – or passion – is the activating and

realising principle; the Idea is the inner essence, and the state is
the reality of ethical life in the present.   (p. 94)

So Hegel would have no time for 'hero worship' in Carlyle's terms.
The primacy of the state, moving towards the 'absolute Idea',
requires that its heroes are those who further its advance. The
rewards of the individual will are therefore denied them – Hegel
says, for instance, they are not happy: 'Their actions are their
entire being, and their whole nature and character are determined
by their ruling passion. When their end is attained, they fall aside
like empty husks' (p. 85). Such, for Hegel, is the fate of Alexander,
Caesar and even Napoleon, who, subject to and dependent on the
advance of the state, is 'only momentary' (p. 20).

   It is the state, then, which harnesses and institutionalises the
rebellious, satanic energies of the exceptional individual, but
Hegel, the former theologian, retains for the highest impulses and
'ends' of both the term 'divine' as seemingly interchangeable with
'absolute'. Near the beginning of his *Introduction* he says, 'divine
providence is wisdom, coupled with infinite power' (p. 35). This is
wholly congruent with Satan's admiration for undiluted power as
a means of achieving ends at others' expense, a power which he
sees as all that distinguishes him from God the Father in *Paradise
Lost*: 'Whom reason hath equalled, force hath made supreme /
Above his equals' (*Paradise Lost*, 1.248–9). Hegel's text entails this
difficult paradox. How are actions which fulfil the absolute *Geist* to
be recognised as distinct from those of the acquisitive 'particular'
will (satanic 'ambition')? Transposing morality to an 'ethical life'
only possible within the state does not overcome the paradox. To
the 'ultimate ends of spirit' all things are possible:

> world history moves on a higher plane than that to which
> morality properly belongs, for the sphere of morality is that of
> private convictions, the conscience of individuals, and their
> own particular will and mode of action; and the latter have their
> value, imputation, and reward or punishment within
> themselves . . . no representations should be made against
> world-historical deeds and those who perform them by moral
> circles to which such individuals do not belong.   (*Introduction*,
> p. 141)

Here is the climax of that 'ends and means' debate over which

Coleridge worries in relation to the actions of Robespierre. The task of philosophy is to understand the actions of these 'world-historical individuals' as 'moments within the universal Idea'; and, since they themselves understand what is to be the new universal, 'whatever they do is right' (p. 84).[5]

It is as if Carlyle, in his *On Heroes and Hero-Worship*, freed from the historical circumstances and nationalist urgencies out of which Fichte and Hegel write, begins from this point – it was Hegel who said the Owl of Minerva flies at dusk. Hero worship, for Carlyle, exists outside temporal contexts. Before his discussion of Luther (who is Fichte's example of the ideal German type), Carlyle can defend the 'Idolatry' which it was Luther's achievement to expel: 'Condemnable Idolatry is *insincere* Idolatry. . . . Souls are no longer *filled* with their Fetish; but only pretend to be filled, and would fain make themselves feel that they are filled. "You do not believe," said Coleridge; "you only believe that you believe"' (p. 122). Again, though he stops short of defending the Divine Right of Kings, Carlyle is insistent that 'there is a Divine Right or else a Diabolic Wrong at the heart of any claim that one man makes upon another' (p. 199). If this recalls Fichte's guarded address to Napoleon – 'We must assume either that the being to whom at the present time the conduct of a great part of the world's affairs has fallen is a truly great soul, or we must assume the contrary; no third assumption is possible' (*Addresses*, p. 186) – it contrasts sharply with Coleridge's assertion that the absolute to be striven for is not a heroic 'spirit' but a moral 'principle'. (Both theories are weakened by a pragmatism in which the theory must be modified in the case of each individual to whom it would seem to apply.)

Carlyle has no theory of the hero. On his first page, having assumed the synonymy of 'Heroes' and 'Great Men', he explicates the chronological structure of his book, 'For, as I take it, Universal History, the history of what man has accomplished in this world, is at bottom the History of the Great Men who have worked here' (*On Heroes*, p. 1). Thus the hero is a type which accommodates, amongst others, Mohammed, Dr Johnson and Napoleon and the book is necessarily most revelatory of the second part of its title: hero worship 'enters deeply, as I think, into the secret of Mankind's ways and vitalest interests in this world' (p. 243). Carlyle's heroes are, to be sure, the embodiment of the best impulses of their respective ages, but he sees such impulses as emanations of an individual spirit separable from a spirit of the age. His epitaph on Cromwell is, 'Let the Hero rest. It was not to *men's* judgment that he appealed; nor have men judged him very well' (p. 237). His admission of Napoleon as a hero is not as grudging as that of Rousseau, but he is by far inferior to Cromwell, the product of a blighted Enlightenment:

> Napoleon lived in an age when God was no longer believed; the meaning of all Silence, Latency, was thought to be Nonentity: he had to begin not out of the Puritan Bible, but out of poor Sceptical *Encyclopédies*. . . . An element of blamable ambition shows itself, from the first, in this man; gets the victory over him at last, and involves him and his work in ruin.   (p. 238)

But ultimately, as in the case of Cromwell, his saving grace is precisely his heroism: 'He has an instinct of Nature better than his culture was.' The actions of Hegel's 'world-historical individual' are removed from history and naturalised, even supernaturalised, as heroism. The eighteenth century values Pym and Hampden, whom Carlyle calls 'dull', above Cromwell. Their concern with Ship Money and so on is for Carlyle merely temporal, limited and ultimately trivial, while he imagines Cromwell saying, '"You may take my purse; but I cannot have my moral Self annihilated"' (p. 210).

Such an absolutism of the spirit is what is common to Carlyle's heroes whether in the category of divinity, prophet, poet, man of letters or king, but, as in his derogation of Pym and Hampden, it is rather this spirit than the ends to which it is put that Carlyle admires. Again speaking of Cromwell, he describes Laud, in insisting on the 'forms', the 'Idolatry of hollow *shows*', as 'like a College-Tutor': 'rather the rigorous formal *Pedant*, intent on his "College-rules", than the earnest Prophet, intent on the essence of the matter!' (p. 206). 'Great Men' presume little men; commanding genius implies a majority who are objects to be commanded. Hegel's dismissal of the Coleridgean equivocation employs the same image. He says that the fact that world-historical individuals gain only the objective ends of spirit may be a consolation for the envious:

> What schoolmaster has not demonstrated of Alexander the Great or Julius Caesar that they were impelled by such passions

[the lust for conquest/power] and were therefore immoral characters? – from which it at once follows that the schoolmaster himself is a more admirable man than they were because he does not have such passions (the proof being that he does not conquer Darius and Porus, but simply lives and lets live). (*Introduction*, p. 87)

Both Hegel and Carlyle also quote the apophthegm that 'no man is a hero to his valet'. Hegel adds that this is 'not because the former is not a hero, but because the latter is a valet' (pp. 87–8 and see *Phenomenology*, p. 404) while Carlyle expands the homely saw into diagnosis of a debilitating *Zeitgeist*: 'Not a Hero only is needed, but a world fit for him; a world not of *Valets*', and this world is 'visible coming'. Meanwhile, there are

Ballot-boxes, suffrages, French Revolutions – if we are as Valets, and do not know the Hero when we see him, what good are all these? . . . We shall either learn to know a Hero, a true Governor and Captain, somewhat better than we see him; or else go on to be for ever governed by the Unheroic; had we ballot-boxes clattering at every street-corner, there were no remedy in these. (*On Heroes*, pp. 216–17)

Despite the disavowal of history in favour of an ahistorical 'spirit', then, the conservatism of such a view of history is more profound even than Fichte's (Fichte's prophesying 'a whole race of heroes' is the nationalist imperative). Denying the dependence of his heroes upon history, Carlyle is led to assert the dependence of history upon its heroes:

Given your Hero, is he to become Conqueror, King, Philosopher, Poet? It is an inexplicably complex controversial-calculation between the world and him! He will read the world and its laws; the world with its laws will be there to be read. What the world, on *this* matter, shall permit and bid is, as we said, the most important fact about the world. (p. 80)

The evidence of decline Carlyle finds in the comparison of Luther with Rousseau and of Cromwell with Napoleon is, for him, irresistible. Yet the very emergence of the two French heroes above the secular, levelling culture of the Enlightenment provides a basis for projecting his nostalgic vision into a realisable future. He determines three great movements in the return to reality, or 'Fact': Luther and the Protestant Reformation; the English Civil War and the Revolution of 1688; and the French Revolution, which is still regarded as apocalyptic, and which 'we may well call the final [act]; for lower than that savage *Sansculottism* man cannot go. They stand there on the nakedest haggard Fact' (p. 237), and yet

> Napoleon, from amid boundless revolt of Sansculottism, became a King. Hero-worship never dies, nor can die. . . . In all this wild revolutionary work, from Protestantism downwards, I see the blessedest result preparing itself: not abolition of Hero-worship, but rather what I would call a whole World of Heroes.   (pp. 126–7)

History is, therefore, providential; indeed it is the rebels that Carlyle's history puts in its pantheon. Despite the enormous difference in the relative weight Hegel and Carlyle give, respectively, to the realisation and the realisers of *Geist* in history, Hegel's attitude is similar:

> This objective interest [i.e. in world rather than parochial history], which affects us both through the general design and through the individual who implements it, is what makes history attractive. Such designs and individuals are the ones whose downfall and destruction we most lament. When we contemplate the struggle of the Greeks against the Persians, or the momentous reign of Alexander, we are fully aware of where our interests lie: we wish to see the Greeks liberated from the barbarians, and feel concern for the preservation of the Greek state and for the ruler who subjugated Asia at the head of a Greek army.   (*Introduction*, p. 45)

Yet this is not to say that, for either man, history enshrines the satanic spirit. Carlyle's version of the ends of the spirit which the Great Man serves is, for his own time, the imposition of Order. The French Revolution was for the Enlightenment a consummation devoutly to be wished – 'A true Apocalypse, though a terrible one, to this false, withered artificial time' (*On Heroes*, p. 201) – but the Great Man resembles Coleridge's man of absolute rather than commanding genius in that the political order he imposes is naturalised:

> it is tragical for us all to be concerned in image-breaking and down-pulling; for the Great Man, *more* a man than we, it is doubly tragical. . . . Disorder is dissolution, death. No chaos but it seeks a *centre* to revolve round. While man is man, some Cromwell or Napoleon is the necessary finish of a Sansculottism. (p. 204)

A distinction has therefore emerged between the 'Fact', pursued by the Sansculottes into apocalyptic disorder, and 'Reality'. The 'Reality' to which Carlyle's history strives is always that seen through the eyes of his heroes. The last category of heroism is kingship:

> he to whose will our wills are to be subordinated, and loyally surrender themselves, and find their welfare in doing so, may be reckoned the most important of Great Men. He is practically the summary for us of *all* the various figures of Heroism; Priest, Teacher, whatsoever of earthly or of spiritual dignity we can fancy to reside in a man, embodies itself here, to *command* over us, to furnish us with constant practical teaching, to tell us for the day and hour what we are to *do*. (p. 196)

This returns to the difficulty posed by Satan. Carlyle has given the etymology of the word 'king' as '*Könning*, which means *Can*-ning, Able-man' (ibid.); but if the hero, and his authority to command, is to be recognised by his active ability it is likely that this will entail a suspension or displacement of morality. Hegel accepts this; Carlyle will not: 'There is no act more moral between men than that of rule and obedience. . . . I say, Find me the true *Könning*, King, or Able-man, and he *has* a divine right over me' (p. 199). Wilfully or otherwise then, Carlyle ignores the paradox attendant on his postulating the hero and hero worship as the motive forces in history. The three great movements of contemporary history that he posits are all revolutions (indeed, the English Civil War and the French Revolution both involved killing a hereditary king), yet such praise as he has for Napoleon is as a counter-revolutionary. Further, the detachment of the heroic spirit from history makes tenable the possibility of two such heroes being mutually opposed, yet Carlyle has nothing to say of the two English military leaders who were celebrated as heroes for defeating Napoleon: Wellington and Nelson. Again, he refers to Washington, to whom Coleridge unfavourably compares Napoleon, only in passing, in dismissing favourable eighteenth-century comparisons to Cromwell.

In wishing to retain morality and displace history, Carlyle can only simplify history so drastically that imperfect states result, simply, from their ignorance of the man primitive societies would have acclaimed as the 'natural' king: 'This is the history of all rebellions, French Revolutions, social explosions in ancient or modern times. You have put the too *Un*able Man at the head of affairs!' (p. 198). So despite its appearance of drastic, even radical simplicity, Carlyle's political formula can only be pragmatic:

> Hustings-speeches, Parliamentary motions, Reform Bills, French Revolutions, all mean at heart this; or else nothing. Find in any country the Ablest Man that exists there; raise *him* to the supreme place, and loyally reverence him: you have a perfect government for that country.   (p. 197)

Carlyle's language is religious: in the posture of 'worship' the epithet 'loyal' can modify 'reverence'. He thereby poses by omission the problem with which Coleridge struggles: of the moral imperative, even when witnessing such active ability, to deny to the fallen angel the 'supreme place'.

13 Plank or Bridge

The history of Napoleon's reception is almost the history of the higher happiness attained by this whole century in its most valuable human beings and moments. (Nietzsche, *Beyond Good and Evil*)

The history of Napoleon presented by Carlyle is a teleological one: his fall is due to his ambition outstripping its unity with history. Carlyle's Napoleon soliloquises on St Helena, a spent egotist, still imagining himself 'Nature' or 'France': 'and yet look how in fact – HERE AM I! He cannot understand it: inconceivable that the reality has not corresponded to his program of it; that France was not all-great, that he was not France' (*On Heroes*, p. 243). In Coleridge's periodical the *Friend* Napoleon is identified only with an unnatural dogma. The egotistical despot is the apotheosis of the Rousseauist state 'which had so marvellously raised and supported him, had marked HIM out for the representative of Reason, and had armed him with irresistible force, in order to realise its laws. In Him therefore MIGHT becomes RIGHT, and HIS cause and that of destiny. . . . HIS cause and the cause of God are one and the same' (*Friend* [*CC*], I, 197). Elsewhere, however, Napoleon's ambition is that of the usurper Satan:

It has been well remarked, that there is something far more shocking in the tyrant's pretensions to the gracious attributes of the Supreme Ruler, than in his most remorseless cruelties. There is a sort of wild grandeur, not ungratifying to the imagination, in the answer of Timar Khan to one who remonstrated with him on the *inhumanity* of his devastations. . . . Why do you deem me a *man*, and not rather the incarnate wrath of God acting on the earth for the ruin of mankind?   (I, 232*)

That even here, claiming to be disabused of Napoleon's greatness,

Coleridge can find in his pretensions to it a 'wild grandeur, not ungratifying to the imagination', is typical of his ambivalence. The terms of Coleridge's admiration come through even beneath condemnation: 'In his usurpation, Bonaparte stabbed his honesty in the vitals; it has perished – we admit, that it has perished – but the mausoleum, where it lies interred, is among the wonders of the world' (*EOT* [*CC*], I, 211).

Before turning to Brissot and to Robespierre in the 1795 passage with which this part began, Coleridge quotes from Milton – not, however, from *Paradise Lost* but from *Samson Agonistes*. His purpose is merely to make an epigram at the expense of 'the Mob': 'Like Sampson, the People were strong – like Sampson, the People were blind' and he affirms that such men as are represented by Brissot *and* Robespierre are more likely to be 'the Victims . . . than the Illuminators, of the Multitude' (*Lectures 1795* [*CC*], p. 34). Even at this early stage, then, such qualified hopes for the Revolution as Coleridge records depend on those few who might combine the 'visionary' ideal with the practical, active will. He sighs over Brissot and passes on to Robespierre. The attraction to Napoleon is of this kind. E. J. Hobsbawm sees the French Revolution as a bourgeois revolution without a vanguard party or specific programme, which 'hardly even threw up "leaders" of the kind to which twentieth-century revolutions have accustomed us, until the post-revolutionary figure of Napoleon'.[1] In Sara Coleridge's edition of her father's journalism she acknowledges that it was the 'character and conduct' of Napoleon which formed the 'plank or bridge' by which Coleridge passed from support for, to opposition to, the French.[2]

His daughter's terminology rightly suggests the judgements of personal morality as central to Coleridge's passage. He is decreasingly inclined to the equivocation over 'ends' and 'means' in which he involves himself when writing of Robespierre in 1795, decreasingly inclined to struggle with the difficulty of disentangling a personal morality from that of the commander. (Schiller's solution, at the end of *The Robbers*, is only provisional, a *coup de théâtre*.) Coleridge's lexis is moral ('shocking', 'honesty') and briefly to return to that debate alluded to in Chapter 2 will be helpful in describing this language. In the second of his *Fifteen Sermons* Bishop Butler says, 'Passion or appetite implies a direct simple tendency towards such and such objects, without distinction of the means by which they are to be obtained . . . how often soever [passion or appetite] happens to prevail, it is mere *usurpation*', and he draws a distinction between '*mere power* and *authority*'.[3] In seeking to reverse 'this suppos'd pre-eminence of reason above passion' Hume asserts that 'Reason is, and ought only to be the slave of the passions, and can never pretend to any other office than to serve and obey them' (*Treatise*, pp. 413, 415 [II.iii.3]).[4] Coleridge, then, is morally more conservative than Hume as in this regard he is aesthetically more conservative than Kames. He sees the tyranny of the passions as an analogue of the tyrant himself. In a notebook entry of June 1810 Coleridge returns to Napoleon's 'autotheism'. Vice, he says, leads to 'practical Atheism' which will be either 'slavish' or 'despotic':

> The slavish Atheism substitutes the vis bruta of Nature, as the cause ab extra of Appetites & passions, for the Lex – or supreme Reason, and of course with the Law removes the will, and with obedience the freedom / the despotic Atheism would make the Will a Law to itself, i.e. itself God. – Buonaparte a fair instance of the latter . . . .

Man must use his free will, Coleridge continues, to act from Reason (the sum of Reason and Will, he says, is Conscience). The occurrence in a moral lexis of such terms as 'slavish', 'despotic' and 'Law' ('natural' law? the Commandments? Mosaic law? the Napoleonic code?), and the instancing of Napoleon, are indicative of Coleridge's admission of no discontinuity between the moral and political worlds. Since Napoleon acts not from no principle but from a negative principle (cf. *Friend* [*CC*] I, 121), he is a species of the domination which will ensue for those who ignore moral 'laws'. Coleridge concludes,

> Where there is no Law, there must be Tyranny – and this will be either ab extra, or a se – the tyranny of Satanic pride, or of bestial Sensuality. Without God Man ceases to be Man, & either soars into a Devil or sinks into a Beast-Spasm, or Dissolution / Napoleon 'not a man; but a Cramp!' / (*CN*, III, 3866)[5]

Eight years earlier, in the *Morning Post*, in the midst of a comparison of the republic of France with that of Rome under the Caesars, Coleridge says that despots emerge in response primarily to a *moral* need:

In both countries, proscriptions and tumults and the most shameless venality had made the very name of liberty odious, and the vices of the leaders of all parties had introduced into the minds even of good men a despair of the Republic, and a disposition to submit to the sober despotism of any individual, rather than the mad tyranny of a multitude.   (*EOT* [*CC*], I, 315–16)

Here Coleridge is projecting his own initial hopes at the rise of Napoleon onto the French. These hopes are qualified but, writing in the *Morning Post* for 11 March 1800, he claims that

it is undeniable, that already his commanding genius has introduced a new tone of morality into France, and that it is now fashionable to assume the rigid and simple character of the Great Consul. . . . In his individual character and conduct, the Chief Consul has hitherto supported the part of a man ambitious of greatness: too intensely preoccupied to be otherwise than austere in morals; too confident in his predestined fortune to be suspicious or cruel; too ambitious of a new greatness for the ordinary ambition of conquest or despotism.   (I, 210–11)

The nature of such 'commanding genius' is disinterested or, at least, as in Hegel, personal ambition is identical with ambition for the state, and to be admired. Yet only a month earlier, in the same paper, Coleridge had seen this tendency as a moral flaw within the state to which its leaders were inevitably subject:

The nature of the French system was nothing but an insatiable love of aggrandisement: that was its governing principle: it was the soul that animated it at its birth, and certainly would not desert it till its extinction: it had been invariably the same at every stage of the Revolution: it equally belonged to Brissot, Robespierre, Reubell, and Barras; but it belonged more than all to Bonaparte, in whom were united all their powers and all their crimes.   (I, 154)

Carlyle, in setting himself against a caricature eighteenth-century view of Cromwell, could be caricaturing Coleridge on Napoleon:

Selfish ambition, dishonesty, duplicity; a fierce, coarse, hypocritical *Tartufe*; turning all that noble Struggle for constitutional Liberty into a sorry farce played for his own benefit. . . . And then there come contrasts with Washington and others . . . the Sceptic of the Eighteenth century looks for regulated respectable Formulas, 'Principles', or what else he may call them . . . . (*On Heroes*, p. 208)[6]

This ambivalence towards Napoleon runs through Coleridge's political journalism. Despite his attaching the terms 'duplicity', 'temerity' and, pre-eminently, 'ambition' to Napoleon, he will still refer to him by the titles Napoleon would choose for himself, as in the first of the two examples above, even where he intends irony in calling him 'the Emperor'. Napoleon's power has to be acknowledged prior to any moral judgement upon it: he is, undeniably, 'the first military genius of the modern world' (*EOT* [*CC*], I, 71). Again, apropos of Addington's ministry which is 'beneath mediocrity', and an inadequate rival to a France almost metonymic of Napoleon, Coleridge says, 'Whether in war or peace, we shall have to struggle with a rival nation, at present the most powerful in Europe, guided by the greatest genius in the world, who is as restless, ambitious, and artful, as he is superior in ability' (I 310). This genius is, however, the 'commanding genius' of the translation of *Wallenstein* and of the *Biographia*, far more ambivalent morally than is implied by this apparent admiration. In the same year as the publication of the former, Coleridge's obituary of Washington in the *Morning Post* speaks of his having 'perfected in himself that character which all are compelled to feel, though few are capable of analysing, the character of a commanding genius. His successes . . . were still greater, still more sublime, from the means, by which they were attained' (*EOT* [*CC*], I, 132). Later Washington's saintliness is explicitly contrasted to the character of Napoleon (II, 198), but, in some highly equivocal comments cited above, Coleridge allows his comments to be interpreted either as admiring or as condemnatory. He refers to the new consul's 'ambition, temerity, and his good luck' in the Revolution and an initial subordinate clause modifies what would otherwise be unqualified praise: 'In conniving at the usurpation of Bonaparte [the French] have seated on the throne of the Republic a man of various talent, of commanding genius, of splendid exploit' (I 207–9).

Coleridge's famous aside on the 'man of genius' (*BL* [*CC*], i, 43) includes the assertion that he 'lives most in the ideal world' in which all time is one. The man of commanding genius, however, is a pragmatist, thinking serially. 'During a Revolution', he writes at the end of a long note, 'confusion and individual impoverishment increase the means and intensify the powers of the existing rulers – who not looking forward to hereditary transmission of their power think only of the present point' (*CN*, iii, 3797). Reworking for a second time a passage from the *Friend* quoted in Chapter 12 (*Friend* [*CC*], ii, 84), Coleridge identifies the power of the latter not as abandonment to 'natural' appetites but as the Satanic resolve 'Evil, be thou my good!':

> All *system* so far is power; and a *systematic* criminal, self-consistent and entire in wickedness, who entrenches villainy within villainy, and barricadoes crime by crime, has removed a world of obstacles by the mere decision, that he will have no obstacles, but those of force and brute matter. (*LS* [*CC*], p. 66)

The passage occurs in Appendix C of *The Statesman's Manual*, which, attempting to account for or effect a co-operation of Reason with Religion, once more ascribes the regulative function to the Will – of which the functions here are akin to the Freudian super-ego. However,

> in its utmost abstraction and consequent state of reprobation, the Will becomes satanic pride and rebellious self-idolatry in the relations of the spirit to itself, and remorseless despotism relatively to others; the more hopeless as the more obdurate by its subjugation of sensual impulses, by its superiority to toil and pain and pleasure; in short, by the fearful resolve to find in itself alone the one absolute motive of action, under which all other motives from within and from without must be either subordinated or crushed.

Coleridge then goes on to list the 'ingredients' of such a character:

> Hope in which there is no Chearfulness; Stedfastness within and immovable Resolve, with outward Restlessness and whirling Activity; Violence with Guile; Temerity with

Cunning; and, as the result of all, Interminableness of Object
with perfect Indifference of Means; these are the qualities that
have constituted the COMMANDING GENIUS! these are the Marks,
that have characterised the Masters of Mischief, the
Liberticides, and mighty Hunters of Mankind, from NIMROD to
NAPOLEON. (*LS* [*CC*], pp. 65–6)[7]

The difference then between the trivial 'egotist' and the man of
'commanding genius' is one of degree: of the force and energy with
which the latter surmounts the moral and material 'obstacles' he
encounters 'in real life'. (Much earlier, even Pitt could be referred
to as 'our State-Nimrod' – *Watchman* [*CC*], p. 39.)

Coleridge is aware of the vicarious attractions of a Napoleon to
others. He quotes a German passage on a very Miltonic God and
adds a series of numbered annotations, the fourth of which is:
'Courage – That courage which the Sold. derives from B – B being
God – His general' (*CN*, I, 1082). He can then be pragmatic. The
editor of the *Essays on his Own Times* reproduces a note: 'More than
any Despot What's in his character of promise?' (*EOT* [*CC*], I,
155n12) – still, at that point, in question. Even by September 1802
Coleridge can write, 'We are not conscious of any feelings of
bitterness towards the First Consul; or, if any, only that venial
prejudice, which naturally results from the having hoped proudly
of any individual, and the having been miserably disappointed'
(I, 319). The 'plank or bridge' is then a fairly rickety structure; but
it is one over which Coleridge crosses. The hardening of his
attitude, though, is once more connected to Napoleon's personal
morality. In 1811 he writes of a decree which forbade women with
an income of 6000 francs or more to marry without his permission:
'Who does not see to what shocking immoralities this outrageous
measure may and must lead? But it is his purpose, his passion, to
wound the feelings of nature, and to demoralize the human race.
He would reduce all to his own level' (*CN*, II, 237). This level is
that at which the personal tyranny of the Will becomes state
despotism:

Often have I reflected with awe on the great and
disproportionate power, which an individual of no
extraordinary talents or attainment may exert, by merely
throwing off all restraint of conscience. What then must not be
the power, where an individual, of consummate wickedness,

can organize, into the unity and rapidity of an individual will all the natural and artificial forces of a populous and wicked nation? (*Friend* [*CC*], ɪ, 120).

Such questions are in the public writings rhetorical.[8] The ambivalence remains throughout. We might compare Blair, noting that the character of Satan is 'not altogether void of some good qualities', with Coleridge's scorn for Napoleon's retreat from Russia. Blair lists Satan's qualities:

> He is brave and faithful to his troops. In the midst of his impiety, he is not without remorse. He is even touched with pity for our first parents, and justifies himself in his design against them from the necessity of his situation. He is actuated by ambition and resentment, rather than by pure malice. In short, Milton's Satan is no worse than many a conspirator or factious chief that makes a figure in history. (*Lectures on Rhetoric*, ɪɪ, 472–3)

Coleridge crows at the 'mighty hunter' having become a 'muffled fugitive' (his editorial is actuated by a Bulletin of the Grand Army in which Napoleon, having abandoned his army to the Russian winter, complains of their 'having lost their gaiety'):

> Never, surely, was any thing so horrible – so unnatural – as this. Our great Bard, even when his sublime imagination was struggling to embody consummate wickedness in the person of *Satan*, never in his bitterest conception, hit upon sentiments so truly diabolical as these. When the rebel champion of Pandemonium has experienced a defeat, even the stern genius of Milton was relaxed, and he represents the great author of human woe, relenting for the moment, and shedding such tears as Angels might, over the fruitless fidelity, the unavailing courage, and fallen fortunes, of his unhappy warriors. Satan's taunts are directed only against his Conqueror – it was reserved for the '*mild and merciful*' Napoleon, to exhibit an original trait of infernal ingratitude, such as poetry could never feign, nor the mind of Milton conceive! (*EOT* [*CC*], ɪɪ, 357)

14　Conclusion

Coleridge's journalism, then, affords another example of the ambivalence towards representation of the self which, under the heading of 'egotism', has been the concern throughout. To end with a reading of a poem as a triumphant resolution of these difficulties would be to patronise his work – yet this is a strategy adopted even by some of the better works on Coleridge. Clearly 'Kubla Khan' could be read in the context I have outlined in Part IV. The Khan's *fiat* is the speech act of a man of commanding genius (whose context is also one of 'tumult'), and in the line and a half 'Kubla heard from far / Ancestral voices prophesying war' 'Kubla' and 'war' are separated by elements – of past aural significance, original 'voices', prophecy and deferment of millennium – on which much of what I have said has a bearing. Again, the Khan is named only twice (compare Gray's 'Elegy'), the second time in the context of this threat to his power. The poem presents rather than reconciles oppositions. The 'sunny pleasure-dome with caves of ice' yokes together what in 'Frost at Midnight' will be a process of metamorphosis from 'eave-drops' to ice; the scene is 'holy and enchanted' and, similarly, 'a miracle of rare device' conjoins the divine and the man-made; and the 'demon-lover' seems to yoke together forces of attraction and repulsion.[1] The 'mazy' course of the 'sacred river' also connects it with 'error' in Satan's view of Eden (*Paradise Lost*, IV.239–46). Conversely, taking Coleridge's attitudes towards, say, the French Revolution or to Napoleon as metaphoric of the language of poems not overtly concerned with politics will be to court the dangers hinted at in the beginning of Part IV. Rather than offer a reading of 'Kubla Khan' I shall sketch some possible conditions for such a reading, but first I must adduce some conclusions from the apotheosis of egotism presented in this part.

　I have suggested Hegel as a resolution of the wider problem represented by 'egotism', but Raymond Benoit's reading of the journey of 'The Ancient Mariner' in terms of Hegel's Unhappy

Consciousness is more ingenious than it is convincing.[2] Hegel does have a direct bearing on the problems of poetic language, however, for example in his annulment of ethical imperatives such as 'Everyone ought to speak the truth.' As he shows, this is a 'commandment' not a 'law', since it is always contingent: 'This contingency of the content has universality merely in the *propositional form* in which it is expressed; but as an ethical proposition it promises a universal and necessary *content* and thus contradicts itself by the content being contingent' (*Phenomenology*, p. 254). It is perhaps not trivially to invoke the notion of category mistake to say that Hegel did not write 'The Ancient Mariner'. The consequences of the problem, though organised around poetic language, clearly lead into wider issues. Still, we are led to those issues by Coleridge's language as we are not by, for example, the language of Bowles or of Cowper. One reason for the problems of Coleridge's language is his extension of the boundaries of discourse, his pushing some of the implications of Young's *Conjectures*, for example, to their logical extreme: Young says that 'ambition is sometimes no Vice in life; it is always a Virtue in Composition' (p. 6) and implies that literary ambition is inextricable from a Satanic will to power, which would rather reign in hell than serve in heaven:

> an *Original*, tho' but indifferent . . . yet has something to boast; it is something to say with him in Horace
>
> Meo *sum Pauper in oere*;
>
> and to share ambition with no less than *Caesar*, who declared he had rather be the First in a Village, than the Second at *Rome*.   (p. 11)

Such assertions can be wittily paradoxical rather than heretical so long as writer and reader share a clear demarcation of the different kinds of composition.

In Chapter 3 I quoted Hazlitt's apophthegm that 'the language of poetry naturally falls in with the language of power' (*HW*, IV, 214). This recognition of the capability of language for affecting by might before right occurs in his essay on Coriolanus. Hazlitt approaches the problem of the artist as hero from the direction taken by Young rather than by Carlyle: 'We may depend upon it that what men delight to read in books, they will put in practice in reality.' It is less important here to reproduce Hazlitt's characterisation of this egotistical hero – who, in his 'consistency' is consistent with others we considered – than to focus on the account of conditions for his rise. Only Providence or some (other) kind of moral law can falsify the natural law of the hero:

> The great have private feelings of their own, to which the interests of humanity and justice must courtesy. Their interests are so far from being the same as those of the community, that they are in direct and necessary opposition to them; their power is at the expense of *our* weakness; their riches of *our* poverty; their pride of *our* degradation; their splendour of *our* wretchedness; their tyranny of *our* servitude. If they had the superior knowledge ascribed to them (which they have not) it would only render them so much more formidable; and from Gods would convert them into Devils. (IV, 216)

In dealing with the problem of Edmund in *King Lear* Coleridge's solution is rather to return within the boundaries, asserting a separation of truth and fiction, for all that fiction may convince us of its truth. Edmund is distinguished by his 'intellectual power' from the outrageous wickedness of Regan and Goneril, but 'truth' and 'goodness' are usually correlative of such power. Therefore, 'it becomes both morally and poetic[ally] unsafe to present what is admirable – what our nature compels us to admire – in the mind, and what is most detestable in the heart, as co-existing in the same individual without any apparent connection, or any modification of the one by the other' (*ShakCrit*, I, 58). The danger is escaped only by contingencies of the plot which in fact argue its truthfulness (Edmund's foreign education, away from Edgar; his pride). Thus the solution is in Shakespeare himself, who is almost a natural force akin to the natural energies of the sublime:

> He had read nature too heedfully not to know that courage, intellect, and strength of character were the most impressive forms of power, and that to power in itself, without reference to any moral end, an inevitable admiration and complacency appertains, whether it be displayed in the conquests of a Napoleon or Tamerlane, or in the foam and thunder of a cataract. (Ibid.)

Wordsworth of course makes a claim for the heroism of the Imagination,

> which, in truth,
> Is but another name for absolute strength
> And clearest insight, amplitude of mind,
> And reason in her most exalted mood.
> (*Prelude*, 1805, xiii.167)

(In 1850, 'strength' has become 'power'.) The problem of the hero and/or the tyrant as it specifically relates to poetic language is posed in terms that reverse the order of, rather than substitute for, the terms of the moral or political problem.

    The implication of much of the writing cited in Part IV is that (revolutionary) heroes are the unacknowledged poets of the world. Nietzsche, though his own *Übermensch* is exemplified rather by Goethe, sees Napoleon as the totalisation of a new world view which, accepting a 'fallen' state, has also seen the fall of God and anticipated the fall of a morality dependent on Him. In such a view, many of the problems which seem to actuate problems in Coleridge's language would have been superseded. The significance of Nietzsche's comment, cited as epigraph to Chapter 13, can be gauged not only by the biographies by Scott and Hazlitt, but by what Napoleon comes to represent for subsequent fictional heroes. Rousseau's *Confessions* chart the rise of a young provincial in bourgeois society, and Stendahl's Julien Sorel, rising and being admired in terms of values which he despises, takes as his 'bibles' the *Confessions*, Napoleon's memoirs, and bulletins of the Grand Army. Becky Sharp, the heroine of *Vanity Fair*, shouts 'Vive Bonaparte!' as she leaves the Pinkerton Academy for Young Ladies, and Thackeray comments, 'In those days, in England, to say "Long live Bonaparte!" was as much as to say, "Long live Lucifer!"' (ch. 2). Later, Tolstoy's Pierre Bezukhov projects his own Werther-like confusions onto Napoleon, whom he meets after attempting to assassinate him, and for Dostoyevsky's Raskolnikov the only moral choice is between being a Napoleon or being a louse. Napoleon, then, is seen as a myth of success or paradigm of ambition, but also represents the limits and nature of humanity.[3] As such he has been taken in this final part as a mythic figure exemplifying the egotistical pole of the dichotomy sketched in the first.

Carlyle says that 'the grand fundamental character is that of Great Man; that the man be great. Napoleon has words in him which are like Austerlitz battles' or that 'Napoleon in Saint-Helena is charmed with the genial veracity of old Homer' (*On Heroes*, pp. 79, 99), and Nietzsche calls Napoleon 'a great artist of government'.[4] In doing so of course he is treating the hero as artist rather than, as in Young and Carlyle (for whom he has contempt), the reverse. My argument has been that Coleridge's poetic language demands consideration in the terms of Hegel and Nietzsche rather than, for instance, in the terms of that honourable-enough Romantic humanism or Burkean conservatism of his *Church and State*. I am aware that this begs the question of value judgements upon, or the authority of, Coleridge's poetry, but in arguing for greater attentiveness to his use of language I have enjoined description rather than prescription. It may be that such an activity is always preliminary but it is also always essential. That is why I offer only some hints towards a fuller reading of Coleridge. Such a reading would also be a history or theory of British Romanticism, but in taking full account of the speech-act theories of J. L. Austin and others it would be a very different enterprise from Abrams's *Natural Supernaturalism* or Engell's *Creative Imagination*. (Paradoxically, the effect of treating poems as documentary evidence of historical change is also a misreading of writing which may explicitly attempt such a documentation. Hegel becomes merely grist to the mill.) Nor need this imply a kind of fetishisation of the poems, since the constant challenge to interpretation they present is akin to the challenge to validation with which Coleridge himself struggles. In refining his theory of speech acts Austin returns to the first person, insisting that 'the utterer must be the performer' and that the performative is only 'happy' if the action performed is 'at the moment of uttering being done by the person uttering'.[5] Definition of the self is as likely as a definitive reading of a poem and the problem is always, rather, of the authority of particular acts as of particular interpretations. Even without the knowledge that in Purchas the Khan merely 'builds' and does not as in Coleridge 'decree', many readers share Carl Woodring's sense of the questions that 'Kubla Khan' imposes on them: 'With what justice did the Khan decree at all? By what authority? And to what purpose?'[6]

In the *Morning Post* on 1 January 1800 Coleridge comments on a letter purportedly written by Napoleon to one of his generals on the day after his installation as First Consul: 'never did epistle from an Oriental Monarch to some slave he meant to honour, affront the principles of Equality with a more stately egotism' (*EOT* [*CC*], I, 63). It is notable that the author of the unpublished 'Kubla Khan' should compare the magnitude of Napoleon's 'egotism' with that of 'an Oriental Monarch'. David Pirie, in the notes to his and Empson's selection of Coleridge's poetry, builds on a suggestion implied in a notebook entry of April 1802, 'Poet Bonaparte – Layer of a World-garden' (*CN*, I, 1166), to suggest himself 'that Coleridge vaguely had Napoleon in mind when writing the poem'. But the answer to his question 'is . . . Kubla supposed to be an ideal creator, or a self-indulgent tyrant who is culpably insensitive to the forces represented by the sacred river?'[7] is that, as in the note, he can be both. As Elisabeth Schneider wrote in 1953, the 'balance or reconciliation of opposite or discordant qualities' in Coleridge's poem 'does not quite occur. . . . It is in fact avoided. What we have instead is the very spirit of "oscillation" itself.'[8] Replacing the word 'spirit' with 'syntax' would bring us to the place at which a reading of Coleridge should begin, as H. W. Piper's learned exegesis of sources for the poem acknowledges. I would however qualify one of Piper's final assertions – that 'any interpretation of "Kubla Khan" as a poem about writing poetry gives to poetic vision what Coleridge gave to the Heavenly vision, and robs the poet–prophet of his more important dimension'[9] – since it is just the uncertainty of that vision and of that dimension which provides the characteristic oscillation. (He mentions neither the advertisement nor the sub-titles.) The 'mingled measure' of the poem is not so different from the 'mingled charm' of the blank-verse poems. It is the 'conversation' rather of dialectic than of overhearing. The community invoked by 'all who hear' is a source of verification and authentication for some very large claims for the 'poet–prophet'. I have treated such appeals as a recurrent problem for Coleridge.

The impossibility of a stable definition of 'egotism' (apparent even in attempting a distinction from 'egoism' at the start) stems from the impossibility of defining the self. If the latter is activity, the former is the only word for the 'pure' activity of the self: an intransitive noun, as it were. Allowing privileged space neither to a Cartesian self nor to a godlike individual actor, Coleridge rewrites his earlier 'querulous egotism' as a question not merely 'querulous' but reconciling that 'desire with loathing strangely mixed' (*PW*, I, 390) which both motivates and results from the poems. It is a reconciliation which only holds within the space of the poem. That space is, I have suggested, circular; its point of departure and its destination are the same point. The self which is an object evident to the consciousness meets the individual who is an object of admiration and desire or of fear and loathing. These recognise each other. It is a circle that Coleridge never breaks. He will detach himself from his own construction, be a spectator even of his own mooted community; and yet those very acts of detachment provide us with a language antagonistic to the closure this suggests. They provide a language that is exemplary but not ideal – sceptical, dialectical, fragmentary. The language promised is like that promise we read out of the very end of *Paradise Lost*. Its promise is made to neither an 'I' nor an 'I AM' but to us.

Notes

PART I: THE BIRTH OF THE SELF

CHAPTER ONE: QUERULOUS EGOTISM

1. *Essays on the Intellectual Powers of Man* (1785), *The Works of Thomas Reid*, 4 vols (Charleston, Mass., 1813–15) II and III, repr. as 1 vol. (Cambridge, Mass., 1969) p. 179 (II.x).
2. Ibid., p. 138 (II.viii).
3. See Coleridge's essay 'On the Philosophic Import of the Words OBJECT and SUBJECT', *Blackwood's Edinburgh Magazine*, x (1821) 246–52: 'The egoist, or ultra-idealist, affirms all objects to be subjective' – though Coleridge distinguishes here between Berkeley and those of his disciples who would hold that 'the objective subsists wholly and solely in the universal subject – God' (p. 249).
4. For a parallel to the distinction made between 'egoism' and 'egotism', see Coleridge's distinction between 'Presumption' and 'Arrogance' (*Friend* [*CC*], I, 26–7).
5. Samuel Johnson, *A Dictionary of the English Language*, 2 vols (London, 1755) I, A–K (no p. nos). The citation of Addison is from *The Spectator*, ed. Donald F. Bond, 4 vols (Oxford, 1965) IV, 519–22 (no. 562). Further references are given after quotations in the text. Addison ascribes the word to 'the Gentlemen of *Port-Royal* . . . [who] banished the way of speaking in the First Person out of all their works, as arising from Vain-Glory and Self-Conceit' (p. 519). However, George Steiner says that 'it appears neither in the *Logique* nor in the *Grammaire de Port Royal* (translated into English in 1676)' – 'Contributions to a Dictionary of Critical Terms: "Egoism" and "Egotism"', *Essays in Criticism*, II (1952) 444–52 (p. 447).
6. *British Critic*, VIII (1796) 527–36 (p. 536).
7. Hugh Blair, *Lectures on Rhetoric and Belles-lettres*, 2 vols (London, 1783) I, 400–1 (Lecture XIX). Further references are given after quotations in the text. Coleridge borrowed vol. II of Blair's *Lectures* between 29 Jan and 26 Feb 1796. See George Whalley, 'The Bristol Library Borrowings of Southey and Coleridge, 1793–8', *Library*, 5th ser., IV (1949) 116–26 (p. 125).
8. Adam Smith, 'A Dissertation on the Origin of Languages', in *The Theory of Moral Sentiments*, 6th edn, with additions and corrections, 2 vols (London and Edinburgh, 1790) II, 434–5. Further references are given after quotations in the text. *The Theory of Moral Sentiments* has appeared as vol. I of the Glasgow

Edn, ed. D. D. Raphael and A. L. Macfie (Oxford, 1976) but the 1790 edn is preferred because it prints the 'Dissertation', to be included in vol. IV of the Glasgow Edn.

9. Coleridge, 'On Faith', *Literary Remains*, ed. H. N. Coleridge, 4 vols (London, 1836–9) IV, 434.

10. Shaftesbury, *An Enquiry Concerning Virtue or Merit*, ed. David Walford, Philosophical Classics (Manchester, 1977) p. 13 (I.iii).

11. Ibid., p. 48 (II.i).

12. On the *Opus Maximum* MS see Laurence S. Lockridge, *Coleridge the Moralist* (Ithaca, NY, and London, 1977) esp. pp. 199–250. On the translation of the terms of eighteenth-century moral debate into the terms of Romantic discourse, see Walter Jackson Bate, *From Classic to Romantic: Premises of Taste in Eighteenth-Century England* (London, 1946) pp. 141–7. It might be said that the dichotomy for which I argue below is such a translation or transmutation, in which 'selfishness' becomes ego(t)ism and the 'sympathy' of Shaftesbury and Adam Smith Keats's 'negative capability'.

13. See Raymond Williams, *Culture and Society, 1780–1950* (London, 1956), and *Keywords: A Vocabulary of Culture and Society* (London, 1976); E. J. Hobsbawm, *The Age of Revolution: Europe 1789—1848* (1962; repr. London, 1977) p. 13. For a study of verbal change in the eighteenth century, see Susie I. Tucker, *Protean Shape: A Study in Eighteenth-Century Vocabulary and Usage* (London, 1967).

14. J. Dykes Campbell, 'Coleridge's Quotations', *Athenaeum*, no. 3382 (20 Aug 1892) 259–60 (p. 259).

15. Charles Pigott, *A Political Dictionary: Explaining the True Meanings of Words* (London, 1795) pp. 19, 65, 56, 118, 64.

16. Lockridge, *Coleridge the Moralist*, p. 149, says that Coleridge coined the term 'self-realization'.

17. Marjorie Hope Nicolson, *The Breaking of the Circle: Studies in the Effect of the 'New Science' upon Seventeenth-Century Poetry* (Evanston, Ill., 1950) p. 149.

18. Cf. *CN*, I, 787 and n; *CL*, I, 386–7.

19. Ian Hacking, *Why Does Language Matter to Philosophy?* (Cambridge, 1975) p. 29. Cf. Coleridge's note in ch. 5 of the *Biographia*, *BL* [*CC*], I, 96–8*.

20. Shaftesbury, *Characteristics of Men, Manners, Opinions, Times, etc.*, ed. John M. Robertson, 2 vols (1900; repr. Gloucester, Mass., 1963) II, 275–6 (Miscellany IV.i).

21. Coleridge, 'On Faith', *Literary Remains*, IV, 426.

22. John Locke, *An Essay Concerning Human Understanding*, ed. Peter H. Nidditch, Clarendon Edn (Oxford, 1975) p. 343 (I. ii. 27). Further references to this edn are given after quotations in the text.

23. 'On Personal Identity', *The Works of Joseph Butler*, ed. W. E. Gladstone, 2 vols (Oxford, 1897) I, 318.

24. Locke has been defended against Butler's charge of circularity by David Wiggins, *Sameness and Substance* (Oxford, 1980) pp. 149–89. See also Geoffrey Madell, *The Identity of the Self* (Edinburgh, 1981), which defends the views of Reid and Butler on 'personal identity' against the 'empiricist' views of Locke and Hume.

25. David Hume, *A Treatise of Human Nature*, ed. L. A. Selby-Bigge, 2nd edn, rev. P. H. Nidditch (Oxford, 1978) p. 630 (Appendix). Further references to

this edn are given after quotations in the text. In this section all but the last, which is again from the Appendix, are from i.iv.6.

26. Cf. Hobbes's *Leviathan*, i.ii, in which 'imagination' and 'fancy' are synonyms, the referent of which is 'nothing but *decaying sense*' — *The English Works of Thomas Hobbes*, ed. Sir William Molesworth, 11 vols (1839; repr. Darmstadt, 1966) iii, 4.

27. Isaac D'Israeli, *An Essay on the Manners and Genius of the Literary Character* (London, 1785) pp. 121–2.

28. *The Anecdotes and Egotisms of Henry Mackenzie 1745–1831*, ed. Harold William Thompson (London, 1927). See, for example, pp. 38, 133, 184, 245. The 'egotisms' were to be a separate book but, according to Thompson, 'evidently . . . [Mackenzie] had no clear idea in his own mind of the distinction between an anecdote and an egotism' (p. xxxii).

29. *Emma Darwin: A Century of Family Letters*, ed. Henrietta Litchfield, 2 vols (London, 1915) ii, 284.

30. John Locke, *The Second Treatise of Government*, ed. J. W. Gough, 3rd edn (Oxford, 1966) p. 67.

31. I discuss some of Coleridge's political journalism in Part IV below, but see the following: E. P. Thompson, 'Disenchantment or Default? A Lay Sermon', in *Power and Consciousness*, ed. C. C. O'Brien and W. D. Vanech (London and New York, 1969) pp. 149–82; George Watson, 'The Revolutionary Youth of Wordsworth and Coleridge', *Critical Quarterly*, xviii (1976) 49–66, and the reply by John Beer, *Critical Quarterly*, xix (1977) 79–87.

32. Edmund Burke, *A Philosophical Enquiry into the Origin of our Ideas of the Sublime and Beautiful*, ed. James T. Boulton (London, 1958) p. 38 (i.vi). Further references are given after quotations in the text.

33. Gilbert Ryle, *The Concept of Mind* (London, 1949) p. 8. In his *The Myth of Metaphor* (New Haven, 1962), Colin Murray Turbayne calls this statement 'about the best definition of metaphor known to me' (p. 18).

CHAPTER TWO: THE CRUCIBLE AND THE FIRE

1. David Hartley, *Observations on Man, his Frame, his Duty and his Expectations* (1749), repr. Scholars' Reprints and Facsimiles, 2 vols in 1 (Gainesville, Fla., 1966), i, 371 (iii.iii.89).

2. For Coleridge on the will, see *CL*, vi, 986; *PL*, p. 362; *BL* [*CC*], i, 293–4; *CN*, ii, 2382. On the will in Tetens's and Schelling's theories of *Dichtkraft*, see the chapter 'Imagination and Will' in James Engell, *The Creative Imagination: Enlightenment to Romanticism* (Cambridge, Mass., 1981) pp. 123–8. On the usurpation of the will, see Coleridge, 'On Faith', *Literary Remains*, iv, 430; *EOT* [*CC*], ii, 80. In general see Michael G. Cooke, *The Romantic Will* (New Haven, Conn., and London, 1976).

3. For the relation of such a statement to an 'ethics of feeling' in Rousseau see Louis I. Bredvold, *The Natural History of Sensibility* (Detroit, 1962) pp. 23–6.

4. *Paradise Lost*, v. 469–88, cited from Alastair Fowler's edn, Longman Annotated English Poets, 6th impression (London, 1981) pp. 286–7. All

quotations are from this edn. Further references will give book and line number after quotations in the text.

5. Johann Gottlieb Fichte, *Science of Knowledge*, ed. and trs. Peter Heath and John Lachs (1970; repr. with corrections, Cambridge, 1982) p. 33. Further references are given after quotations in the text.

6. F. W. J. Schelling, *System of Transcendental Idealism* (1800), trs. Peter Heath (Charlottesville, Va., 1978) p. 36. Further references are given after quotations in the text.

7. Coleridge, *Biographia Literaria*, ed. H. N. and Sara Coleridge, 2 vols in 3 (London, 1847) I.i, 271–3n.

8. Coleridge and Southey, *Omniana*, ed. Robert Gittings (Fontwell, Sussex, 1969) p. 29.

9. For the way in which our responses to the art object are affected by its fragmentariness, see the very suggestive discussion of the history of responses to the Venus de Milo in Peter Fuller's *Art and Psychoanalysis* (London, 1980) ch. 2, esp. pp. 104–129. Cf. Tzvetan Todorov, *Theories of the Symbol*, trs. Catherine Porter (Oxford, 1982) p. 170: 'Let us recall . . . that the romantics' favorite genres are specifically the dialogue and the fragment, the one for its unfinished character, the other for the way it stages the search for and the elaboration of ideas: both share in the same valorization of production with respect to the product.' See also Thomas MacFarland, *Romanticism and the Forms of Ruin: Wordsworth, Coleridge, and Modalities of Fragmentation* (Princeton, NJ, 1981), which hints at a theory of much Romantic writing being 'diasparactive'.

10. Cf. Fichte's attempts at rewriting the *Cogito* in the first pages of the *Science of Knowledge*, pp. 99–101. The attempt 'to express that *Act* which does not and cannot appear among the empirical states of our consciousness, but rather lies at the basis of all consciousness, and alone makes it possible' (p. 93) is, unavoidably, circular.

11. Immanuel Kant, *Anthropology from a Pragmatic Point of View* trs. Mary J. Gregor (The Hague, 1974) p. 9.

12. Immanuel Kant, *Critique of Pure Reason*, trs. N. Kemp-Smith, 2nd edn (London, 1933) p. 329 (A341, B399). Further references are given after quotations in the text.

13. Kant, *Anthropology*, p. 9.

14. *The Logic of Hegel, translated from The Encyclopaedia of the Sciences*, trs. William Wallace, 2nd edn (1892; repr. Oxford, 1975) pp. 68–70 (section 42).

15. Kant, *Anthropology*, p. 10. Kant's word is *der Egoism*, rather than the more usual *Egoismus* with its Fichtean associations.

16. See John D. Boyd, SJ, *The Function of Mimesis and its Decline* (Cambridge, Mass., 1968) pp. 183–217.

17. *The Works of George Berkeley*, ed. A. A. Luce and T. E. Jessop, 9 vols (London, 1949–57) II, 37–8.

18. Robert Lowth, *Lectures on the Sacred Poetry of the Hebrews*, trs. G. Gregory, 2 vols (London, 1787) I, 309 (XIV). Further references are given after quotations in the text. Coleridge borrowed a volume of Lowth's original Latin lectures in September 1796. See Whalley, 'Bristol Library Borrowings', *Library*, 5th ser., IV, 123. I have glossed 'subject' as 'object' here on the authority of G. E. M. Anscombe, quoted in Hacking, *Why Does*

Language Matter to Philosophy?, p. 30: 'That word "object" . . . has suffered a certain reversal of meaning in the history of philosophy, and so has the connected word "subject", though the two reversals aren't historically connected. The subject used to be what the proposition, say, is about, the thing itself as it is in reality . . . objects on the other hand were formerly always objects *of*.' See also *BL* [*CC*] I, 172n3.

19. Hegel, Preface to *Phenomenology of Spirit*, trs. A. V. Miller (Oxford, 1977) p. 8. Further references are given after quotations in the text.

20. See Rosemary Ashton, *The German Idea: Four English Writers and the Reception of German Thought, 1800–1860* (Cambridge, 1980).

CHAPTER THREE: PROTEAN AND EGOTISTICAL

1. Kant, *Anthropology*, p. 10.

2. *First Defence of the English People*, ch. 5, in *The Works of John Milton*, Columbia Edn, ed. F. A. Patterson, A. Abbott and H. M. Ayres, 18 vols and suppl. (New York, 1931–8) VII, 327.

3. Samuel Johnson, *Lives of the English Poets*, World's Classics, 2 vols (London, 1952) I, 74.

4. Ibid., p. 102.

5. Ibid., p. 109.

6. D'Israeli, *Essay on the Literary Character*, p. 147.

7. William Richardson, *A Philosophical Analysis and Illustration of some of Shakespeare's Remarkable Characters* (London, 1774) p. 26.

8. Ibid., pp. 27–8.

9. Ibid., p. 40.

10. Augustus William Schlegel, *A Course of Lectures on Dramatic Art and Literature*, trs. John Black, 2 vols (London, 1815) II, 128, 153 (XII). Schlegel has said that 'this Prometheus not merely forms men' but spirits, and characters like Caliban, 'and these beings existing only in imagination possess such truth and consistency that . . . he exorts the assenting conviction, if there should be such beings they would so conduct themselves' (II, 130).

11. On 'under consciousness' see the gloss by Elinor Shaffer, *'Kubla Khan' and the Fall of Jerusalem: The Mythological School in Biblical Criticism and Secular Literature, 1770–1880* (Cambridge, 1975) pp. 156 and 336n21. Wordsworth also uses the term in the account of the ascent of Snowdon in MS A of *The Prelude* (variant of 1805, XIII.71). See the Preamble to Part II below.

12. Richard Payne Knight, *An Analytical Enquiry into the Principles of Taste* (London, 1805) pp. 333–4 (III.i.). Coleridge's annotations of the 3rd (1806) edn of Knight's *Enquiry* (in Wordsworth's hand) are of extraordinary interest. See Edna Aston Shearer, 'Wordsworth and Coleridge Marginalia in a Copy of Richard Payne Knight's *Analytical Enquiry into the Principles of Taste*', *Huntingdon Library Quarterly*, I (Oct 1937) 63–94.

13. Note cited in *The Romantics on Milton: Formal Essays and Critical Asides*, ed. Joseph Anthony Wittreich (Cleveland, Ohio, and London, 1970) p. 250. In the *Biographia* Coleridge says, 'The very words, *objective* and *subjective*, of such constant recurrence in the schools of yore, I have ventured to re-introduce,

because I could not as briefly or conveniently by any more familiar terms distinguish the percipere from the percipi' (*BL* [*CC*], I, 172).

14. Cf. Novalis: '[The] power of truly awaking in one's self a foreign individuality – and not to be deceived by an imitation of superficialities – is still wholly unfamiliar and rests on the most extremely wonderful *penetration* [of the object], on a spiritual mimesis. The artist conforms himself to all he sees and wishes to be' – quoted in Engell, *The Creative Imagination*, p. 242.

15. See also *CL*, II, 810, 1054; *CN*, III, 4111, 4112. This is the fundamental relation which must obtain in the state as well: see *Lectures 1795* [*CC*], p. 122n.

16. Collier reports Coleridge opining that 'it was in characters of complete moral depravity, but of first-rate wit and talents, that Shakespeare delighted; and [he] instanced Richard the Third, Falstaff, and Iago' (*ShakCrit*, II, 29–30).

17. Shaftesbury, *Advice to an Author*, I.iii, in *Characteristics*, I, 129–34.

18. Cf. Walter Pater: 'In Coleridge we feel already that faintness and obscure dejection which cling like some contagious damp to all his writings', in contrast to Wordsworth's 'flawless temperament'; Coleridge 'is the victim of a division of the will, often showing itself in trivial things: he could never choose on which side of the garden path he would walk' – 'Coleridge's Writings', in *Essays on Literature and Art*, ed. Jennifer Uglow (London, 1973) pp. 3, 4, 11.

19. Patricia M. Ball, *The Central Self: A Study in Romantic and Victorian Imagination* (London, 1968), also traces the dichotomy of an 'egotistical' and a 'protean' or 'chameleon' poet, but believes that one or other term can be simply applied to any given poem, speaking of 'the egotistical "Frost at Midnight" and the protean *Ancient Mariner*' (p. 99).

CHAPTER FOUR : WHO WROTE GRAY'S 'ELEGY'?

1. *The Poems of Gray, Collins and Goldsmith*, ed. Roger Lonsdale, Longman Annotated English Poets (London, 1969) pp. 130–1, 1.72n. The text of the 'Elegy' is quoted from this edn, pp. 117–40.

2. Ibid. p. 115.

3. It is at this point that the new ending is added.

4. John Walker, *A Rhetorical Grammar* (1785), repr. English Linguistics Facsimile Reprints, 266 (Menston, Yorks, 1971) p. 202.

5. Ibid., p. 198.

6. See *Twentieth Century Interpretations of Gray's Elegy: A Collection of Critical Essays*, ed. Herbert W. Starr (Englewood Cliffs, NJ, 1968), pp. 41–81. Lonsdale rejects the problem of the 'swain' in a terse footnote to his edn (*Poems of Gray, Collins and Goldsmith*, p. 135, 1.93n), yet in his essay 'The Poetry of Thomas Gray: Versions of the Self', *Proceedings of the British Academy*, LIX (1973) 105–23, he recognises exactly this instability, though chiefly in the earlier version (pp. 107–8).

7. Frank Hale Ellis, 'Gray's *Elegy*: The Biographical Problem in Literary Criticism', in *Twentieth Century Interpretations*, pp. 51–75 (p. 63).

8. Cf. Byron's exasperated reply when Dallas asked who was the 'he' in the elegy which closes canto II of *Childe Harold*: 'the "he" refers to "Wanderer" and anything is better than the *I I I I* always I' – *The Works of Lord Byron*, ed. E. H. Coleridge, 13 vols (London, 1898–1904) II, 161n.

9. Thompson's line is of course taken as a title by John Barrell, *English Literature in History, 1730–1780: An Equal, Wide Survey* (London, 1983), the argument of which (pp. 17–109) I am here paraphrasing.

10. Crabb Robinson reports Coleridge later praising Goethe's novel for its 'powers of exhibiting man in a state of exalted sensibility' – *Henry Crabb Robinson on Books and their Writers*, ed. E. J. Morley, 3 vols (London, 1938) I, 122. A reference to 'the author of the Sorrows of Werter' as one who, like himself, had retracted his early republicanism, in a letter to Poole from Germany in 1798 (*CL*, I, 435), suggests that Coleridge was familiar with it before this date.

11. J. W. von Goethe, *The Sorrows of Werter: A German Story*, trs. attrib. to Daniel Malthus, 3rd edn, 2 vols (London, 1782) I, 29, 22–3. This is a translation from French rather than the original (see Preface, p. vi.). Further references are given after quotations in the text.

12. J. W. von Goethe, *Gedenkausgabe der Werke, Briefe und Gespräche*, ed. Ernst Beutler, 24 vols (Zurich, 1948–53) IV, 389.

13. Cited in *Hegel's Philosophy of Nature*, ed. and trs. Michael John Petry, 3 vols (London, 1970) I, 96–7.

14. *Schiller's Werke*, ed. J. Petersen and H. Schneider, Nationalausgabe, 42 vols (Weimar, 1943–) XXVII, 24–7.

15. Friedrich Schiller, *'Naive and Sentimental Poetry' and 'On the Sublime': Two Essays*, trs. Julius A. Elias (New York, 1966) p. 137. Further references are given after quotations in the text. A. C. Dunstan, 'The German Influence on Coleridge', *Modern Language Review*, XVII (1922) 272–81, and XVIII (1923) 183–201, furnishes 'definite proof' by evidence of parallels 'that Coleridge was familiar with *Über naïve und sentimentalische Dichtung*' (XVII, 274), but he fails to observe his own caution that 'a similarity need not imply a borrowing' (XVIII, 191).

16. Raymond Benoit, *Single Nature's Double Name: The Collectedness of the Conflicting in British and American Romanticism*, De Proprietatibus Litterarum, Series Maior, 26 (The Hague, 1973) p. 7.

17. Edward Young, *Conjectures on Original Composition. In a Letter to the Author of Sir Charles Grandison* (1759), repr. Scolar Press Facsimile (Leeds, 1966) p. 21. Further references are given after quotations in the text. Coleridge borrowed Young's *Works* in the spring of 1795. See Whalley, 'Bristol Library Borrowings', *Library*, 5th ser., IV, 119.

18. Friedrich Schlegel, *'Lucinde' and the Fragments*, trs. Peter Firchow (Minneapolis, 1971) p. 175 (Athenäum Fragment, 116). See commentary in Todorov, *Theories of the Symbol*, pp. 194–8 (cf. pp. 77–8).

19. J. W. von Goethe, *Wilhelm Meister's Apprenticeship and Travels*, in *The Works of Thomas Carlyle*, Centenary Edn, 30 vols (London, 1897) XXIII, 281–2.

20. Pater calls Coleridge 'the perfect flower of the romantic type. More than Childe Harold, more than Werther, more than René, Coleridge, by what he did, what he was, and what he failed to do, represents that inexhaustible discontent, languor, and homesickness, the chords of which ring all through

our modern literature' – 'Coleridge's Writings', in *Essays on Literature and Art*,
    p. 26.
21. Coleridge and Southey, *Omniana*, p. 123.

PART II: THE CIRCLE OF THE I

CHAPTER FIVE: THAT DESPOTISM OF THE EYE

1. G. W. F. Hegel, *Aesthetics: Lectures on Fine Art*, trs. T. M. Knox, 2 vols
   (Oxford, 1975) I, 375 (II.ii.3). (Psalm 104 is discussed as an example of
   sublimity of expression in Lowth, *Lectures*, I, 340; II, 280–2.)
2. Immanuel Kant, *The Critique of Judgement*, trs. James Creed Meredith (1928;
   repr. Oxford, 1957) p. 120 ('Analytic of the Sublime', A29).
3. 'Auguries of Innocence', ll.125–6, in *The Poetry and Prose of William Blake*, ed.
   David V. Erdman (Garden City, NY, 1965) p. 484. The emendation is made
   with the authority of the conclusion to *A Vision of the Last Judgment* (ibid., p.
   555) and this reading occurs in the first (Pickering) manuscript and in 'The
   Everlasting Gospel' (ibid., p. 512). For Blake on the eye, see also annotation
   to Reynolds's Discourse II (ibid., p. 634); letter to the Revd Dr Trusler, 23
   Aug 1799 (ibid., pp. 676–7); *There is No Natural Religion*, v and vi (ibid., p. 1);
   The Marriage of Heaven and Hell, Plate 12 (ibid., p. 38). In *Jerusalem*, ch. 3,
   Blake speaks of 'the Vegetated Mortal Eye's perverted & single vision'
   (ibid., p. 200), which, in the poem in a letter to Thomas Butts, 22 Nov 1802,
   he would replace by a 'fourfold vision' as repelling 'Single vision & Newton's
   sleep!' (ibid., pp. 692–3). See also the poem by Coleridge that Ernest Hartley
   Coleridge found in a notebook and titled 'Phantom' (*PW*, I, 393), in which
   'all accident' of a woman's material (and mortal) reality has been
   superseded by 'one spirit all her own' which 'Shone in her body visibly'. In
   copying the poem three years later, Coleridge writes this line as 'Shone
   thro' her body visibly'. See Edward Kessler, *Coleridge's Metaphors of Being*
   (Princeton, NJ, 1979), p. 40–4.
4. Smith uses the same image for the development of language in the
   'Dissertation' (*Theory*, II, 455).
5. *The Letters of Anna Seward*, 6 vols (Edinburgh, 1811) VI, 367.
6. Coleridge's criticism of the poem differs from this account of Wordsworth's
   only by its severity and in adding a criticism of bathos: that the poem sinks
   'most abruptly, not to say burlesquely' to the final couplet (*BL* [*CC*], II,
   136–7).
7. Cf. Addison: 'Our Sight . . . may be considered as a more delicate and
   diffusive kind of Touch, that spreads it self over an infinite Multitude of
   Bodies, comprehends the largest Figures, and brings into our reach some of
   the most remote Parts of the Universe' – *Spectator*, III, 536 (no. 411). The
   connection thereby suggested between sight and desire has echoes in
   Coleridge: 'The first education which we receive, that from our mothers, is
   given to us by touch; the whole of its process is nothing more than, to express
   myself boldly, an extended touch by promise. The sense itself, the sense of

vision itself, is only acquired by a continued recollection of touch' (*PL*, p. 115 [III]. See also *LS* [*CC*], p. 71; and the *Opus Maximum* MS, quoted in MacFarland, *Romanticism and the Forms of Ruin*, p. 150.

8. Berkeley, *Works*, I, 264. As it is expanded into the notion, in the *Alciphron*, of the Divine Alphabet, this has been claimed to lie behind both Coleridge's contention in 'The Destiny of Nations' that all sensory experience is 'Symbolical, one mighty alphabet' (*PW*, I, 132) and his benediction to the child in 'Frost at Midnight' of 'The lovely shapes and sounds intelligible, which thy God / Utters' (I, 242). See J. A. Appleyard, *Coleridge's Philosophy of Literature: The Development of a Concept of Poetry 1791–1819* (Cambridge, Mass., 1965) p. 49. See Ch. 8 below.

9. Coleridge, writing to Poole that he is reading the *Opticks* inclines to the consignment of Newton, familiar in Blake, to a group of perniciously Cartesian materialists (*CL*, II, 709). For Coleridge's actual interest in optics, see Trevor H. Levere, *Poetry Realized in Nature: Samuel Taylor Coleridge and Early Nineteenth-Century Science* (Cambridge, 1981) pp. 149–56.

10. T. H. Green, Introduction to *The Philosophical Works of David Hume*, ed. T. H. Green and T. H. Grose, 4 vols (London, 1874) I, 11 (para. 14).

11. Lord Kames (Henry Home), Appendix to *Elements of Criticism*, 6th edn, 2 vols (Edinburgh, 1785) II, 518–20.

12. Samuel H. Monk, *The Sublime: A Study of Critical Theories in Eighteenth-Century England* (1935; repr. Ann Arbor, Mich., 1960). The most stimulating study of the sublime known to me is by Thomas Weiskel, *The Romantic Sublime: Studies in the Structure and Psychology of Transcendence* (Baltimore and London, 1976). An article of rare acuity is Frances Ferguson's 'The Sublime of Edmund Burke; or, The Bathos of Experience', *Glyph*, VIII (1981) 62–78.

13. Kames, *Elements of Criticism*, I, 211 (ch. 4).

14. John Baillie, *Essay on the Sublime* (1747), Augustan Reprints, 43 (Los Angeles, 1953) p. 3. Further references are given after quotations in the text.

15. See Clarence DeWitt Thorpe, 'Coleridge on the Sublime', in *Wordsworth and Coleridge: Studies in Honor of George McLean Harper*, ed. Earl Leslie Griggs (Princeton, NJ, 1939) pp. 192–219; Raimonda Modiano, 'Coleridge and the Sublime', *Wordsworth Circle*, IX, no. 1 (Winter 1973) 110–20.

16. Archibald Alison, *Essays on the Nature and Principles of Taste* (Edinburgh, 1790) p. 2 (I.i.1).

17. Ibid., pp. 17, 46 (I.i.3), 49 (I.ii.1).

18. Berkeley, *Works*, I, 175, 194, 211, 234. Cf. Jacques Lacan: 'The whole trick, the hey presto!, of the classic dialectic around perception, derives from the fact that it deals with geometral vision, that is to say, with vision in so far as it is situated in a space that is not in its essence the visual' – *The Four Fundamental Concepts of Psycho-Analysis*, ed. Jacques-Alain Miller, trs. Alan Sheridan (Harmondsworth, 1979) p. 94. (It is a happy coincidence for me that the translator renders Lacan's *regard* as 'gazing'.) See also Turbayne, *The Myth of Metaphor*, pp. 141–202.

19. Kant, *Critique of Judgement*, p. 104 ('Analytic of the Sublime', A26).

20. Shaftesbury, 'A Letter Concerning Enthusiasm', vii, in *Characteristics*, I, 37–8.

21. *The Grounds of Criticism*, ch. 4, in *The Critical Works of John Dennis*, ed. Edward Niles Hooker, 2 vols (Baltimore, 1939) I, 338–9, 345.

22. Kant, *Critique of Judgement*, p. 128 ('Analytic of the Sublime', A29). On the amelioration of 'enthusiasm' from the eighteenth century to the present, see Susie I. Tucker, *Enthusiasm: A Study in Semantic Change* (Cambridge, 1972).
23. Jeremy Taylor, Bishop of Down, *Via Intelligentiae. A Sermon Preached to the University of Dublin* (London, 1662) pp. 12–13. Cf. Kant: 'The poet assays the task of interpreting to sense the rational ideas of invisible beings' (*Critique of Judgement*, p. 176 ['Analytic of the Sublime' A49).
24. Nevertheless, 'the old man' can, syntactically, be the complement of 'Time'. In this instance the baffled 'reader' is not a critical fiction. Edward Kessler, in *Coleridge's Metaphors of Being*, says that the old man achieves a state 'in which physical passivity and spiritual activity are combined' (p. 102), but that his gaze 'becomes a fusion of physical action and spiritual stillness' (p. 103). On the barren reciprocity of this gaze, cf. Keats, *The Fall of Hyperion*, I.257–71, where the poet is finally afforded a glimpse of Moneta – *Keats: Poetical Works*, ed. H. W. Garrod, Oxford Standard Authors (London, 1956) p. 409.
25. See *CL.* I, 649. Also cf. Kames, on 'ideal presence', which, as an effect of fictions, is distinguished from both 'real presence' and 'reflective remembrance' and thus 'may properly be termed a *waking dream*; because, like a dream, it vanisheth the moment we reflect upon our present situation: real presence, on the contrary, vouched by eye-sight, commands our belief, not only during the direct perception, but in reflecting afterward upon the object . . . when ideal presence is complete, we perceive every object as in our sight; and the mind, totally occupied with an interesting event, finds no leisure for reflection' (*Elements of Criticism*, I, 91, 95 (vii).
26. Arthur Symons, *The Symbolist Movement in Literature* (London, 1899) pp. 82, 90.
27. Lane Cooper collected several examples, mainly from *The Ancient Mariner*, of the verbal proximity of the verb 'to fix' and the 'eye', a determining power for one eye over another which he connected with Coleridge's interest in the phenomenon of animal magnetism – Lane Cooper, 'The Power of the Eye in Coleridge', in his *Late Harvest* (Ithaca, NY, 1952) pp. 65–95. See also Andrew J. Green, 'Essays in Miniature: The Restless Eye', *College English*, III (1942) 722–3. Keats's Belle Dame Sans Merci disarms the knight-at-arms just by looking at him. David Simpson, in *Irony and Authority in Romantic Poetry* (London, 1979) pp. 197–8, follows Cooper in relating the 'thraldom' of the knight to animal magnetism. Simpson's speculation on the relation of the phenomenon to the contract of writer and reader is germane to my argument.
28. Cf. Coleridge's sonnet of 1790, 'On the Evening Star' (*PW*, I, 16–17): 'On thee full oft with fixed eye I gaze / Till I, methinks, all spirit seem to grow'; and see Geoffrey Hartman, 'Evening Star and Evening Land', in *New Perspectives on Coleridge and Wordsworth: Selected Papers from the English Institute*, ed. G. Hartman (New York and London, 1972) pp. 85–131; repr. in his *The Fate of Reading and Other Essays* (Chicago, 1975) pp. 147–78.
29. Blake, *Poetry and Prose*, p. 656.
30. G. N. G. Orsini, in *Coleridge and German Idealism* (Carbondale, Ill., 1969), finds a source for this reflection in Fichte's lectures of 1799, where the example adduced of the most recalcitrant materiality was also a wall (pp.

178–83). More convincingly to me, Daniel Stempel, in 'Revelation on Mount Snowdon: Wordsworth, Coleridge and the Fichtean Imagination', *Journal of Aesthetics and Art Criticism*, xxix, (1970–1) 371–84, discusses the stasis of the 'eye made quiet' which 'sees into the life of things' in terms of Fichte's *Anschauung* (intuition without awareness or reflection, in which the ego and non-ego can be synthesised). He finds sources in Fichte, including the phrase *dunkle Gefühle* ('dark feelings' – 'dim sympathies'?) (pp. 372–6).

31. See Descartes, 'Principles of Philosophy', 45, in *Philosophical Works*, trs. Elizabeth S. Haldane and G. R. T. Ross, 2 vols (Cambridge, 1911) I, 237; Locke, *Essay*, p. 363 (II.xxix.2).

32. Richard Rorty, *Philosophy and the Mirror of Nature* (Oxford, 1981), p. 373. See pp. 38–69 on this ocular metaphor within the Western philosophical tradition, and pp. 131–64 for the way theories of knowledge in Descartes, Locke and Kant share a common foundation on such a metaphor.

CHAPTER SIX: BLEST OUTSTARTING

1. Karsten Harries, 'The Infinite Sphere: Comments on the History of a Metaphor', *Journal of the History of Philosophy*, xiii (1975) 5–15.

2. M. H. Abrams, *Natural Supernaturalism: Tradition and Revolution in Romantic Literature* (London, 1971) pp. 12–13.

3. J. Hillis Miller, 'Tradition and Difference', *Diacritics*, ii (Winter 1972) 6–13 (p. 12). Hillis Miller's review of *Natural Supernaturalism* led eventually to an illuminating exchange between Abrams, Wayne Booth and himself. See Wayne C. Booth, 'M. H. Abrams: Historian as Critic, Critic as Pluralist', *Critical Inquiry*, ii (Spring 1976) 411–45; Abrams, 'Rationality and Imagination in Cultural History: A Reply to Wayne Booth', ibid., pp. 447–64; Booth, '"Preserving the Exemplar": or, How not to Dig our Own Graves', *Critical Inquiry*, iii (Spring 1977) 407–23; Abrams, 'The Deconstructive Angel', ibid., pp. 425–38; Hillis Miller, 'The Critic as Host', ibid., pp. 439–47.

4. Abrams, *Natural Supernaturalism*, pp. 225–37, 454.

5. Coleridge, 'On Poesy or Art', in *Biographia Literaria*, ed. J. Shawcross, 2 vols (1907; repr. with corrections, Oxford, 1954) II, 262. On this 'death' as imaginative (Wordsworth's 'we murder to dissect' – *WPW* IV, 57), see Alison, *Essays on Taste*, pp. 7–9 (I.i.2[2]); Reid, 'Of Taste': 'A philosophical analysis of the objects of taste is like applying the anatomical knife to a fine face' – *Essays on the Intellectual Powers*, p. 762 (VIII.ii). Cf. Peter Firchow's beautiful translation of Schlegel: 'If some mystical art lovers who think of every criticism as a dissection and every dissection as a destruction of pleasure were to think logically, then "wow" would be the best criticism of the greatest work of art. To be sure, there are critiques which say nothing more, but only take much longer to say it' – *'Lucinde' and the Fragments*, pp. 149–50 (Critical Fragment 57).

6. For an anthology of texts on the aesthetic uses of Primitivism, see *The Rise of Modern Mythology*, ed. Burton Feldman and Robert D. Richardson (Bloomington, Ind., 1972).

7. See J. W. Milley, 'Some Notes on Coleridge's "Eolian Harp"', *Modern Philology*, xxxvi (1939) 359–75.
8. Cf.: 'Poetry itself is indebted for its origin, character, complexion, emphasis and application, to the effects which are produced upon the mind and body, upon the imagination, the senses, the voice, and respiration by the agitation of passion' (Lowth, *Lectures* I, 366 [xvii]).
9. Cited in *The Poetical Works of Samuel Taylor Coleridge*, ed. J. Dykes Campbell (London, 1893) p. 578. By the time of the *Biographia* Coleridge is willing to concede to the reviewers that the labour is more apparent than the deserts (*BL [CC]*, I, 6–7), but a fortnight before publication of the *Poems* he ends a letter to Benjamin Flower in a manner which, incidentally, reflects once more on the difficulty expressed in Chapter 1 above: 'I suppose you have heard that I am married. I was married on the 4th of October. I rest for all my poetical credit on the *Religious Musings*' (*CL*, I, 197).
10. Cf.: 'Christ must become Man – but he cannot become *us*, except as far as we become *him* – & this we cannot do but by *assimilation*: and assimilation is a *vital real* act, not a notional or merely intellective one' (*CL*, v, 48).
11. Hartley, *Observations on Man*, I, 497 (IV.vi.99). Georges Poulet, in *The Metamorphoses of the Circle*, trs. Carley Dawson and Elliott Coleman (Baltimore, 1966), quotes a pseudo-hermetic manuscript of the twelfth century: 'Deus est sphaera cujus centrum ubique' (p. xi) – a metaphor which, as his book shows, is itself ubiquitous. (The aphorism itself is quoted by Coleridge – *AR*, p. 226.) For Poulet, the circle's 'simplicity . . . perfection . . . [and] ceaseless universal application' (*Metamorphoses*, p. vii) liberates a constant or timeless plenitude of 'being'. That before it is anything else the metaphor of the circle *is* a metaphor, which is to say a linguistic construct which can, therefore, be negatively applied, is unproblematic as he completes a movement in which 'the circle is the form of the perfection of true being' (p. 350).
12. Hegel, *On Christianity: Early Theological Writings*, trs. T. M. Knox (Gloucester, Mass., 1970) p. 285; quoted by Simpson, *Irony and Authority*, p. 186.
13. On Coleridge's Unitarianism, see *CL*. I, 147, 178, 377. On the dissenting tradition, see Abrams, *Natural Supernaturalism*, pp. 46–65.
14. Christopher Hill, *The Century of Revolution: 1603–1741* (London, 1961) p. 253.
15. 'The Moral Teaching of Jesus Christ', in *The Complete Works of Percy Bysshe Shelley*, ed. R. Ingpen and W. E. Peck, 10 vols (New York, 1965) VI, 255; quoted by Simpson, *Irony and Authority*, p. 187.
16. Cf. Schelling: 'Through art, divine creation is presented objectively, since it rests on the same idea of the infinite ideal dwelling in the real on which the creation of art rests. The exquisite German word *Einbildungskraft* actually means the power of forming into one, an act on which all creation is founded. It is the power through which an ideal is also something real, the soul the body; it is the power of individuation, which of all is the truly creative one' – quoted in Engell, *The Creative Imagination*, p. 304.
17. Cf. Hegel: 'Nor *is* there such a thing as the false, any more than there *is* something evil. The evil and the false, to be sure, are not as bad as the devil, for in the devil they are even made into a particular *subjective agent*; as the false and the evil, they are mere *universals*, though each has its own essence as against the other' (Preface to *Phenomenology*, p. 22).

Notes

18. Thomas Burnet, *Archaeologicae Philosophicae*, pt II; or, *The Theory of the Visible World*, trs. Mr Foxton (London, 1729) p. 17 (ch. 2).
19. Geoffrey H. Hartman, 'Romanticism and Anti-Self-Consciousness', in *Beyond Formalism: Literary Essays, 1958–1970* (New Haven, Conn., and London, 1970) p. 307. Cf. Abrams, *Natural Supernaturalism, passim*, esp. pp. 113–14. In his essay, Hartman locates *Werther* as the '*terminus a quo* of thought as a disease' (p. 298n2).
20. Dennis, *Grounds of Criticism*, ch. 2, in *Critical Works*, I, 336.
21. Hegel, *Logic*, p. 43 (II.xxiv).
22. See *BL* [*CC*], I, 98. For Coleridge's attempt to create a 'system' in the *Magnum Opus*, see MacFarland, *Romanticism and the Forms of Ruin*, pp. 342–81. For one definition of 'process' in relation to Coleridge, see Kathleen M. Wheeler, *Sources, Processes and Methods in Coleridge's 'Biographia Literaria'* (Cambridge, 1980) p. ix.
23. See, for example, Abrams, *Natural Supernaturalism*, pp. 235–37; Walter Kaufmann, *Hegel: Reinterpretation, Texts and Commentary* (London, 1966) pp. 242–3.
24. For Spinoza, substance is 'that which is in itself and is conceived through itself: in other words, that, the conception of which does not need the conception of another thing from which it must be formed' – Benedict de Spinoza, *Ethic*, trs. W. Hale White, 4th edn, rev. Amelia Hutchison (London, 1910) p. 1 (I.iii). Furthermore, 'there cannot be any substance excepting God, and consequently none other can be conceived' (p. 13 [I.xiv]).
25. Hegel, Introduction to *Aesthetics*, I, 31.
26. Martin Heidegger, *Poetry, Language, Thought*, trs. Albert Hofstadter (New York, 1971) p. 18. Of course, there are only two nouns in the German title, since 'work of art' is *Kunstwerk*. It is worth pointing out too that the German *Ursprung* (origin) can be literally translated 'primal leap'.
27. Ibid., p. 78.
28. Heinrich von Kleist, *Sämtliche Werke und Briefe*, ed. Helmut Sembdner, 6th edn, 2 vols (Munich, 1977) II, 342–3. Translation cited from Idris Parry, *'Hand to Mouth' and Other Essays* (Manchester, 1981) p. 16.
29. Kleist, *Sämtliche Werke*, II, 345; Parry, *Hand to Mouth*, p. 18.
30. George MacLean Harper, 'Coleridge's Conversation Poems' (1928), in *English Romantic Poets: Modern Essays in Criticism*, ed. M. H. Abrams, 2nd edn (New York, 1975) pp. 188–201.
31. B. Ifor Evans, 'Coleridge's Copy of "Fears in Solitude"', *The Times Literary Supplement*, no. 1733 (18 Apr 1935) 255.
32. The snake with its tail in its mouth, self-enfolding and autogenetic, appears in Egyptian and other primitive mythologies, often as a symbol for eternity. (It is as such that it is painted on Clarissa's coffin at the end of Richardson's novel.) The pre-Socratic Greeks knew it as the *ouroborous*. See Erich Neumann, *The Origins and History of Consciousness*, trs. R. F. C. Hull, Bollingen Series XLII, 2nd edn, corrected (New York, 1964), pp. 10–11 and illus. 5–9. Cf. *Church and State* [*CC*], 179–80.
33. Paul de Man, *Allegories of Reading: Figural Language in Rousseau, Nietzsche, Rilke, and Proust* (New Haven, Conn., and London, 1979) pp. 26–7.

PART III: SARA, HARTLEY, PORLOCK

PREAMBLE

1. Cf. Wordsworth, in the Preface to the *Poems* of 1815, speaking of *The Task* as exemplifying the 'composite order' of the descriptive 'Idyllium', the didactic and philosophical satire (*WPr*, III, 28). Coleridge says that Cowper's poem was unknown to him in 1796 (*BL* [*CC*], I, 25n), but Lamb, writing to him in July of that year, encloses a sonnet in praise of 'Cowper, of England's Bards the wisest and the best', then demurs, 'I fear you will not *accord* entirely with my sentiments of Cowper, as *exprest* above, (perhaps scarcely just) but the poor Gentleman has just recovered from his lunacies, & that begets pity, & pity love, & love admiration' – *The Letters of Charles and Mary Anne Lamb*, ed. Edwin W. Marrs, Jr, 2 vols (Ithaca, NY, and London, 1975) I, 41. In 1798, the year 'Frost at Midnight' was written, Hazlitt reports that Coleridge 'spoke of Cowper as the best modern poet' (*HW*, XVII, 120).

CHAPTER SEVEN: A MINGLED CHARM

1. Thomas Lisle Bowles, *Sonnets, Written Chiefly on Picturesque Spots, during a Tour*, 2nd edn (Bath, 1789); *Monody Written at Matlock, October 1791* (London and Bath, 1791).
2. M. H. Abrams, 'Structure and Style in the Greater Romantic Lyric', in *From Sensibility to Romanticism: Essays Presented to Frederick A. Pottle*, ed. Frederick W. Hilles and Harold Bloom (New York, 1965) pp. 527–60 (pp. 533–44).
3. In justification of the analogy here assumed between spatial and psychological 'superiority', consider Paul de Man, 'The Rhetoric of Temporality', in *Interpretation: Theory and Practice*, ed. Charles S. Singleton (Baltimore, 1969) pp. 173–209; now repr. in his *Blindness and Insight: Essays in the Rhetoric of Contemporary Criticism*, 2nd edn, rev. (London, 1983) pp. 187–228. Speaking of irony, which issues 'at the cost of the empirical self' (p. 214), de Man says, 'when the concept of "superiority" is still being used when the self is engaged in a relationship not to other subjects, but to what is precisely not a self, then the so-called superiority merely designates the *distance* constitutive of all acts of reflection. Superiority and inferiority then become merely spatial metaphors to indicate a discontinuity and a plurality of levels within a subject that comes to know itself by an increasing differentiation from what it is not' (pp. 212–13).
4. Abrams, 'Structure and Style', in *From Sensibility to Romanticism*, p. 540.
5. These lines (5 and 6) were omitted from the 3rd edn of the *Poems* but later reinstated.
6. Humphry House, *Coleridge: The Clark Lectures, 1951–2* (London, 1953) pp. 78–9. See also Norman Fruman, *Coleridge, the Damaged Archangel* (London, 1972) pp. 305–9. The passage from Cowper is from *The Task*, IV ('The Winter Evening') 291–5 – Cowper, *Poetical Works*, ed. H. S. Milford, Oxford Standard Authors, 4th edn, corrections and additions by Norma Russell (London, 1967) pp. 188–9.

7. This is certainly the interpretation at least one eighteenth-century reader put upon it: in Jane Austen's *Emma*, Knightley thinks of Cowper's line when he wonders whether his suspicion that Frank Churchill may be planning to 'trifle' with Jane Fairfax while wooing Emma is any more than a jealous self-deception – *Emma*, ed. David Lodge, Oxford English Novels (London, 1971) p. 310 (III.v).

8. Kant, *Critique of Judgement*, p. 89 ('Analytic of the Beautiful', A244).

9. A good summary of sources for this speculation is Levere's *Poetry Realised in Nature*, pp. 156–8.

10. George Watson, *Coleridge the Poet* (London, 1966) p. 66; House, *Coleridge*, p. 77.

11. It would be a nice point to make if 'aye' were homophonous with eye/I. It is not. However, as Dr Joan Beal of the University of Newcastle-upon-Tyne writes to me, 'Coleridge has chosen to spell it *aye* and therefore some reference to aye = yes may be here to be seen with the eye if not heard with the ear – the equivalent in puns of an "eye-rhyme" perhaps.'

12. J. Dykes Campbell says that this footnote is 'of no interest' (Coleridge, *Poetical Works*, ed. Dykes Campbell, p. 578).

13. Hartley, *Observations on Man*, II, 214 (III.ii.50).

14. Thomas McFarland, *Coleridge and the Pantheist Tradition* (Oxford, 1969) p. 166.

15. *Coleridge's Verse: A Selection*, ed. William Empson and David Pirie (London, 1972) p. 18.

16. In all editions of *Sibylline Leaves* was a section headed 'Meditative Poems in Blank Verse' containing all the poems usually discussed as 'conversation poems'.

17. Empson, in *Coleridge's Verse*, p. 21.

18. Cf. J. Robert Barth, SJ, *The Symbolic Imagination: Coleridge and the Romantic Tradition* (Princeton, NJ, 1977): 'Symbol leaves the mystery intact' (p. 55). Empson's comment seems robustly English but the difficulty he identifies is a version of that with which Romantic aestheticians struggled too. In Appendix C of *The Statesman's Manual*, from which I quoted, Coleridge insists on God being the signified of the symbol but that it inscribes 'the translucence of the Eternal through and in the Temporal. It always partakes of the Reality which it renders intelligible . . .' (*LS* [*CC*], p. 30). Hegel speaks of a disjunction between signifier and signified in the artistic symbol: 'art appropriates a substantial content grasped through the spirit, a content that does not appear externally, but in an externality which is not only present immediately but is first *produced* by the *spirit* as an existent comprising that content in itself and expressing it' (*Aesthetics*, I, 316 [II.i, Introduction]). He means of course an absolute spirit whose relation to 'ego' is not obvious: even here he is speaking of the advance of spirit, through art, in history. Kant opposes the symbolic to the schematic, both of which stem from intuition: it is 'Taste' which makes the 'transition from the charm of sense to a habitual moral interest possible without too violent a leap' and he assumes a simple correspondence of sensuous and moral beauty, of freedom and conformity to the laws of Reason (*Critique of Judgement*, p. 225 ['Dialectic of Aesthetic Judgement', 59]). This is a problem that will be met with again. On the symbol, see de Man, 'Rhetoric of Temporality', in *Blindness and*

Insight; Todorov, *Theories of the Symbol*, esp. ch. 6, pp. 147–221; M. Jadwiga Swiatecka OP, *The Idea of the Symbol: Some Nineteenth-Century Comparisons with Coleridge* (Cambridge, 1980).

CHAPTER EIGHT: THE FROST PERFORMS

1. Paul Hamilton, *Coleridge's Poetics* (Oxford, 1983) p. 20.
2. The term, like others I am using here, is of course drawn from J. L. Austin, *How to Do Things with Words*, ed. J. O. Urmson and Marina Sbisà, 2nd edn (London, 1980). At their simplest level, a constative is what is generally held to be a 'statement', while examples of performatives are 'I bet', 'I apologise', 'I promise', in which 'it seems clear that to utter the sentences (in, of course, the appropriate circumstances) is not to *describe* my doing of what I should be said in so uttering to be doing or to state that I am doing it: it is to do it' (p. 6). Thus, 'we might justify the "performative–constative" distinction . . . as a distinction between doing and saying' (p. 47); and the 'performative is happy or unhappy [i.e. appropriate or otherwise] as opposed to true or false' (p. 133). The last sentence quoted bears on much of what I have said, especially in Chapter 6. Austin excludes what he calls 'parasitic' or 'etiolated' performatives (p. 22), for example when spoken by an actor on a stage. Such a point is one where his 'ordinary language' becomes notoriously problematic. Taking account of the nebulosity of the term 'statement' itself, he then revises the initial distinction into a shifting one between locutionary and illocutionary (including perlocutionary) utterances, none of which are context-free. This is analogous to the problem dealt with here, where the status of the act by which the promise is made or the contract proffered is at issue.
3. *Prelude*, 1805, I. 490–4. See also: 'The natural sun is . . . a symbol of the spiritual. . . . [It] converts the air itself into the minister of its own purification' (*BL* [*CC*], II, 243); and Coleridge's comment (still apparently persuaded by Burnet's *Sacred Theory of the Earth*) that 'the Earth with its scarred face is the symbol of the Past; the Air and Heaven, of Futurity' (*TT*, 2 June 1824).
4. M. J. Petry, in *Hegel's Philosophy of Nature* p. 15, opines that the Hegelian 'synthesis' derives from a concept of the Trinity.
5. 'To Wordsworth . . . the vision on Mount Snowdon is a revelation of the structure and operation of the mind – not the limited mind of the individual but mind itself, the three levels of the absolute self corresponding to the three functions of the Fichtean imagination' – Stempel, 'Revelation on Mount Snowdon', *Journal of Aesthetics and Art Criticism*, XXIX, 381. This is what comes, in a valuable essay, of translating 'the hieroglyphics of Wordsworth's description into the prosaic terms of philosophy' (p. 372).
6. This is less obviously ironic than the self-reproach implied by the 'abstruse research' in 'Dejection', where it is also claimed as something like the Hegelian hand that may heal the self-inflicted wound. See Chapter 6 above. The phrase also occurs in *BL* [*CC*], I, 17.
7. The *OED* cites Coleridge, in *The Ancient Mariner*, as the earliest authority for this usage.
8. Cf. 'Tintern Abbey': 'yet a little while / May I behold in thee what I was once'.

216   *Notes*

9. *Samuel Taylor Coleridge: Poems*, ed. John Beer, Everyman's Library, 2nd edn (London, 1974) pp. 272–80, see p. 274.
10. Dennis, *Advancement and Reformation of Poetry*, ch. 5, in *Critical Works* I, 215.
11. Satan's mood is dispelled by 'the hot hell that always in him burns'. This Satanic inherence of conscience within consciousness – of consciousness of evil – will be discussed in Part IV.
12. Bourn(e): 'boundary, bound, limit or terminus, destination, goal' (*OED*). Probably from *Hamlet*, in which death is 'The undiscover'd country, from whose bourn / No traveller returns'.
13. See Stephen K. Land, *From Signs to Propositions: The Concept of Form in Eighteenth-Century Semantic Theory* (London, 1974). Schiller's positing of a universal conceptual division between 'naive' and 'sentimental' is clearly also relevant.
14. Cooke, *The Romantic Will*, p. 119.
15. Coleridge, *Biographia*, ed. Shawcross, II, 263.
16. See C. S. Lewis, *Studies in Words*, 2nd edn (Cambridge, 1967) pp. 181–213.
17. On the need for awareness of the self as unifying subject and therefore as object, see *CL*, V, 117.

CHAPTER NINE: COMMUNION

1. For a study of 'egoism' as sentiment in the tradition from 'Il Penseroso' which includes the 'Elegy', see Eleanor M. Sickels, *The Gloomy Egoist: Moods and Themes of Melancholy from Gray to Keats* (1932; repr. New York, 1969).
2. *The Letters of William and Dorothy Wordsworth: The Early Years 1787–1805*, ed. Ernest de Selincourt, rev. Chester L. Shaver, 2nd edn (Oxford, 1967) p. 594.
3. William Empson, *Milton's God* (London, 1961) p. 94. Cf. *MiscCrit*, p. 162.
4. I cannot agree with Irene H. Chayes, 'Kubla Khan and the Creative Process', *Studies in Romanticism*, V (1966) 1–21, that 'in the verse text . . . there is nothing to correspond to the transcription of the dream poem from memory, in which the poet is interrupted by the arrival of the "person on business from Porlock"' (p. 4), since the whole of the sixth section of the poem seems to me such a correspondence.
5. See Hamilton, *Coleridge's Poetics*, pp. 196–9.
6. I owe these ideas to Frances Loe, and to her unpublished dissertation '"The Soul in Paraphrase": A Study of the Operation of Religious Language in Herbert's *The Temple* and Milton's *Paradise Regained*' (University of Cambridge, 1984). See also, Barbara Leah Harman, *Costly Monuments: Representations of the Self in George Herbert's Poetry* (Cambridge, Mass., and London, 1982); Barbara Kiefer Lowalski, *Protestant Poetics and the Seventeenth-Century Religious Lyric* (Princeton, NJ, 1979).
7. Hegel, *On Christianity*, p. 251. Cf. Hegel's advice, in the first part of the *Phenomenology*, to 'those who assert the truth and certainty of the reality of sense-objects' that 'they should go back to the most elementary school of wisdom, viz. the ancient Eleusinian Mysteries of Ceres and Bacchus, and that they have still to learn the secret meaning of the eating of bread and the drinking of wine. For he who is initiated into these Mysteries, not only comes

to doubt the being of sensuous things, but to despair of it; in part he brings
about the nothingness of such things himself in his dealings with them, and
in part he sees them reduce themselves to nothingness' (p. 65).
8. A virtuoso reading reportedly performed, for demonstration purposes, by
Mr J. H. Prynne of Gonville and Caius College, Cambridge.
9. Leslie Brisman, *Romantic Origins* (Ithaca, NY, and London, 1978) p. 30.
10. Cf. 'the iron goad of Destiny' (*Friend* [CC], I, 106).

PART IV: THE LANGUAGE OF POWER

PREAMBLE

1. I. A. Richards, *Coleridge's Minor Poems* (1960: repr. n.p., 1970) p. 16.
2. 'Hope' recurs as a capitalised abstraction in several later poems. Cf. 'Hope
without an object cannot live' (*PW*, I, 447).
3. The term used of the histories Hume and Adam Smith proposed, by Smith's
friend and editor Dugald Stewart, in his *Account of the Life and Writings of Adam
Smith*, in *The Collected Works of Dugald Stewart*, ed. Sir William Hamilton, 10
vols and suppl. (Edinburgh, 1854–60) x, 33–4.
4. Joseph Warton, *An Essay on the Genius and Writings of Pope*, 2 vols, 5th edn,
corrected (London, 1806) I, 47.
5. Hayden White, *Metahistory: The Historical Imagination in Nineteenth-Century
Europe* (Baltimore, 1973) pp. 4, 13. For an exhaustive but ultimately
unconvincing reply to such textualising, see Fredric Jameson, *The Political
Unconscious: Narrative as a Socially Symbolic Act* (Ithaca, NY, 1981) pp. 17–102.
For a fine study of the interinanimation of history and novel in the eighteenth
century, see Leo Braudy, *Narrative Form in History and Fiction* (Princeton, NJ,
1970).
6. David Hume, *Enquiries Concerning the Human Understanding and Concerning the
Principles of Morals*, ed. L. A. Selby-Bigge, 2nd edn (1902; repr. Oxford, 1961)
p. 314 (Appendix IV).

CHAPTER TEN: GREAT BAD MEN

1. 'Sonnet: England in 1819', *Poetical Works of P. B. Shelley*, ed. Thomas
Hutchinson, Oxford Standard Authors, 2nd edn. rev. G. M. Matthews
(Oxford, 1970) pp. 574–5.
2. Harold Bloom, *The Anxiety of Influence* (New York, 1975) p. 20.
3. See J. M. Thompson, *Robespierre*, 2 vols (Oxford, 1935) I, 264–8.
4. See Brissot's *Mémoires*, quoted in Harold T. Parker, *The Cult of Antiquity and
the French Revolutionaries* (Chicago, 1937) p. 175.
5. From Robespierre's weekly paper *Le Défenseur de la Constitution*, 19 May 1792;
quoted in Thompson, *Robespierre*, I, 237.
6. See Carl R. Woodring, *Politics in the Poetry of Coleridge* (Madison, Wis., 1961)
pp. 194–8.

7. Longinus, *A Treatise on the Sublime*, trs. Mr Welsted, 3rd edn, corrected (Dublin, 1727) p. 112.
8. Dennis, *Critical Works*, II, 221.
9. James Beattie, *Dissertations Moral and Critical* (London, 1783), p. 612.
10. Ibid., pp. 612–13.
11. Ibid., p. 614.
12. Kames, *Elements of Criticism*, I, 243 (ch. 4).
13. William Godwin, *Enquiry Concerning Political Justice and its Influence on General Virtue and Happiness*, 2 vols (London, 1793) I, 261–2.
14. The textualisation of history has consequences for history as well as for the text, as Marx, citing Hegel in *The Eighteenth Brumaire of Louis Bonaparte*, realises. See *Karl Marx and Frederick Engels: Selected Works* (Moscow, 1968) pp. 96–104.
15. Hegel, *Aesthetics*, I, 195 (I.iii [BxI.i(c)]).
16. Friedrich Schiller, *The Robbers. A Tragedy*, trs. (anonymously) Alexander F. Tytler, Lord Woodhouselee (London, 1792) p. 217.
17. Ibid., p. 97.
18. Marilyn Butler, *Romantics, Rebels and Reactionaries: English Literature and its Background 1760–1830* (Oxford, 1981) p. 73.
19. Schiller, *The Robbers*, p. 163.
20. See Peter L. Thorslev, *The Byronic Hero: Types and Prototypes* (Minneapolis, 1962), and 'The Romantic Mind is its Own Place', *Comparative Literature*, xv (1963) 250–68.
21. Cf. D'Israeli: 'Genius is a perilous gift of Nature; for it is acknowledged that the same materials she employs to form a Cataline and a Cromwell, make a Cicero and a Bacon' – *Essay on the Literary Character*, p. 114.
22. *Schiller's Werke*, III 6–7.
23. Friedrich Schiller, *On the Aesthetic Education of Man: In a Series of Letters*, ed. and trs. E. M. Wilkinson and L. A. Willoughby (Oxford, 1967) p. 17.
24. Cf. Blake, in 'The Keys of the Gates', accompanying the engravings *For the Sexes: The Gates of Paradise*. The white-bearded patriarch of the engraving, his hand on a sword he looks too frail to lift, is threatened by a naked youth with a raised spear. He is saying 'My Son! My Son! thou treatest me / But as I have instructed thee' – *Poetry and Prose*, p. 266.
25. Walter Benjamin, *The Origin of German Tragic Drama*, trs. John Osborne (London, 1977) p. 69.
26. Hegel, *Aesthetics*, pp. 195–6.
27. Shaftesbury, *Characteristics*, I, 128 (I.iii). Thus I disagree with Woodring, *Politics in the Poetry of Coleridge*, pp. 87, 199–200, that *Wallenstein* is the source of the phrase. *LS* [*CC*], pp. 65–6n1, and *BL* [*CC*], I, 32n1, repeat Woodring's attribution.
28. On this term see Maurice Mandelbaum, *History, Man, and Reason: A Study in Nineteenth-Century Thought* (Baltimore, 1981) pp. 428–9 (n. 3 to p. 164).

CHAPTER ELEVEN: THE GENERAL WILL

1. Thomas Carlyle, *On Heroes, Hero-Worship and the Heroic in History*, in *Works*, V,

188. Further references to this volume of the *Works* will be given after quotations in the text.

2. See *Du contrat social*, II. 3, in *Oeuvres Complètes de Jean-Jacques Rousseau*, ed. Bernard Gagnebin and Marcel Raymond, Bibliothèque de la Pléiade (1959–), III (1964) 289–94.

3. Wordsworth, *Letters: The Early Years*, pp. 586–7; Rousseau, *Oeuvres Complètes*, I (1959). 5.

4. *A Letter from Mr Burke, to a Member of the National Assembly; in Answer to Some Objections to his Book on French Affairs* (Paris; repr. London, 1796) pp. 33, 35.

5. Cf. Hume on his reading of moralists: 'of a sudden I am surpriz'd to find, that instead of the usual copulations of propositions, *is* and *is not*, I meet with no proposition that is not connected with an *ought*, or an *ought not*. This change is imperceptible; but is, however, of the last consequence' (*Treatise*, p. 469 [III.i.1]).

6. M. J. Petry says in *Hegel's Philosophy of Nature*, p. 171, that the word came into English through John Ellistone's translations of Boehme in the mid seventeenth century and that 'Hegel simply uses the word to generalise the concept of "self"'.

7. Stanley Cavell, 'Genteel Responses to Kant? In Emerson's "Fate" and Coleridge's *Biographia Literaria*', *Raritan*, III, no. 2 (Fall 1983) 38. Kant himself seems to be saying much the same thing at the start of the *Critique of Pure Reason*, p. 7 (Avii).

CHAPTER TWELVE: WHATEVER THEY DO IS RIGHT

1. See the connection made between 'loyalty' and 'property' in *BL* [*CC*], I, 213.

2. Quoted in J. G. Fichte, *Addresses to the German Nation*, trs. R. F. Jones and G. H. Turnbull, ed. G. A. Kelly (New York and Evanston, Ill., 1968) p. xi. Further references are given after quotations in the text.

3. G. W. F. Hegel, *Lectures on the Philosophy of World History: Introduction: Reason in History*, trs. H. B. Nisbet (Cambridge, 1975) p. 21. Further references to this edn are given after quotations in the text.

4. I have amended the translation at this point. Nisbet translates *geistreich* as 'resourceful' where I prefer 'inspired'.

5. Cf. '*What is rational is actual and what is actual is rational*' – Hegel, Preface to *Philosophy of Right*, trs. T. M. Knox, 2nd edn, corrected (Oxford, 1945) p. 10; 'the abolition of the antithesis in the *means*' (Hegel, *Phenomenology*, p. 240).

CHAPTER THIRTEEN: PLANK OR BRIDGE

1. E. J. Hobsbawm, *The Age of Revolution: Europe 1789–1848* (London, 1962) p. 79.

2. Coleridge, *Essays on His Own Times, Forming a Second Series of The Friend*, ed. Sara Coleridge, 3 vols (London, 1850) I, xxviii.

3. *Works of Joseph Butler*, II, 54.

4. Cf. Reid, for whom this is a 'gross and palpable abuse of words', a conflation

of 'reason' to 'passion' in order that Hume can defend 'his favourite paradox, that reason is, and ought to be, the servant of the passions' – *Essays on the Active Powers of the Human Mind*, in *Works*, III and IV (1815), repr. as 1 vol. (Cambridge, Mass., 1969) p. 208 (III, ii).

5. The reference is to *The Tempest*, v.i.286. The editor of the New Arden edn explains it as either a simple hyperbole, perhaps a pun on Stephano's name which means 'lashed' or 'flayed' or, in Neapolitan slang, 'stomach' – *The Tempest*, ed. Frank Kermode, New Arden Shakespeare, 5th edn, rev. (London, 1954) p. 129. Coleridge's sense of the insult is clearly that it means an irritating, perhaps disabling, affliction that passes.

6. For Coleridge's Burkean appeal to 'Principles' see the sub-title to the *Friend*. See also *Lectures 1795* [*CC*], p. 5, where 'bottoming on fixed Principles' is necessarily against 'the disgusting Egotisms of an affected Humility'; *BL* [*CC*], I, 190–1; *CL*, III, 181; *TT*, 21 Sept 1830; *Church and State* [*CC*], p. 19. See also David V. Erdman, 'Coleridge as Editorial Writer', in *Power and Consciousness*, pp. 183–201 (p. 189); E. P. Thompson, reviewing Erdman's *CC* edition of *EOT*, *Wordsworth Circle*, x (1979) 261–5 (pp. 262–3).

7. Cf. Burke, who calls the 'cannibal philosophers' of Jacobin France 'a misallied and disparaged branch of the house of Nimrod. They are the Duke of Bedford's natural hunters; and he is their natural game' – *A Letter from the Right Honourable Edmund Burke to a Noble Lord* (London, 1796) pp. 56–7.

8. Cf. *CN*, III, 3845; *Friend* [*CC*], II, 215; *EOT* [*CC*], II, 198–9.

CHAPTER FOURTEEN: CONCLUSION

1. The reading in the Crewe MS is 'Daemon'.

2. Benoit, *Single Nature's Double Name*, pp. 23–9. A more convincing and suggestive reading of the poem as an attempt to imagine the transgression of Kantian limits is Cavell's 'Genteel responses to Kant', *Raritan*, III, no. 2.

3. See *Europe*, XLVII, special issue: 'Napoléon et la littérature' (Apr–May 1969).

4. Friedrich Nietzsche, *The Will to Power*, trs. Walter Kaufman and R. J. Hollingdale, ed Walter Kaufmann (New York, 1968) p. 79 (no. 179). Cf. Napoleon: 'J'aime l'art comme pouvoir' – quoted in Kaufmann, *Nietzsche: Philosopher, Psychologist, Antichrist* (Princeton, NJ, 1950) p. 9.

5. Austin, *How to Do Things with Words*, p. 60.

6. Carl Woodring, 'Coleridge and the Khan', *Essays in Criticism*, IX (1959) 361–8 (p. 364).

7. Pirie, in *Coleridge's Verse*, ed. Empson and Pirie, p. 249.

8. Elisabeth Schneider, *Coleridge, Opium and 'Kubla Khan'* (Chicago, 1953) p. 286.

9. H. W. Piper, 'The Two Paradises in "Kubla Khan"', *Review of English Studies*, XXVII (1976) 148–58 (p. 157).

Select Bibliography

I PRIMARY WORKS

Addison, Joseph, *The Spectator*, ed. Donald F. Bond, 4 vols (Oxford, 1965).

Alison, Archibald, *Essays on the Nature and Principles of Taste* (Edinburgh, 1790).

Austen, Jane, *Emma*, ed. David Lodge, Oxford English Novels (London, 1971).

Baillie, John, *An Essay on the Sublime* (1747), Augustan Reprints, 43 (Los Angeles, 1953).

Beattie, James, *Dissertations Moral and Critical* (London, 1783).

Berkeley, George, *Works*, ed. A. A. Luce and T. E. Jessop, 9 vols (London, 1949–57).

Blair, Hugh, *Lectures on Rhetoric and Belles Lettres*, 2 vols (London, 1783).

Blake, William, *The Illuminated Blake*, annotated by David V. Erdman (Garden City, NY, 1974).

——, *Poetry and Prose*, ed. David V. Erdman (Garden City, NY, 1965).

Bowles, Thomas Lisle, *Monody Written at Matlock, October 1791* (London and Bath, 1791).

——, *Sonnets, Written Chiefly on Picturesque Spots, during a Tour*, 2nd edn (Bath, 1789).

Burke, Edmund, *A Letter from Mr Burke to a Member of the National Assembly; in Answer to Some Objections to his Book on French Affairs* (London, 1796).

——, *A Letter from the Right Honourable Edmund Burke to a Noble Lord* (London, 1796).

——, *A Philosophical Enquiry into the Origin of our Ideas of the Sublime and Beautiful*, ed. J. T. Boulton (London, 1958).

Burnet, Thomas, *Archaeologicae Philosophicae; or, the Ancient Doctrine Concerning the Originals of Things*, trs. Mr Foxton (London, 1729).

——, *The Sacred Theory of the Earth*, Centaur Classics (Fontwell, Sussex, 1965).

Butler, Joseph, *Works*, ed. W. E. Gladstone, 2 vols (Oxford, 1897).

Byron, George Gordon, Lord, *Works*, ed. E. H. Coleridge, 13 vols (London, 1898–1904).

Carlyle, Thomas, *Works*, Centenary Edn, 30 vols (London, 1897).

Coleridge, Samuel Taylor, *Aids to Reflection, in the Formation of a Manly Character on the General Grounds of Prudence, Morality and Religion* (London, 1825).

——, *Biographia Literaria*, ed. J. Shawcross, 2 vols (1907; corrected, Oxford, 1954).

——, *Coleridge on the Seventeenth Century*, ed. Roberta Florence Brinkley (Durham, NC, 1955).

——, *Collected Letters*, ed. Earl Leslie Griggs, 6 vols (Oxford, 1956–71).

——, *Collected Works*, general editor Kathleen Coburn (with Bart Winer), Bollingen Series LXXV, in progress (London and Princeton, NJ, 1969–).

——, *Complete Poetical Works*, ed. Ernest Hartley Coleridge, 2 vols (Oxford, 1912).

——, *Essays on his Own Times, Forming a Second Series of the 'Friend'*, ed. Sara Coleridge, 3 vols (London, 1850).

——, *Literary Remains*, ed. H. N. Coleridge, 4 vols (London, 1836–9).

——, *Miscellaneous Criticism*, ed. Thomas Middleton Raysor (London, 1936).

——, *Notebooks*, ed. Kathleen Coburn, Bollingen Series L, in progress (London, New York and Princeton, 1957–).

——, 'On the Philosophic Import of the Words, OBJECT and SUBJECT', *Blackwood's Edinburgh Magazine*, x (1821) 246–52.

——, *Philosophical Lectures*, ed. Kathleen Coburn (London, 1949).

——, *Poems, to which are Now Added, Poems by Charles Lamb and Charles Lloyd* (Bristol and London, 1797).

——, *Poetical Works*, ed. J. Dykes Campbell (London, 1893).

——, *Shakespearean Criticism*, ed. Thomas Middleton Raysor, 2nd edn, 2 vols (London, 1960).

——, *Specimens of the Table Talk*, ed. H. N. Coleridge, 2nd edn, rev. (Oxford, 1836).

——, and Southey, Robert, *Omniana*, ed. Robert Gittings (Fontwell, Sussex, 1969).

——, *Table Talk and Omniana* (Oxford, 1917).

Cowper, William, *Poetical Works*, ed. H. S. Milford, Oxford Standard Authors, 4th edn, corrections and additions by Norma Russell (London, 1967).

Crabb Robinson, Henry, *On Books and their Writers*, ed. E. J. Morley, 3 vols (London, 1938).

Darwin, Emma, *A Century of Family Letters*, ed. H. Litchfield, 2 vols (London, 1915).

Dennis, John, *Critical Works*, ed. Edward Niles Hooker, 2 vols (Baltimore, 1939).

De Quincey, Thomas, *Collected Writings*, ed. David Masson, 14 vols (Edinburgh, 1889–90).

Descartes, René, *Philosophical Works*, trs. E. S. Haldane and G. R. T. Ross, 2 vols (Cambridge, 1911).

D'Israeli, Isaac, *Essay on the Manners and Genius of the Literary Character* (London, 1795).

Fichte, Johann Gottlieb, *Addresses to the German Nation*, trs. R. F. Jones and G. H. Turnbull, ed. G. A. Kelly (New York and Evanston, Ill., 1968).

——, *The Popular Works*, trs. William Smith, 2nd edn, 2 vols (London, 1848).

——, *Science of Knowledge (Wissenschaftslehre)*, ed. and trs. P. Heath and J. Lachs (1970; repr with corrections, Cambridge, 1982).

Godwin, William, *Enquiry Concerning Political Justice and its Influence on General Virtue and Happiness*, 2 vols (London, 1793).

Goethe, Johann Wolfgang von, *Gedenkausgabe der Werke, Briefe und Gespräche*, ed. Ernst Beutler, 24 vols (Zürich, 1948–53).

——, *The Sorrows of Werter: A German Story*, trs. attrib. to Daniel Malthus, 3rd edn, 2 vols (London, 1782).

Gray, Thomas, *The Poems of Gray, Collins and Goldsmith*, ed. Roger Lonsdale, Longman Annotated English Poets (London, 1969).

Hartley, David, *Observations on Man, his Frame, his Duty, And his Expectations* (1749), Scholars' Facsimiles and Reprints, 2 vols in 1 (Gainesville, Fla., 1966).

Hazlitt, William, *Complete Works*, ed. P. P. Howe, Centenary Edition, 21 vols (London and Toronto, 1930–4).

Hegel, G. W. F., *Aesthetics: Lectures on Fine Art*, trs. T. M. Knox, 2 vols (Oxford, 1975).

——, *Lectures on the Philosophy of World History: Introduction: Reason in History*, trs. H. B. Nisbet (Cambridge, 1975).

——, *The Logic of Hegel, translated from 'The Encyclopaedia of the Sciences'*, trs. William Wallace, 2nd edn (1892; repr. Oxford, 1975).

——, *On Christianity: Early Theological Writings*, trs. T. M. Knox and Richard Kroner (Gloucester, Mass., 1970).

——, *Phenomenology of Spirit*, trs. A. V. Miller (Oxford, 1977).

——, *Philosophy of Nature*, ed. and trs. M. J. Petry, 3 vols (London and New York, 1970).

——, *Philosophy of Right*, trs. T. M. Knox, 2nd edn, corrected (Oxford, 1945).

Hobbes, Thomas, *English Works*, ed. Sir W. Molesworth, 11 vols (1839; repr. Darmstadt, 1966).

Hume, David, *Enquiries Concerning the Human Understanding and Concerning the Principals of Morals*, ed. L. A. Selby-Bigge, 2nd edn (1902; repr. Oxford, 1961).

——, *Treatise of Human Nature*, ed. L. A. Selby-Bigge, 2nd edn, rev. P. H. Nidditch (Oxford, 1978).

Johnson, Samuel, *Dictionary of the English Language*, 2 vols (London, 1755).

——, *Lives of the English Poets*, World's Classics, 2 vols (London, 1952).

Kames, Lord (Henry Home), *Elements of Criticism*, 6th edn, 2 vols (Edinburgh, 1785).

Kant, Immanuel, *Anthropology from a Pragmatic Point of View*, trs. Mary J. Gregor (The Hague, 1974).

——, *Critique of Judgement*, trs. J. C. Meredith (1928; repr. Oxford, 1957).

——, *Critique of Pure Reason*, trs. N. Kemp-Smith, 2nd edn (London, 1933).

——, *Prolegomena to any Future Metaphysics that will be able to Present Itself as a Science*, trs. P. Gray-Lucas, Philosophical Classics (Manchester, 1953).

Keats, John, *Letters*, ed. Hyder Edward Rollins, 2 vols (Cambridge, Mass., 1958).

——, *Poetical Works*, ed. H. W. Garrod, Oxford Standard Authors (London, 1956).

Kleist, Heinrich von, *Sämtlich Werke und Briefe*, ed. H. Sembdner, 6th edn, 2 vols (Munich, 1977).

Knight, Richard Payne, *Analytical Enquiry into the Principles of Taste* (London, 1805).

Lamb, Charles, *Letters of Charles and Mary Anne Lamb*, ed. E. W. Marrs, Jr, 2 vols (Ithaca, NY, and London, 1975).

Locke, John, *Essay Concerning Human Understanding*, ed. P. H. Nidditch, Clarendon Edn (Oxford, 1975).

——, *Second Treatise of Government*, ed. J. W. Gough, 3rd edn (Oxford, 1966).

Longinus, *Treatise on the Sublime*, trs. Mr Welsted, 3rd edn, corrected (Dublin, 1727).

Lowth, Robert, *Lectures on the Sacred Poetry of the Hebrews*, trs. G. Gregory, 2 vols (London, 1787).

MacKenzie, Henry, *Anecdotes and Egotisms*, ed. H. W. Thompson (London, 1927).

Milton, John, *Paradise Lost*, ed. Alastair Fowler, Longman Annotated English Poets, 6th impression (London, 1981).

——, *Works*, Columbia Edn, ed. F. A. Patterson, A. Abbott and H. M. Ayres, 18 vols and suppl. (New York, 1931–8).

Nidecker, Henri, 'Notes Marginales de S. T. Coleridge', *Revue de Littérature Comparée*, x (1930) 163–9.

Pigott, Charles, *A Political Dictionary: Explaining the True Meanings of Words* (London, 1795).

Reid, Thomas, *Essays on the Active Powers of the Human Mind*, in *Works*, 4 vols (Charleston, Mass., 1813–15), iii and iv (1815), repr. as 1 vol. (Cambridge, Mass., 1969).

——, *Essays on the Intellectual Powers of Man*, in *Works*, ii and iii (1815), repr. as 1 vol. (Cambridge, Mass., 1969).

Richardson, William, *A Philosophical Analysis and Illustration of some of Shakespeare's Remarkable Characters* (London, 1774).

Rousseau, Jean-Jacques, *Oeuvres Complètes*, ed. B. Gagnebin and M. Raymond, Bibliothèque de la Pléiade, in progress (1959–).

Schelling, F. W. J., *System of Transcendental Idealism* (1800), trs. P. Heath (Charlottesville, Va, 1978).

Schiller, Friedrich, *'Naive and Sentimental Poetry' and 'On the Sublime': Two Essays*, trs. Julius A. Elias (New York, 1966).

——, *On the Aesthetic Education of Man: In a Series of Letters*, ed. and trs. E. M. Wilkinson and L. A. Willoughby (Oxford, 1967).

——, *The Robbers. A Tragedy*, trs. anonymously Alexander F. Tytler, Lord Woodhouselee (London, 1792).

——, *Werke*, ed. J. Petersen and H. Schneider, Nationalausgabe, 42 vols, in progress (Weimar, 1943–).

Schlegel, August Wilhelm, *Course of Lectures on Dramatic Art and Literature*, trs. John Black, 2 vols (London, 1815).

Schlegel, Friedrich, *'Lucinde' and the Fragments*, trs. P. Firchow (Minneapolis, 1971).

Seward, Anna, *Letters*, 6 vols (Edinburgh, 1811).

Shaftesbury, Third Earl of (Anthony Ashley Cooper), *Characteristics of Men, Manners, Opinions, Times, etc.*, ed. John M. Robertson (1900; repr. Gloucester, Mass., 1963).

——, *Inquiry Concerning Virtue or Merit*, ed. David Walford, Philosophical Classics (Manchester, 1977).

Shakespeare, William, *The Tempest*, ed. Frank Kermode, New Arden Shakespeare, 5th edn, rev. (London, 1954).

Shearer, Edna Aston, 'Wordsworth and Coleridge Marginalia in a Copy of Richard Payne Knight's *Analytical Enquiry into the Principles of Taste*', *Huntingdon Library Quarterly*, i (1937) 63–94.

Shelley, Percy Bysshe, *Complete Works*, ed. R. Ingpen and W. E. Peck, 10 vols (New York, 1965).

——, *Poetical Works*, ed. T. Hutchinson, corrected G. M. Matthews, Oxford Standard Authors (Oxford, 1970).

Smith, Adam, *Theory of Moral Sentiments*, 6th edn, with corrections and additions (London and Edinburgh, 1790).

Spinoza, Benedict de, *Ethic*, trs. W. Hale White, rev. A. Hutchison (London, 1910).
Stewart, Dugald, *Collected Works*, ed. Sir W. Hamilton, 10 vols and suppl. (Edinburgh, 1854–60).
Taylor, Jeremy, *Via Intelligentiae. A Sermon Preached to the University of Dublin* (London, 1662).
Walker, John, *Rhetorical Grammar* (1785), English Linguistics Facsimile Reprints, 266 (Menston, Yorks, 1971).
Warton, Joseph, *Essay on the Genius and Writings of Pope*, 2 vols, 5th edn, corrected (London, 1806).
Wittreich, Joseph Anthony (ed.), *The Romantics on Milton: Formal Essays and Critical Asides* (Cleveland, Ohio, 1970).
Wordsworth, William, *Letters: The Early Years, 1787–1805*, ed. Ernest de Selincourt, rev. C. L. Shaver, 2nd edn (Oxford, 1967).
——, *Poetical Works*, ed. Ernest de Selincourt and Helen Darbishire, 5 vols (Oxford, 1940–9).
——, *The Prelude 1799, 1805, 1850*, ed. Jonathan Wordsworth, M. H. Abrams and Stephen Gill, Norton Critical Editions (New York, 1979).
——, *Prose Works*, ed. W. J. B. Owen and Jane W. Smyser, 3 vols (Oxford, 1974).
Young, Edward, *Conjectures on Original Composition. In a Letter to the Author of Sir Charles Grandison*, Scolar Press Facsimile (Leeds, 1966).

II SECONDARY WORKS

Abrams, M. H., 'The Deconstructive Angel', *Critical Inquiry*, III (1977) 425–38.
——, *The Mirror and the Lamp* (New York, 1958).
——, *Natural Supernaturalism: Tradition and Revolution in Romantic Literature* (London, 1971).
——, 'Rationality and Imagination in Cultural History: A Reply to Wayne Booth', *Critical Inquiry*, II (1976) 447–64.
——, 'Structure and Style in the Greater Romantic Lyric', in *From Sensibility to Romanticism: Essays Presented to Frederick A. Pottle*, ed. F. W. Hilles and H. Bloom (New York, 1965) pp. 527–60.
—— (ed.), *English Romantic Poets: Modern Essays in Criticism*, 2nd edn (New York, 1975).
Appleyard, J. A., *Coleridge's Philosophy of Literature: The Development of a Concept of Poetry, 1791–1819* (Cambridge, Mass., 1965).
Ashton, Rosemary, *The German Idea: Four English Writers and the Reception of German Thought, 1800–1860* (Cambridge, 1980).
Austin, J. L., *How to Do Things with Words*, ed. J. O. Urmson and Marina Sbisà, 2nd edn (London, 1980).
Ball, Patricia M., *The Central Self: A Study in Romantic and Victorian Imagination* (London, 1968).
Barker, Arthur, '"... And on his Crest Sat Horror": Eighteenth-Century Interpretations of Milton's Sublimity and his Satan', *University of Toronto Quarterly*, XI (1942) 421–36.
Barrell, John, *English Literature in History, 1730–1780: An Equal, Wide Survey* (London, 1983).

Barth, J. Robert, sj, *Coleridge and Christian Doctrine* (Cambridge, Mass., 1969).
——, *The Symbolic Imagination: Coleridge and the Romantic Tradition* (Princeton, NJ, 1977). .

Bate, Walter Jackson, *From Classic to Romantic: Premises of Taste in Eighteenth-Century England* (London, 1946).

Beer, John, *Coleridge's Poetic Intelligence* (London, 1977).
——, *Coleridge the Visionary* (London, 1959).
——, ' "The Revolutionary Youth of Wordsworth and Coleridge": A Reply', *Critical Quarterly*, xix (1977) 79–87.
—— (ed.), *Coleridge's Variety* (London, 1974).

Benjamin, Walter, *The Origin of German Tragic Drama*, trs. John Osborne (London, 1977).

Benoit, Raymond, *Single Nature's Double Name: The Collectedness of the Conflicting in British and American Romanticism*, De Proprietatibus Litterarum, Series Maior, 26 (The Hague, 1973).

Bloom, Harold, *The Anxiety of Influence* (New York, 1975).

Booth, Wayne C., 'M. H. Abrams: Historian as Critic, Critic as Pluralist', *Critical Inquiry*, ii (1976) 411–45.
——, ' "Preserving the Exemplar"; or, How Not to Dig Our Own Graves', *Critical Inquiry*, iii (1977) 407–23.

Boyd, John D., sj, *The Function of Mimesis and its Decline* (Cambridge, Mass., 1968).

Braudy, Leo, *Narrative Form in History and Fiction* (Princeton, NJ, 1970).

Bredvold, Louis I., *The Natural History of Sensibility* (Detroit, 1962).

Brisman, Leslie, *Romantic Origins* (Ithaca, NY, 1978).

Butler, Marilyn, *Romantics, Rebels and Reactionaries: English Literature and its Background, 1760–1830* (Oxford, 1981).

Campbell, J. Dykes, 'Coleridge's Quotations', *Athenaeum*, no. 3382 (20 Aug 1892) 259–60.

Caskey, Jefferson D., and Stapper, Melinda M., *Samuel Taylor Coleridge: A Selective Bibliography of Criticism, 1935–1977* (Westport, Conn., 1978).

Cavell, Stanley, 'Genteel Responses to Kant? In Emerson's "Fate" and in Coleridge's *Biographia Literaria*', *Raritan*, iii, no. 2 (Fall 1983) 34–61.

Chayes, Irene H., 'Kubla Khan and the Creative Process', *Studies in Romanticism*, vi (1966) 1–21.

Coburn, Kathleen (ed.), *Coleridge: A Collection of Critical Essays* (Englewood Cliffs, NJ, 1967).

Cooke, Michael G., *Acts of Inclusion: Studies Bearing on an Elementary Theory of Romanticism* (New Haven, Conn., 1979).
——, *The Romantic Will* (New Haven, Conn., 1976).
——, ' "Quisque Sui Faber" ': Coleridge in the *Biographia Literaria*', *Philological Quarterly*, l (Apr 1971) 208–29.

Cooper, Lane, *Late Harvest* (Ithaca, NY, 1952).

De Man, Paul, *Allegories of Reading: Figural Language in Rousseau, Nietzsche, Rilke and Proust* (New Haven, Conn., 1979).
——, 'The Rhetoric of Temporality', in *Interpretation: Theory and Practice*, ed. C. S. Singleton (Baltimore, 1969) pp. 173–209; repr. in his *Blindness and Insight: Essays in the Rhetoric of Contemporary Criticism*, 2nd edn, rev. (London, 1983) pp. 187–228.

Draper, John W., *Eighteenth-Century English Aesthetics: A Bibliography* (1931; repr. New York, 1968).

Dunstan, A. C., 'The German Influence on Coleridge', *Modern Language Review*, XVII (1922) 272–81; XVIII (1923) 183–201.

Ellis, Frank Hale, 'Gray's *Elegy*: The Biographical Problem in Literary Criticism', in *Twentieth Century Interpretations*, ed. Starr, pp. 51–75.

Empson, William, *Milton's God* (London, 1961).

—— and Pirie, David (eds), *Coleridge's Verse: A Selection* (London, 1972).

Engell, James, *The Creative Imagination: Enlightenment to Romanticism* (Cambridge, Mass., 1981).

Evans, B. Ifor, 'Coleridge's Copy of "Fears in Solitude"', *Times Literary Supplement*, no. 1733 (18 Apr 1935) p. 255.

Feldman, Burton, and Richardson, Robert D. (eds), *The Rise of Modern Mythology* (Bloomington, Ind., 1972).

Ferguson, Frances, 'Coleridge and the Deluded Reader: "The Rime of the Ancient Mariner"', *Georgia Review*, XXXI (1977) 617–35.

——, 'The Sublime of Edmund Burke; or, The Bathos of Experience', *Glyph*, VIII (1981) 62–78.

Fruman, Norman, *Coleridge, the Damaged Archangel* (London, 1972).

Green, Andrew J., 'Essays in Miniature: The Restless Eye', *College English*, III (1942) 722–3.

Green, T. H., Introduction to *The Philosophical Works of David Hume*, ed. T. H. Green and T. H. Grose, 4 vols (London, 1874) I, 1–299.

Hacking, Ian, *Why Does Language Matter to Philosophy?* (Cambridge, 1975).

Hamilton, Paul, *Coleridge's Poetics* (Oxford, 1983).

Harman, Barbara Leah, *Costly Monuments: Representations of the Self in George Herbert's Poetry* (Cambridge, Mass., and London, 1982).

Harper, G. M., 'Coleridge's Conversation Poems', in *English Romantic Poets*, ed. Abrams, pp. 188–201.

Harries, Karsten, 'Descartes, Perspective and the Angelic Eye', *Yale French Studies*, XLIX (1973) 28–42.

——, 'The Infinite Sphere: Comments on the History of a Metaphor', *Journal of the History of Philosophy*, XIII (1975) 5–15.

Hartman, Geoffrey, *'The Fate of Reading' and Other Essays* (Chicago, 1975).

——, 'Romanticism and Anti-Self-Consciousness', in *Beyond Formalism: Literary Essays, 1958–1970* (New Haven, Conn., 1970) pp. 298–310.

—— (ed.), *New Perspectives on Coleridge and Wordsworth: Selected Papers from the English Institute* (New York, 1972).

Heidegger, Martin, *Poetry, Language, Thought*, trs. Albert Hofstadter (New York, 1971).

Hill, Christopher, *The Century of Revolution, 1603–1714* (London, 1961).

Hobsbawm, E. J., *The Age of Revolution: Europe 1789–1848* (London, 1962).

House, Humphry, *Coleridge: The Clark Lectures, 1951–2* (London, 1953).

Jameson, Fredric, *The Political Unconscious: Narrative as a Socially Symbolic Act* (Ithaca, NY, 1981).

Kaplan, Fred, 'Coleridge's Aesthetic Ministry', in *Miracles of Rare Device: The Poet's Sense of Self in Nineteenth-Century Poetry* (Detroit, 1972) pp. 44–61.

Kaufmann, Walter A., *Nietzsche: Philosopher, Psychologist, Antichrist* (Princeton, NJ, 1950).

Kaufmann, Walter A., *Hegel: Reinterpretation, Texts, and Commentary* (London, 1966).

Kessler, Edward, *Coleridge's Metaphors of Being* (Princeton, NJ, 1979).

Lacan, Jacques, *The Four Fundamental Concepts of Psycho-Analysis*, ed. Jacques-Alain Miller, trs. Alan Sheridan (Harmondsworth, 1979).

Land, Stephen K., *From Signs to Propositions: The Concept of Form in Eighteenth-Century Semantic Theory* (London, 1974).

Levere, Trevor H., *Poetry Realized in Nature: Samuel Taylor Coleridge and Early Nineteenth-Century Science* (Cambridge, 1981).

Lewis, C. S., *Studies in Words*, 2nd edn (Cambridge, 1967).

Lockridge, Laurence S., *Coleridge the Moralist* (Ithaca, NY, 1977).

Loe, Frances, ' "The Soul in Paraphrase": A Study of the Operation of Religious Language in Herbert's *The Temple* and Milton's *Paradise Regained*' (unpublished Part II English dissertation, University of Cambridge, 1984).

Lonsdale, Roger, 'The Poetry of Thomas Gray: Versions of the Self', *Proceedings of the British Academy*, LIX (1973) 105–23.

Lowalski, Barbara Kiefer, *Protestant Poetics and the Seventeenth-Century Religious Lyric* (Princeton, NJ, 1979).

Lyons, John O., *The Invention of the Self: The Hinge of Consciousness in the Eighteenth Century* (Carbondale, Ill., 1978).

McFarland, Thomas, *Coleridge and the Pantheist Tradition* (Oxford, 1969).

——, *Romanticism and the Forms of Ruin: Wordsworth, Coleridge, and Modalities of Fragmentation* (Princeton, NJ, 1981).

Madell, Geoffrey, *The Identity of the Self* (Edinburgh, 1981).

Mandelbaum, Maurice, *History, Man and Reason: A Study in Nineteenth-Century Thought* (Baltimore, 1981).

Marx, Karl, *The Eighteenth Brumaire of Louis Bonaparte*, in *Karl Marx and Frederick Engels: Selected Works* (Moscow, 1968) pp. 96–179.

Miller, J. Hillis, 'The Critic as Host', *Critical Inquiry*, III (1977) 439–47.

——, 'Tradition and Difference', *Diacritics*, II (1972) 6–13.

Milley, Henry J. W., 'Some Notes on Coleridge's "Eolian Harp" ', *Modern Philology*, XXXVI (1939) 359–75.

Modiano, Raimonda, 'Coleridge and the Sublime', *Wordsworth Circle*, IX, no. 1 (Winter 1973) 110–20.

Monk, Samuel H., *The Sublime: A Study of Critical Theories in Eighteenth-Century England* (1935; repr. Ann Arbor, Mich., 1960).

Neumann, Erich, *The Origins and History of Consciousness*, trs. R. F. C. Hull, Bollingen Series XLII, 2nd printing with corrections (New York, 1964).

Nicolson, Marjorie Hope, *The Breaking of the Circle: Studies in the Effect of the 'New Science' upon Seventeenth-Century Poetry* (Evanston, Ill., 1950).

Nietzsche, Friedrich, *Beyond Good and Evil: Prelude to a Philosophy of the Future*, trs. Walter Kaufmann (New York, 1966).

——, *The Will to Power*, ed. Walter Kaufmann, trs. Walter Kaufmann and R. J. Hollingdale (New York, 1968).

Orsini, G. N. G., *Coleridge and German Idealism: A Study in the History of Philosophy with Unpublished Materials from Coleridge's Manuscripts* (Carbondale, Ill., 1969).

Parker, Harold T., *The Cult of Antiquity and the French Revolutionaries* (Chicago, 1937).

Parry, Idris, *Hand to Mouth and Other Essays* (Manchester, 1981).

Pater, Walter, 'Coleridge's Writings', in *Essays on Literature and Art*, ed. Jennifer Uglow (London, 1973) pp. 1–26.

Piper, H. W., 'The Two Paradises in "Kubla Khan" ', *Review of English Studies*, XXVII (1976) 148–58.

Poulet, Georges, *The Metamorphoses of the Circle*, trs. Carley Dawson and Elliott Coleman (Baltimore, 1966).

Richards, I. A., *Coleridge's Minor Poems* (1960; repr. n.p., 1970).

Rorty, Richard, *Philosophy and the Mirror of Nature* (Oxford, 1981).

Ryle, Gilbert, *The Concept of Mind* (London, 1949).

Shaffer, E. S., *'Kubla Khan' and the Fall of Jerusalem: The Mythological School in Biblical Criticism and Secular Literature, 1770–1880* (Cambridge, 1975).

Sickels, Eleanor M., *The Gloomy Egoist: Moods and Themes of Melancholy from Gray to Keats* (1932; repr. New York, 1969).

Simpson, David, *Irony and Authority in Romantic Poetry* (London, 1979).

Starr, Herbert W. (ed.), *Twentieth Century Interpretations of Gray's 'Elegy': A Collection of Critical Essays* (Englewood Cliffs, NJ, 1968).

Steiner, F. George, 'Contributions to a Dictionary of Critical Terms: "Egoism" and "Egotism"', *Essays in Criticism*, II (1952) 444–52.

Stempel, Daniel, 'Revelation on Mount Snowdon: Wordsworth, Coleridge, and the Fichtean Imagination', *Journal of Aesthetics and Art Criticism*, XXIX (1970–1) 371–84.

Swiatecka, M. Jadwiga, OP, *The Idea of the Symbol: Some Nineteenth-Century Comparisons with Coleridge* (Cambridge, 1980).

Symons, Arthur, *The Symbolist Movement in Literature* (London, 1899).

Tennyson, Hallam, Lord, *Alfred Lord Tennyson. A Memoir by his Son*, 2 vols (London, 1897).

Thompson, E. P., Review of *EOT [CC]*, *Wordsworth Circle*, X (1979) 261–5.

Thompson, J. M., *Robespierre*, 2 vols (Oxford, 1935).

Thorpe, Clarence DeWitt, 'Coleridge on the Sublime', in *Wordsworth and Coleridge: Studies in Honour of George McLean Harper*, ed. Earl Leslie Griggs (Princeton, NJ, 1939) pp. 192–219.

Thorslev, Peter L., *The Byronic Hero: Types and Prototypes* (Minneapolis, 1962).

——, 'The Romantic Mind is its own Place', *Comparative Literature*, XV (1963) 250–68.

Todorov, Tzvetan, *Theories of the Symbol*, trs. Catherine Porter (Oxford, 1982).

Tucker, Susie I., *Enthusiasm: A Study in Semantic Change* (Cambridge, 1972).

——, *Protean Shape: A Study in Eighteenth-Century Vocabulary and Usage* (London, 1967).

Turbayne, Colin Murray, *The Myth of Metaphor* (New Haven, Conn., 1962).

Watson, George, *Coleridge the Poet* (London, 1966).

——, 'The Revolutionary Youth of Wordsworth and Coleridge', *Critical Quarterly*, XVIII (1976) 49–66.

Weiskel, Thomas, *The Romantic Sublime: Studies in the Structure and Psychology of Transcendence* (Baltimore, 1976).

Whalley, George, 'The Bristol Library Borrowings of Southey and Coleridge, 1793–8', *Library*, 5th ser., IV (1949) 116–26.

Wheeler, Kathleen M., *Sources, Processes and Methods in Coleridge's 'Biographia Literaria'* (Cambridge, 1980).

White, Hayden, *Metahistory: The Historical Imagination in Nineteenth-Century Europe* (Baltimore, 1973).

Wiggins, David, *Sameness and Substance* (Oxford, 1980).

Williams, Raymond, *Culture and Society, 1780–1950* (London, 1956).

——, *Keywords: A Vocabulary of Culture and Society* (London, 1976).

Woodring, Carl R., 'Coleridge and the Khan', *Essays in Criticism*, ix (1959) 361–8.

——, *Politics in the Poetry of Coleridge* (Madison, Wis., 1961).

Index